THE SHOCK
Tunbridge Wells: Life o1
1914-19

*Don't be Alarmed,
the "Queen's" are on guard
at Tunbridge Wells*

Edited by John Cunningham

Royal Tunbridge Wells Civic Society
Local History Group Monograph No.13

November 2014

Published in Great Britain in November 2014
by the Local History Group of the
Royal Tunbridge Wells Civic Society

All rights reserved

No part of this publication may be reproduced,
stored in a retrieval system, or transmitted,
in any form or by any means,
without the prior permission
of the copyright holder.

Within the UK, exceptions are allowed
in respect of any 'fair dealing' for the purpose of
research or private study, or criticism or review,
as permitted under
The Copyright, Design and Patents Act, 1988.

© Royal Tunbridge Wells Civic Society, 2014

The authors have asserted their right to be identified
as the authors of this work in accordance
with the Copyright, Design and Patents Act, 1988

The Publishers have made every effort to establish the copyright
of all extracts and illustrations in this monograph
and apologise for any unwitting oversight or omission.

ISBN 978-09560944-8-3

The text is set in Bookman Old Style 10 pt.
and the cover in Bookman Old Style 10 – 20 pt

Edited by John Cunningham

Printed and bound by
DPI Print & Production Ltd.,
Tonbridge, Kent TN9 1BB

Front cover:
a patriotic 1914 postcard designed to reassure,
'The Queen's' being the Town's local regiment,
the Royal West Kent Regiment.

Title page:
The patriotic 1914 postcard

CONTENTS

		Page
Introduction		1

Chapter
1.	Tunbridge Wells before 1914	3
2.	1914 : The Early Days	30
3.	1915 : The End of the Beginning	49
4.	The response of the Borough Council	68
5.	The Army in Tunbridge Wells	87
	Box: The Canadian Forestry Corps	104
	Box: The YMCA	109
6.	How Tunbridge Wells coped with the Wounded	110
7.	Tunbridge Wells Women in the First World War	132
	Box: Women and the Peace Movement	163
8.	Belgian Refugees in Tunbridge Wells	165
9.	Tunbridge Wells in 1916 : Hope and Despair	189
10.	1917-1918 : The Worsening Situation	207
11.	1918-1919 : The Beginning of the End – and the End	230
12.	Tunbridge Wells after the War	255
	Appendix 1 Sir John and Lady Bromhead Matthews	268
	Appendix 2 Census: Population and Employment: 1911, 1921, 1931	271
	Acknowledgements/Abbreviations/ Acronyms	273
	Sources and Bibliography	274
	Biographical notes on Contributors	278
	Index	281

The Lady Grocer

BEFORE the war we had 1,000 women in our employ, mainly engaged in clerical work. To-day we have nearly 3,000, and they not only do duty at the desk, but at the counter too, and all praise is due to them for the manner in which they have shouldered the extra burden.

¶ Their assistance has enabled us to release nearly 2,000 men for the army.

¶ Despite this enormous upheaval in our organisation, we are still able to satisfy our customers—a most ample tribute to the Lady Grocer.

INTERNATIONAL STORES

THE BIGGEST GROCERS IN THE WORLD
TEA :: COFFEE :: GROCERIES :: PROVISIONS

INTRODUCTION

This book is about Tunbridge Wells in the First World War - what it was like before, what happened there during, and to what it extent it changed afterwards.

It is not a book about the First World War as such. The Western and Eastern Fronts, the Dardanelles and Gallipoli, or submarine warfare and other similar issues, only come into the book insofar as they help to explain how Tunbridge Wells reacted or was affected and changed. However, to give the reader a comparative perspective on what was actually happening outside the narrow confines of Tunbridge Wells, a Chronology of national and international events is provided during the course of the book.

It has been researched and written by a group of fourteen people – mostly members of the Local History Group of the Royal Tunbridge Wells Civic Society, but with the addition of other outside specialists such as from the University of Kent and The Open University, and the Editor of the *Kent & Sussex Courier*. Some ten members of the group both researched and wrote Chapters, while the remaining four researched.

Because it is written by a group, readers may think that it is essentially a collection of essays on the subject and therefore uncoordinated, but it has been written to a precise plan and structure, designed to cover its subject, both over time and in content/matter.

As the reader will see, the book presents its findings, assessments and opinion in both a chronological and a thematic way. Some chapters deal with the individual years, others with broad themes over the whole period, such as how the Borough Council responded to the War; the impact of the Army, whether in training, in transit or just recuperating, on the town; the changing role of women in Tunbridge Wells as a result of the War; how the town coped with the large numbers of convalescent troops; and how the town responded to the 250 Belgian refugees who came to live in the town.

Each writer has been given the freedom to write in their own style and the prime purpose of any editing has been to eliminate any *unnecessary* duplication of detail which is inevitable when a subject is treated both chronologically and thematically.

Sources: For this history of Tunbridge Wells in the First World War, we have been very fortunate, besides the usual sources of newspapers, and Council and Committee minutes, to discover two contemporary, very local and unique sources which have never been published before, for what happened in the Town.

The first is a Diary of some 400 pages written over the four years by Lady Matthews, the wife of Sir John Bromhead Mathews, a Colonial lawyer and administrator. They came to live in Tunbridge Wells in 1910 and both would die there – Sir John in 1934, Lady Matthews in 1957. She came from a Liberal Yorkshire family; was very involved with female emancipation as a Suffragist, rather than a Suffragette; and would be one of the first women JPs in Tunbridge Wells. She had three young children and when the War started, she kept a detailed diary of life during the War, in order that her children who were too young to understand at the time, would have a perspective of what they had unwittingly lived through as children.

We are very grateful to the Executors of the Estate of Lady Matthews and the Imperial War Museum, where the Diaries are deposited, for permission to reproduce from them. Biographical information about Sir John and Lady Matthews will be found in Appendix 1.

The second contemporary source is a remarkable collection of some ten volumes of scrapbook, which include press-cuttings, photographs, and all sorts of printed ephemera. They were kept by Robert Gower, initially Mr. and subsequently Sir, who was Mayor of Tunbridge Wells from 1917-1919 and would go on to be the MP for Hackney Central and subsequently Gillingham. They provide a contemporary record which must be unique.

Nomenclature: The Conflict of 1914-1918 has been referred to throughout this book as World War I (or as WWI), because that is what it is normally called today, but at the time it was generally referred to as "The Great War" and the term "World War I" was only 'invented' in 1919 and would not have any validity until 1939. It is interesting to note that the Royal Tunbridge Wells Borough Council referred to it in 1919 in the testimonial which they gave to every returning soldier, as 'the Great European War'.

About the book: Where a subject is relatively self-contained and separate from the Chapter into which it would normally fit, we have sometimes put it in a box on its own, either within the Chapter or at the end of a Chapter. There are also footnotes throughout the book, the purpose of which is essentially to offer background or more explanatory information. For reasons of space, footnotes which are purely source data have been mostly *but not entirely* deleted, and can be accessed from the Civic Society's website – www.thecivicsociety.org

Illustrations: We have been fortunate to find some 200 mainly contemporary illustrations for the book, but the quality of them does vary, particularly when they are scanned from 100-year-old newspapers.

The writers and researchers: Biographical details of the fourteen researchers and writers will be found at the end of the book on pages 278-280 and very warm thanks must be expressed to them all for the work they have done in making this book possible.

John Cunningham
Chairman, RTWCS Local History Group;
Project Manager and Editor

CHRONOLOGY OF EVENTS PRE-1914

1814-1815 The Congress of Vienna concluded the **Napoleonic Wars** and established both new countries and new boundaries for many countries in Europe. It also established a German Confederation which brought together, although loosely, many of the highly-fragmented states of the former Holy Roman Empire. Prussia, Austria and Russia made major territorial gains.

1830 The Kingdom of the Netherlands had been created in 1815. Its two southern provinces, Flanders which spoke Flemish/Dutch and Wallonia which was French-speaking, were Catholic and in 1830 they separated from the Netherlands following a revolution, to become the new Kingdom of Belgium. The Dutch tried unsuccessfully to recover these provinces, but Belgian independence was eventually guaranteed by an international treaty in 1839, brokered by the United Kingdom (whose Queen Victoria was the favourite niece-by-marriage of the new King of the Belgians, Leopold of Saxe-Coburg); this treaty would be a significant factor in Britain's entry into World War I.

1830 July. Revolution in France reflected the unsettled nature of the 1815 settlement.

1830s-1860s. The 'Zollverein' (a Customs Union, i.e. a Free Trade Area association) established among many of the States of the Germanic Confederation, and this led to much closer cooperation. It is possibly the earliest example of economic union between States without political federation.

1848 General unrest throughout Europe, including Chartist riots in Britain.

1848 February. Revolution in France reflected the continuing unsettled nature of the 1815 settlement, and led to the election of Napoleon Bonaparte's nephew, first as the President of the Second Republic, and then in 1851, he made himself the Emperor Napoleon III. He survived as such until 1870, when he was forced to abdicate, following his defeat and capture by Prussia at the Battle of Sedan.

1848-1861 The movement for the re-unification of Italy had started after the Congress of Vienna, but it was particularly Mazzini and Garibaldi, leading the Risorgimento movement, who 'liberated' and united a myriad of States between 1848-1861 into a new Kingdom of Italy, which was declared in 1861.

1853-56 The Crimean War, fought by Russia against Turkey, Britain, France and Piedmont.

From 1860, Bismarck as the Chancellor (Chief Minister) of Prussia was forging the North German Confederation of States into what would become the new German Empire by 1871; and the Emperor Franz Joseph I of Austria was doing likewise in south-eastern Europe, creating the so-called 'Dual Monarchy' of the Austro-Hungarian Empire in 1867.

1864 Prussian-Denmark War over Schleswig-Holstein: Prussia won decisively after a nine-month war.

1866 Prussian-Austrian War over 'German' supremacy: Prussia won after a seven-week war.

1870 Franco-Prussian War essentially over the European Balance of Power. France was technically the aggressor since they made the declaration of war. Prussia won after a ten-month war, incorporating much of Alsace and Lorraine into Germany. The War was a key factor in bringing together the North German Federation of States with the Southern German States and the creation of a united Germany.

1871 January	Wilhelm I of Prussia became the first Kaiser – the Emperor – of Germany.	
1873 May	First *Dreikaiserbund* (League of the three Emperors) formed –	
	Hohenzollern, Prussia	Hapsburg Austria	and Romanov Russia
1879 October	The Dual *Alliance* signed by Germany and Austria.	
1881 June	Second *Dreikaiserbund* formed.	
1882 May	Italy joined Germany and Austria-Hungary to create the Triple *Alliance*.	
1888 June	Wilhelm II of Prussia became Kaiser at the age of 29, following his father who ruled for only 99 days.	
1890 March	Bismarck (aged 74) dismissed as Chancellor of Germany by Wilhelm II	
1894 January	Franco-Russian Military Convention signed	

1899 (October) -1902 (May) The Boer War in South Africa, where the Boers had the moral support of both the Netherlands and Germany, but it was won *technically* by Britain.

1901 (January) Death of Queen Victoria; accession of King Edward VII

1904 (February)-1905(September) Russo-Japanese War over Manchuria and Korea, won by Japan, with the 'moral' support of Great Britain.

1904 April The Anglo-French Entente removed many issues of disagreement, , particularly over North Africa.

1907 August Anglo-Russian Convention removed many issues of disagreement, particularly over Persia, Afghanistan, Tibet and India. This in effect created the Triple *Entente* between Russia, France and Britain.

1908 Herbert Asquith, Liberal Prime Minister of Britain until December 1916, succeeded Liberal Prime Minister, Sir Henry Campbell-Bannerman (1905-1908)

1908 Britain: Old Age Pensions Act – the start of the Welfare State

1911 Britain: National Insurance Act - the start of self-funding for the Welfare State

1912 (October) -1913 (May) First Balkan War:
Bulgaria. Greece and Serbia attack Turkey.

1913 (June–August) Second Balkan War:
Bulgaria attacks Greece and Serbia.

1914 (August) Third Balkan War
Austria attacks Serbia, after assassination of Arch-Duke Franz Ferdinand, heir to Austro-Hungarian Empire.
Russia comes to aid of Serbia,
Germany attacks Russia and also France.
Britain comes to aid of Belgium, which is invaded by Germany ostensibly as the route to attack France. (See 1839 Treaty above)

START OF 'THE GREAT WAR'.

CHAPTER 1
TUNBRIDGE WELLS BEFORE 1914
by John Cunningham

Introduction

Before the First World War, Tunbridge Wells, or to give it the title granted to it in 1909 by King Edward VII, **Royal** Tunbridge Wells, was a town which had only really become a town in the previous century, after over two centuries of being a successful but highly seasonal tourist village. It had also only recently - within the previous 25 years, in 1889 – become a Borough in its own right and it displayed much self-confidence in itself and its future, following a period of about 50 years in which it had fought for its independence and its 'rights'. But it was still a town in which the original and still-existing landowners of most of its site – the Marquess of Abergavenny, the Marquess Camden, and the Lords of the Manors of Rusthall and South Frith – exerted enormous influence, if not power, and commanded huge respect from the populace.

In changing from village to self-governing town, it had changed its moral character from being a somewhat libertine place in the 17th and 18th centuries, akin to that of Brighton in the 20th, to being in the 19th century a very proper God-fearing community, whose basic religious outlook was Low Church and Evangelical, whether Anglican or Nonconformist.

It had a disproportionately large number of older people in its population and a significantly disproportionate number of women, and unmarried women. Despite the disproportion between the sexes, it was still a town controlled very much by men, which was not surprising in view of what were the prevailing social attitudes.

It was also a town which until 1894, when County boundaries were marginally changed, was literally on the border of two Counties – Kent and Sussex – with half the town in one County and half in the other (and even after the change, the whole of it was only just within the County of Kent); and this has caused problems then and since.

The 1911 Census showed that Tunbridge Wells had a larger population than any other town within a 15-mile radius which includes Sevenoaks, Tonbridge, Southborough, Cranbrook, Edenbridge and East Grinstead[1], despite it being a relative newcomer compared with all of them.

---

[1] Maidstone, the County town of Kent, is some 17 miles by road from Tunbridge Wells and on a comparative 'town' basis, was also marginally smaller in population than Tunbridge Wells in 1911.

The development of Tunbridge Wells.

The Wells at Tunbridge, as they were originally known – Tonbridge, then spelt with a U, being the nearest town to them and about five miles away - had been discovered in 1606 and were one of many wells and springs being 'discovered' all over England about this time. They survived, when many others just disappeared, because of a 'chance' Royal visit in 1629 by the French princess, Henrietta Maria, wife of King Charles I, and they were also helped by being only 35 miles from London. The outcome of her visit 'to take the waters' was the birth nine months after her departure form the Wells, of a boy who would later become King Charles II. The Wells immediately acquired a gynaecological reputation which combined with its proximity to London, made it a fashionable place for the Court to visit; and it became The Courtiers' Spa.

It would continue for nearly the next two centuries as a smart and increasingly libertine[2] venue in which essentially the upper classes could mingle in an informal manner, although it would be overtaken in the 18th century by Bath, and by Brighton and other seaside resorts in the 19th. However Tunbridge Wells can arguably claim to be England's first tourist resort, in time if not in rank.

It was the relative decline of the highly-seasonal tourism from the end of the 18th century, coupled with an increasing number of 'settlers' in the form of retired East India Company nabobs and refugees from the French Revolution, which began to change the nature of Tunbridge Wells. The population grew from an estimated 1,000 in 1801 to 5,929 in 1831. But it was the arrival of the South Eastern Railway in 1846 and the London, Brighton and South Coast Railway in 1866, which gave Tunbridge Wells not only two stations (the Central, and the West [Brighton] Station) but a large increase in population as well. Its population was 13,807 by 1861, 24,309 by 1881, and 33,373 by 1901.

Boundary flagstone still to be seen outside King Charles the Martyr.

Its growth led to problems about who should run the growing town because the site of Tunbridge Wells was on the boundary of two counties – Kent and Sussex; and at the junction of three manors - South Frith, Speldhurst and Rusthall; and three parishes – Tonbridge, Speldhurst and Frant. These boundaries were generally similar, but not always contiguous and somewhat inconveniently, the development of the 'town' refused to conform to county, manor or parish

---

[2] In the 18th century, the principal occupation of visitors to Tunbridge Wells was described somewhat cynically as 'basket –making' - a euphemism, according to the Dictionary of the Vulgar Tongue published in 1811, for bastard-making i.e. copulation.

boundaries. For example, the Common was in Rusthall Manor, Mount Ephraim was in Speldhurst Manor and Mount Sion was in South Frith. Speldhurst Manor was in two parishes – Speldhurst and Tonbridge but South Frith was in only one – Tonbridge. The site of the Pantiles was in two parishes – Speldhurst and Frant – besides being owned by two different families – the Lords of Rusthall Manor (whose ownership has changed over time) and the Abergavennys, who have remained owners throughout. Is the reader confused? He or she should be.

The problems were compounded by much (but not all) of the developed land of Tunbridge Wells being in Tonbridge Parish, which therefore took the lead as the principal parish in the civil administration of the area, and this caused resentment among the others. This became a much bigger problem in the 19th century when the population of the sibling, Tunbridge Wells, rapidly outstripped that of its 'legal' parent, the oligarchic Tonbridge Parish Vestry,[3] and the inhabitants of Tunbridge Wells understandably resented being 'ruled' and dictated to, by a much smaller 'authority'[4].

The problem was partially resolved in 1835 when, as a result of considerable lobbying, the Tunbridge Wells Improvement Act was passed in Parliament, which appointed a Local Board of Improvement Commissioners (eventually to be 24 in number), who were not elected but were men of property, who would be responsible for 'lighting, watching (i.e. policing), cleansing, regulating and otherwise improving the town of Tunbridge Wells...and for regulating the supply of water and establishing a market within the said town'.

The infrastructure of the growing town began to fit together: a Police Station was established in Calverley Market; it was resolved that the streets should be lit by gas and a Gas Company was formed in 1843; the Fire Brigade was inaugurated in 1845; a Municipal Water Supply Company was formed in 1864, with a great deal of difficulty, to merge the several water supplies in the town; the General Hospital was moved and rebuilt in 1869; the Eye and Ear Hospital was established in 1878.

The Commissioners, in theory elected democratically, were in fact to become a self-perpetuating oligarchy kept in office by a small and elite

---

[3] The Tonbridge Parish Vestry was replaced as the local authority in 1871 by a Local Board of Commissioners, similar to that introduced in Tunbridge Wells in 1835, and in their turn, they were replaced in 1895 by an Urban District Council (UDC).
[4] The population of Tonbridge was estimated as 3,400 in 1801, 4,228 in 1841, and despite the coming of the railway in 1842, had only reached 12,736 by 1901.

electorate of only 200-300, most of whom did not bother to vote[5]. By the time the population of Tunbridge Wells had grown to over 24,000 in 1881, there was considerable demand for wider and more democratic representation as well as for incorporation as a borough.

This was strongly opposed by the incumbent Commissioners, led by John Stone-Wigg, the Chairman of the Local Board, until they discovered in 1888 that the new Local Government Act about to be introduced, would establish a two-tier system dividing powers between incorporated boroughs and county councils; and this would leave the Commissioners 'out in the cold'. So the Board had an immediate volte-face, which reveals their motivation, and they petitioned immediately for incorporation as a borough, which was granted on 16th January 1889.

John Stone-Wigg

Some 16 of the 24 Commissioners immediately became Aldermen and Councillors and the Chairman of the Board became the town's first Mayor. So in reality, there was little change except in name and the 'Old Guard' was still in effective control. Their autocratic attitude to, and complacent behaviour about, the government of the town would not change significantly with the creation of the independent Metropolitan Borough of Tunbridge Wells.

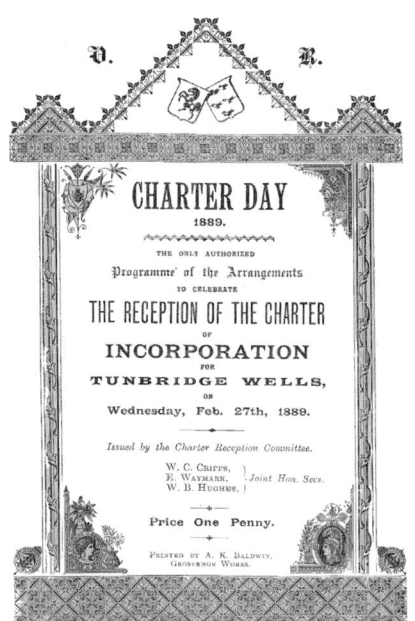

The Borough of Tunbridge Wells

The Incorporation of the Borough in 1889 did however give Tunbridge Wells more independence – not only from what had been the diminishing residual control of Tonbridge Parish, but also from the unspoken yet real power of its noble landlords. While it may have reduced their influence, it does not however seem to have reduced the deference which it had traditionally given to these noble landlords.

The new Borough followed broadly the

Official 4-page Programme for Charter Day. Price: 1d

---

[5] Those entitled to vote had a varying number of votes. For example, the Marquess of Abergavenny had 6 votes as an owner, 4 as a ratepayer; Henry Hollamby of 17 Frant Road had 4 and 2, but William Delves had only 2 as a ratepayer. Such was democracy.

boundaries laid down by the 1835 Improvement Act and so, while Rusthall was included, Southborough and Pembury were not, as they were still physically separated from Tunbridge Wells by farmland. It had four Wards, then named practically if somewhat prosaically North, South, East and West. Its Council consisted of 32 members: a Mayor, who did not have to be an Alderman or Councillor and who was elected annually; eight Aldermen, elected for six years; and 24 Councillors, eight of whom retired each year.

The Borough also had its own Bench, of some 10 members, which was largely made up of Aldermen of the Borough and the Mayor was usually its Chairman. It worked closely with the Town Council, to give legal endorsement to decisions (usually to do with licensing) made by the Town Council.

Because of its location, Tunbridge Wells came under the jurisdiction of three Benches – Kent, Sussex and Borough. The Kent Justices of the Peace met at 11 am on alternate Fridays in the Town Hall; the Sussex Petty Sessions were held at 11 am on the second and fourth Tuesdays of each month; and the Borough magistrates met at 11 am every Monday, although they could meet every day if necessary, for the purpose of summary jurisdiction. By comparison, the Town Council met monthly. All this required a good deal of juggling of issues and dates, but the good juggler could soon learn to control the situation.

First Reading of Town Charter by Town Clerk

There was much euphoria in the town at the time of the Incorporation. Large crowds greeted the arrival of the Charter from London by special train. It then processed with marching bands to the old Town Hall in Calverley Road where the first public reading of the Charter was made outside the Town Hall by the new Town Clerk, William Charles Cripps, who had been the Clerk to the Local Board of Commissioners since 1887. To the general public, it seemed that a new era was opening for Tunbridge Wells but in many respects, it was 'Plus ça change, plus c'est la même chose'.

When one looks back in retrospect at the period after Incorporation, there seems to have been a very definite vigour and entrepreneurial drive in the town and it is easy to attribute this to the stimulus of the Charter. Such an interpretation may not be entirely correct. There were indeed some new men coming forward with progressive ideas, more forward policies were being adopted and everyone took pride in the new borough, but the Old Guard was still very much in control. A more likely explanation is that this vigour was the result of what had been going on before the Charter, and that was the cause of what followed after.

It should also be recognised that there was a mood of confidence and initiative throughout Britain in the 1880s and 1890s. Britain felt itself to be on top of the world, with an Empire with a fifth of the world's population and with its commercial and industrial success. Tunbridge Wells would be no exception to this mood, despite or maybe because of, the bias in its population profile to older age groups and women.

Tunbridge Wells demonstrated this pro-active and progressive attitude in a number of ways. In 1890, the Council was one of the first Councils to raise money for improvements by issuing £126,000 of Corporation Stock. In 1894, it sought to solve the perennial water shortage, by successfully sinking deep-bore wells at Pembury. In 1895, it set up its own electricity monopoly, building a power station by Grosvenor Bridge, supplying electricity for both street lighting and dwellings. In the same year, the Nevill Cricket, Football and Athletic Company was formed to create the Nevill Ground; the Council bought the land on which today's Civic Centre and Adult Education Centre are built; and the very first Motor Show in the United Kingdom was held on what was then the Agricultural Showground, but is now the Showfields housing estate.

Sir David Salomons, Bt.

A major contributor to these developments was Tunbridge Wells' third Mayor, Sir David Salomons, Bt., who lived at Broomhill (now Salomons) and was a noted engineer, electrician, photographer, pioneer of horseless carriages and philanthropist. He was not an Alderman or Councillor, but was invited by the Council to be its Mayor for 1894-5, displacing (temporarily) the Alderman who expected to be elected. He had a major impact on both Council and inhabitants and his year of office was described by the *Courier* as an 'Annus Mirabilis'. His experience, possibly of the Old Guard, was such that he refused a second term of office.

Tunbridge Wells however continued to innovate. In 1897, the company was formed which would open the Opera House in 1902, and in 1901, the

Council opened the first *municipal* telephone exchange in England with 500 subscribers. This proved to be problematic with competition from a private company, the National Telephone Company, and the Council found that they had burnt their fingers. Opposition also came from ratepayers who could not understand why the Council should practice municipal trading, which led to the Council becoming much more cautious in its approach to municipal developments. It also led to the establishment of the Ratepayers' League which would play an active part in Council activities and elections up to the First World War. However it is indicative of something – Complacency? Indifference? Lack of Issues? Or the control of the Old Guard? – that none of the eight elections for Council in 1914 were contested.

Chief Constable Prior

The Town also had in 1914 a police force of 59 – a Chief Constable, two Inspectors, seven Sergeants and 49 constables – and no less than two Fire Brigades – a paid one of 28 men, which consisted of a Captain, a Second Officer, a Superintendent, two Engineers and 23 men; and a Volunteer Fire Brigade of 17 – three Officers, 12 men and two messengers. In an interesting example of control, the Chief Constable was also in command of both Fire Brigades.

Political Parties

One of the fears about the incorporation of Tunbridge Wells as a Borough was that it would bring national party politics into the local government of Tunbridge Wells. In fact, although party politics did enter Tunbridge Wells Council before the First World War, it did not really take over local government until after the War and that situation was also true for most of Britain. Until then, candidates came from local organisations such as the Ratepayers' League (formed in 1902), the Tunbridge Wells Tradesmen's Association (established in 1858), or from groupings of individuals who might not be given a formal name or title except perhaps 'Independent', but who could be broadly categorised on the political spectrum as 'progressive', or 'moderate/conservative', or (dreaded word!) 'socialist'. This last category would however remain virtually unknown in Tunbridge Wells for some time to come. The politics of these 'Independents' was generally well-recognised and understood in a community, where it would be widely-known that Alderman Col. Sladen was also the Chairman of the Tunbridge Wells Conservative Association and Alderman William Delves its Vice-Chairman, even if they did call themselves 'Independents'.

Religion
Religion was probably the greatest influence of all in the Tunbridge Wells of the 19th and early 20th centuries and it was predominantly at the Low Church / Nonconformist /Fundamental end of the spectrum of religious belief and practice. What is so surprising is the complete reversal of moral attitude and behaviour in Tunbridge Wells between the 17th / 18th century and the 19th. The Low Church/Nonconformist presence and influence seems to have been there since the earliest times, despite the 'town's' Royalist and Court associations, witness the somewhat Biblical location names of Mount Ephraim, Mount Sion and Mount Pleasant, but it was only with the Evangelical Revival[6] which began *within* the Anglican Church in the last third of the 18th century, that it began to take hold of the town. By 1900, Tunbridge Wells had had 28 places of worship - 10 Anglican churches, with seating for over 8,800; 17 Nonconformist chapels with seating for over 5,000; and just one Catholic Church with seating for 300.

Canon Edward Hoare

A prime influence on the religious life and morasl tone of the town was the Rev. (later Canon) Edward Hoare who came to Tunbridge Wells in 1853 and stayed active in his ministry until his death at the age of 82 in 1894. The Hoare family were Quakers and City Bankers; and Edward's aunt was Elizabeth Fry, the Quaker prison reformer. He and his family were received into the Anglican Church and it is somewhat surprising, in view of the Quaker tradition of tolerance, that Canon Hoare was so aggressively adverse to any religious beliefs other than his own Evangelical ones.

Royal Tunbridge Wells
English towns with a Royal prefix or a Regis suffix are few in number and the origin of, or reason for their prefix/suffix can be obscure. Lyme Regis became so through a Royal Charter of King Edward I in 1284; Leamington became Royal and a Spa in 1838 and the only connection seems to be that Victoria, when a Princess, visited in 1830; and Bognor seems to have become Regis after King George V recuperated nearby in 1929 and there are a number of well-known, if apocryphal, stories about that.

Tunbridge Wells' acquisition of its Royal title in 1909 is slightly better documented. Trade in Tunbridge Wells, as represented by the powerful

---

[6] John Wesley, the founder of Methodism, was a major inspiration in the Evangelical Movement or Revival, and while he and his followers eventually left the Anglican Church, many with similar views stayed within the Established Church. John Wesley and George Whitefield preached on a number of occasions in Tunbridge Wells.

Tradesmen's Association, was concerned about a perceived fall in the number of visitors and the possibility of advertising the town was raised in 1908. As a result, the Tunbridge Wells Advertising Association was formed in July 1908 with Albert Dennis, a director of Waymark, the drapers of Calverley Road, as Chairman. The Association was very active from the start, which alarmed some of the residents who had to be reassured that 'nothing will be done which may introduce any undesirable element in the shape of holiday trippers'.

Mr. H. M. Caley.

Early in 1909, the Association came up with the idea of renaming the town because they felt that many people were not sure where Tunbridge Wells was – the first name was confused with Tonbridge and the second with a cathedral city in the West Country – and they felt not enough had been made of the town's association with Royalty since its foundation. So they devised a new name – Royal Kentish Spa – which had, they felt, all the right associations and they persuaded the Mayor, Alderman Herbert Murkin Caley, to petition the King and the Home Secretary on 10th. February 1909 to be allowed to use it.

The reaction of the Home Office was very negative but that of the King was surprisingly more accommodating. The King's Private Secretary, Lord Knollys, wrote to the Home Office that 'owing to the historical associations of Tunbridge Wells,...and... the fact that Queen Victoria visited the town in her youth, the King thinks that the Spa might be allowed to have the prefix of 'Royal'' but it was to be called Royal Tunbridge Wells Spa and not Royal Kentish Spa, since half the town was in any case in Sussex. The Home Secretary pointed out that the use of Wells and Spa was tautological and so the King agreed to The Royal Tunbridge Wells, which decision was conveyed to the Mayor on 1st April 1909, less than two months after the submission of the application. It seems possible that the Mayor's petition had been made without the formal blessing of, or discussion within the Council, since he was asked to confirm that his application had the approval of the Town Council and the Town Council then passed a retrospective motion to this effect on 7th April.

The reaction of the town to this singular honour was relatively muted. *The Courier* and *The Advertiser* welcomed it without much enthusiasm and the public did not seem particularly impressed. Perhaps it was all too sudden, too commercial in its application and presentation, and was seen to be as the result of manipulation and therefore was faintly unscrupulous? To this day, there seems to be a certain detachment or reservation among most of the inhabitants of the town about their Royal prefix and the subject is generally kept at arm's length.

Population
The 1911 Census recorded a population for the Borough of 35,697 - 21,147 (or 60%) female and 14,550 (or 40%) male - and a total of 7,955 families. Some 33% of these families live in four rooms or less - 191 (2.4%) lived in just one room, 396 (5%) in two, 534 (7%) in three and 1,527 (19%) in four. (Comparative data from the 1911, 1921 and 1931 Censuses for England & Wales, the County of Kent and Royal Tunbridge Wells, will be found in Appendix 2.)

Population Profile
Tunbridge Wells has been and always will be different from everywhere else. Typical is not an adjective which can be used to describe it and a significant factor in 1914 was the nature of its population.

First, it had a considerably disproportionate number of women – 60% of its population were women, compared with the National and the Kent county average of 51%. If it had had a similar proportion to the National and Kent figure, there would have been approximately 3,170 fewer women in Tunbridge Wells.

Second, largely as a result of this first factor, it also had a disproportionate number of unmarried women – 56% of women compared with the National and Kent county average of 46-47%.

These two factors were linked strongly with a third which was, that it had a disproportionate number of women who worked – 40% of females in Tunbridge Wells over the age of 10 worked, compared with 33% nationally and 29% in the County of Kent.

The explanation of these differences is relatively straightforward. Tunbridge Wells was an affluent town which appealed particularly to retired people (who were 19% of the population of Tunbridge Wells, compared with 16% in England & Wales) and it had a slightly higher proportion (about 10% more) of widows. Clearly the climate and ambience of Tunbridge Wells suited retired people and encouraged longevity. It is entirely understandable that its affluence would support more servants (and principally indoor servants, who would be mainly female, and mostly unmarried). Hence an excess of about 1,250 unmarried women in Tunbridge Wells compared with the National and Kent averages.

Employment

Much of the employment in the town was associated with maintaining the life-style of its inhabitants and its visitors. The 1911 Census shows 81% of men and 40% of women in employment and there are considerable differences between the types and nature of employment for the sexes.

The largest employment for men was in Building & Construction[7] with 1,324; followed by Food, Tobacco, Food & Lodging in second place with 1,280; and 630 defined as Professional in third, which category interestingly did not include in those days anyone employed in Accountancy, Banking or Insurance (*directly* dealing with money was not then sufficiently 'respectable' to be regarded as 'Professional').

The fourth place was taken by 'Domestic Outdoor Service' i.e. Gardeners, Coachmen, Grooms, Chauffeurs, and Gamekeepers, with 610, but if one combines them with Domestic Indoor Service i.e. Butlers, Footmen and 'Boys', with 299, then *Male* Domestic Service at 909 takes third place. Fifth overall place was taken by those 'working on the roads' i.e. everyone from engineers, workmen to a new category – bus conductors – with 595, but if one combines this figure with the 246 working on the railways and the 360 working as porters and messengers together with another 66 working in travel-related roles, then those involved in travel in one form or another, take second place with 1,267 employees, ahead of *male* Domestic Service. It is worth noting that Agriculture with 517 employed, is only the sixth largest individual category in what could be regarded as an agricultural region.

The employment roles of women in Tunbridge Wells were very different from those of their menfolk and were essentially domestic (i.e. concerned with the family and home). The largest single category of employment was at 3,357, Domestic Indoor Service i.e. as Housekeepers, Cooks, and Maids and this was numerically *more than double* the largest single category of employment for men. If different, but similar work-roles such as laundry worker (455), hotel staff (388), charwoman (154) and other domestic categories (87) are added, then this 'service' role increased to 4,441, which was 61% of all female employment in Tunbridge Wells.

The second overall Census category for women was termed 'Professional', nominally but not the same as it male counterpart, and totalled 645. These included 273 teachers, 261 midwives and nurses and 111 defined as 'literary, scientific and political', whose exact role is not immediately apparent today. Depending on how categories are grouped, there is

---

[7] There were 20 broad categories for employment in the 1911 Census, numbered from I to XX, each with several subdivisions. They were slightly reorganised in subsequent Censii, to meet the changing needs of statistical analysis.

another group which could claim to be the second largest for women. That is what might be termed today Fashion & Furnishing – some 513 dressmakers[8], 247 working in drapery, 97 milliners, and 61 staymakers, shirtmakers and seamstresses, making a total of 918 or 13% of the female workforce. So about 75% of employed women were in jobs which were paid extensions of what could be regarded as their domestic role.

Tourism

What we now call tourism was the original *raison d'être* of Tunbridge Wells and the economy of Tunbridge Wells was still based on it at the beginning of the 20th century. The nature of its tourism had however changed and it had lost some of its popularity and its market to other resorts, particularly seaside resorts, in the 19th century. Nonetheless, visitors to Tunbridge Wells still came to stay for long periods – a week or a fortnight was quite usual, unlike today when 97% of visitors are day-visitors.

Tourism still played a very important part in the town's economy – 16 Hotels were listed in the Directories for 1881, and 11 in 1911. In 1917 during the middle of the War, there would still be 11, as well as many boarding houses. The town was not however totally reliant on tourism. It was in the heart of 'the Garden of Kent' which for centuries had been a major provider of fruit and vegetables to the growing metropolis of London. The surrounding agricultural economy, based particularly on hops and fruit, provided a subsidiary and alternative, if somewhat less interesting, source of income.

The position of women in the town

The position of women in Tunbridge Wells before the First World War was very much the same as it was elsewhere in the United Kingdom. Four Acts of Parliament in 1857, 1870, 1882 and 1893 had been needed to give married women the same rights as unmarried women in terms of their earnings and income, property and inheritance. Women who were property *owners* were first given the right to vote in 1894 but only in Municipal elections. Women were still second-class citizens insofar as they did not have the right to vote in National elections.

In the 1890-1900s, there was a growing movement, both passive and active, for female suffrage. Today, historians distinguish between them by calling the passive movement suffragist and the active movement suffragette. Tunbridge Wells certainly had its suffragist members and

---

[8] 'Dressmaker' was often a euphemism in Census returns to describe unmarried daughters, who had no employment but nonetheless could earn a little as 'freelance' dressmakers for friends and neighbours.

may have had suffragette members as well. (See Chapter 7 for a detailed discussion of this subject).

Very early in the morning of Friday 13th April 1913, the Cricket Pavilion at the Nevill Ground was burnt down. It would seem that everybody at the time accepted that the fire was deliberate and was caused by militant suffragettes, largely on the grounds that suffragette literature was found scattered nearby. The suffragettes were referred to as 'these wild women' and the Mayor, Cllr. James Silcock, who lived in Warwick Park only about 200 yards from the Nevill Ground, said that Tunbridge Wells was 'a hotbed of militants'. A public protest meeting was held in the Great Hall, and was addressed by Sir Arthur Conan Doyle, who had an audience of over 1,500 people. The meeting had 'frequent interruptions from a posse of young ladies' who were booed and hustled, had eggs 'in a somewhat advanced state of decadence' thrown at them and had their hats pulled off and clothes torn.

The burnt-out stands

The Courier described all this as 'just horseplay', even though the police had to intervene and rescue the 'young ladies' and take them to the Police Station 'for their own safety'. No one was ever arrested for the 'crime' and a more objective (or would it be more cynical) 21st century view could be that it was the work of an *agent provocateur* seeking to discredit the suffragette movement.

Education

Local Education Authorities (LEAs) were established by the Education Act of 1902 and ended the role and rule of locally elected school boards which had until then controlled all schools, except those run by the Church of England or the Catholic Church. The LEAs introduced State funding of elementary schools through national and local taxation. The Tunbridge Wells Borough Education Committee consisted of 14 Councillors/Aldermen and 6 lay members, of whom two were clergymen and two women.

Tunbridge Wells in 1914 had some 19 Public Elementary Schools with a capacity for 5,225 pupils, mainly provided and run by the Church of England and other religious organisations. Actual attendance in the school year 1913-14 was an average of 4,673. Most of the Public

WILLIAM STAMFORD, Esq. L.R.C.P., M.R.C.S., F.R.I.P.H.

Elementary Schools educated children up to the age of 14, although compulsory education was then only until the age of 11.[9]

Secondary education for boys was provided by the Skinners' School, which had opened in St. John's Road, Tunbridge Wells in 1887 with 52 pupils, following a 17-year struggle between the residents of Tunbridge Wells and Tonbridge about the siting of the new School. Tunbridge Wells had also had Rosehill School in Romanoff House on the London Road since 1832. It was a fee-paying preparatory school for boys up to the age of 13.[10]

Secondary education for girls started in 1883 when at the request of Francis Molyneux, the Girls' Public Day School Trust opened the Tunbridge Wells High School for Girls at Fairlawn in Mount Sion.[11] It was followed by the Tunbridge Wells Grammar School for Girls which was founded in 1905.

Children's health also came under the control of Local Authority School Medical Officers. All schools were inspected at least once a year and all children were inspected at least twice – on entry to the school and at the age of 12-13. School inspections in Tunbridge Wells in 1914 reported that 3% of children were infected with vermin and 20% with nits.

Health and Health Care

The Annual Reports of the Medical Officer of Health for the Borough from 1912 – 1920 are a mine of information, not only about vital statistics and disease, but also about the weather (hours of sunshine, inches of rain, high and low temperatures), the water supply, sanitation, food contamination, the schools and the well-being of children. They also show conflict between the Medical Officer of Health (who was also the School Medical Officer) and the Health Committee of the Council, which consisted of eight male Aldermen and Councillors.

The Medical Officer of Health (MOH) for thirty years from 1881 to September 1911 had been William Stamford, Esq., LRCP, MRCS,

---

[9] The *compulsory* education age was originally 10 in 1880, increased to 11 in 1893, 12 in 1921, 14 in 1931, 15 in 1944 and 16 in 1973.
[10] One of it's most famous pupils was Robert Baden-Powell, the founder of the Boy Scouts, who attended from 1868.
[11] The School premises moved in 1902 to Cambridge House in Camden Park (later Cambridge Gardens). The School was closed in 1945.

FRIPH.[12] Obviously of the Old School and probably of the Old Guard. he was succeeded, after a temporary filling of the post by Dr. John Rix[13], by a much younger man, Dr. Edward Burnet, BA, MB, ChB, BSc (PH) who took over in 1912. He was clearly 'a new broom', being much more progressive in medical and social welfare matters than his predecessor and he had a staff of nine.

From Dr. Burnet's first report for 1912, it is clear that he was appalled by some of the health and social welfare conditions in the Borough and his report is outspoken, as far as the good manners of those times allowed. His report offended the Health Committee, whom he accused of thinking that 'the Public Health administration of the Borough was now an expensive luxury'. He had come to the conclusion that in Tunbridge Wells 'the only cottages available for the labouring class have preposterously high rents compared with the total income of the tenants' and many of 'these cottages were not fit to house cattle in.... When so large a proportion of a worker's income is absorbed in rent, the children are either underfed and badly clothed, or the earnings have to be supplemented by so-called charity. If social conditions in Tunbridge Wells are such that labourers can only earn from 18s. to 21s. a week, good habitable homes should be provided at rents not exceeding 3sd. to 3s.6d.' He goes on to say 'the fact that both members of the Health Committee and officials of the Council are themselves financially interested in the class of property which it is frequently the duty of the Medical Officer of Health to condemn, is sufficient to account for much of the bitterness which has been exhibited on many occasions.'

At a distance of over 100 years, it is somewhat difficult to assess the rights and wrongs of the conflict, particularly since pages 9-10 of the official copy of the 1912 Report have been *literally* torn out. When? Why? And by whom? But the writer must confess that he thinks he is on Dr. Burnet's side.

Whatever the rights or wrongs, it would seem that the Health Committee decided to sack him and his second and last Annual Report (for 1913) and his covering letter submitting this report is very outspoken, ending with a paragraph which reads "I hope to see the time when Public Health officials will be servants of the State, solely responsible to the Central Authority, and independent of the parochial pettiness which has been characteristic of the attitude of some of those, under whom it has been my misfortune to serve in the Borough of Tunbridge Wells." Strong words

---

[12] William Stamford ostensibly retired in 1911 on the grounds of ill-health, but Kelly's Directory records him as being still in private practice in 1918.
[13] John Rix, who was the son of a Tunbridge Wells medical practitioner, joined the RAMC in April 1915 and would be killed in action on 5th July 1916.

indeed. What is not known is whether this was printed because the Borough Council could not prevent it, or whether the Council generously allowed Dr. Burnet to have his say.

He was succeeded by Dr. Frederick Linton, MA, MB, ChB, DPH, who would be called up into the RAMC in 1916, but who would return as Medical Officer of Health after the War. Dr. Linton in the covering letter to his first report referred to important but unspecified changes in the structure and staffing of his department, which had clearly been created by Burnet's criticisms.

Tunbridge Wells, like everywhere else, suffered at this time from diseases which are now relatively rare, or have even died out.

Tuberculosis (TB) was a constant presence and deaths from it in Tunbridge Wells fluctuated between 27-50 every year between 1900 - 1914. Diphtheria was also prevalent. There seem to have been epidemics of diptheria, lasting about 3-5 years, every 10-15 years, with cases fluctuating between 67- 278 each year, but with the annual death rate from it much lower at between 1- 8, although it peaked at 31 in 1896 when there were 278 cases. Other frequent 'epidemic' diseases were scarlet fever and whooping cough. Tunbridge Wells was however quite a healthy place – it was after all, a spa, was it not? – and life expectancy was above the national average. About a fifth (about 100 a year) of all deaths were at the age of 80 or over and about a half of all deaths were above the age of 64.

To cope with the health needs of its population of 36,000, Tunbridge Wells had five local hospitals:

- The General Hospital, founded in 1842, in Grosvenor Road on the island site where the Post Office now is, and opposite to what is now Tesco's, but which was then the site of St. Augustine's Catholic Church. In 1914, it had 71 beds and treated 735 In-patients and 6,379 Out-patients, with a total of 28,794 Attendances by them.
- The Homeopathic Hospital, founded in 1902 from an amalgamation of Dispensaries, in Church Road. It treated 91 In-patients in 1914, with 6,066 attendances by Out-patients.
- The Eye and Ear Hospital, founded in 1878 in the Pantiles, but was situated since 1900 in Mount Sion. It was essentially for Out-Patients, but nonetheless had 20 beds and had treated 31 In-patients and 2,346 Out-patients in 1914.
- The Fever Hospital, (also called the Isolation Hospital and the Sanatorium) in Benhall Mill Road, next door to what was then

called the Frant Forest Cemetery, but is now known as Hawkenbury Cemetery. It received mainly Diphtheria and Scarlet Fever patients [14] and had a 57-bed capacity.
- There was also just outside the Royal Borough boundary the Sandhill Infirmary (later to be called Pembury Hospital), which was a hospital with about 100 beds, which was part of the Pembury Workhouse and used then almost exclusively by the inmates of the Workhouse[15]. It still exists today as the site of the new Tunbridge Wells Hospital[16].

Besides the hospitals, Tunbridge Wells in 1914 had a number of other support services: the Provident Dispensary at 106, Upper Grosvenor Road, had 2,937 members on its books; the District Nursing Association at Holly Lodge, Crescent Road, made 16,493 visits to patients in their homes; and the Tunbridge Wells branch of the Royal Surgical Aid Society, at 66 Grove Hill Road, relieved 1,126 patients and supplied 1,426 appliances.

Although the beginnings of today's Social Services and Benefits had started with the introduction of Old Age Pensions in 1906, there was still a very great need to care for the poor, the homeless and the indigent, and in 1914, the Tonbridge Union, which still had its Workhouse at Pembury, incurred costs of £1,860-12s-6d for what was then called Outdoor Relief.

Public Buildings, Cinemas and Banks
Tunbridge Wells had a number of public buildings with a large capacity for events and meetings. The largest was the Opera House, opened in 1902, which could seat 1,200, followed by the Pump Room in the Pantiles which could hold 800 and the Great Hall in Mount Pleasant which could seat 600-700.

Besides these, the town would have four cinemas by 1914, but the cinema was possibly a little slow in coming to Tunbridge Wells. It first reached the town in 1909, a good 10-13 years after it had reached

---

[14] The site of the Fever Hospital is now occupied by residential housing.
[15] The Pembury Workhouse had been built in 1836 at Sand Hill, Pembury, with a capacity for 400 inmates, as the Workhouse for the Tonbridge Union. The Union had been created by the Poor Law Amendment Act of 1834 which merged individual parish Poor Law administration into 'Unions' of about ten parishes. Hence the Tonbridge Union of which Tunbridge Wells was part. Workhouse inmates, by their nature, were understandably more prone to illness and disease and it was soon realised that a separate building for the sick and ill was required and a dedicated infirmary building was built in 1856, with beds for 55. This was expanded in 1890-3 with the building of four new blocks – three for the sick, and one for the aged and infirm – and it was given a new name – the Sandhill Infirmary – but it was still part of the Workhouse, which had 533 inmates in the 1911 Census, and would eventually close in 1930.
[16] Opened with 512 beds in 2011 at a cost of £226 million.

London. It is for the reader to judge whether this delay was because the population was initially thought to be not large enough for the commercial investment, or whether cinema with its strong early associations with the Music Hall, was considered too down-market for upper-class Tunbridge Wells.

The earliest cinemas were in Music Halls and converted halls and shops. Purpose-built cinemas did not start to arrive until the end of the first decade of the century and would not actually arrive in Tunbridge Wells until 1934. Camden Hall in Camden Road was situated between Calverley Road and Garden Street[17] and existed before it became Tonbridge Wells's first cinema in 1909. It was far from purpose-built, but it was sufficiently successful for it to be altered in 1910, by incorporating an adjacent building into what would be referred to, from then on, as a 'bijou theatre' called the Camden Electric Theatre. It had 300 tip-up seats and would survive until 1925.

The Picture Palace in Camden Road was the Town's second cinema and opened at 97, Camden Road in 1912 in a converted premise and would survive until 1922. It was originally called Ambrose Adams' Picture Palace.

The third cinema was relatively short-lived. Called the Cinema de Luxe, it opened in August 1913 in the building in Culverden Down, which had been opened as an Ice Skating Rink in 1909. The building reverted to being an Ice Skating Rink during the First World War, but closed in 1921.

The fourth and longest-lasting cinema was the Kosmos Kinema at 40-42 Calverley Road. Until 1912, it had been the Calverley Penny Bazaar and then it became a fishmonger's shop for a short time, but in February 1914, it became the Kosmos, or 'Kozzy' as it was familiarly known. It remained in operation until February 1960 – a life of some 46 years.

The Kosmos Cinema, with its 13 staff

There can be no doubt that the belated arrival of cinemas in Tunbridge Wells would prove a boon during the First World War, when the Town had a regular influx of several thousand soldiers, who needed to be kept interested and amused and 'out of trouble'.

---

[17] On the site already mainly occupied by the Camden Hotel and the old Town Hall, which would be redeveloped by NPI in 1965 as Calverley House.

The town also had six banks – all except one were in Mount Pleasant Road, with some familiar and also not so familiar names: Barclays; Capital & Counties; Lloyds; London, County & Westminster; London, City & Midland; and Union of London & Smith's.

Rail Services

The coming of the railway to Tunbridge Wells in 1846 was a very significant factor in the growth of Tunbridge Wells in the 19th century. The original route via Redhill and Tonbridge was shortened by about 13 miles in 1866 to a new route via Sevenoaks and Tonbridge. Tunbridge Wells was then thought to be such an attractive prospect for the railways that two railway companies, the South Eastern Railway (SER) and the London, Brighton and South Coast Railway (LB&SCR), provided two separate railway stations for the town – the Central station which still exists; and the West or Brighton station, which was closed as recently as 1982. The journey time was reduced from its original duration of 2-2½ hours to just under 1 hour by the 1880's; and residents of Tunbridge Wells could then travel to four London Termini - Victoria, Charing Cross, Waterloo and Cannon Street – *without changing trains*. Today that number is down to three.

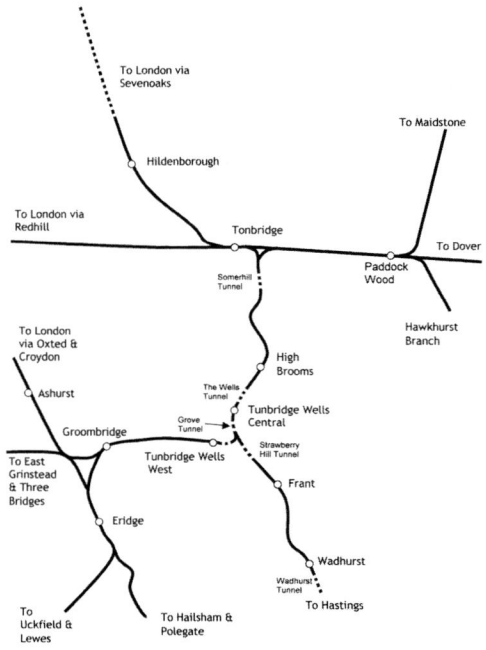

Newspapers

Tunbridge Wells has been served over time by many local newspapers – *The Kent and Sussex Courier, The Tunbridge Wells Advertiser, The Tunbridge Wells Gazette, Tunbridge Wells Society, the Argus, the Sussex Daily News, the Southern Weekly \News and the Tonbridge Free Press*. Only *The Courier* survives today, but one daily and three weekly newspapers were in circulation before and during the First World War.

The daily papers were the *Argus*, priced ½d, which had a morning and an evening edition and the *Sussex Daily News*, priced 1d, both of which were published by the Southern Publishing Co. of Vale Road, which also published the *Southern*

Weekly News on Saturdays, price 1d. The Southern Publishing Co. declared its publications to be 'Independent'.

The oldest newspaper was the *Tunbridge Wells Gazette*, first published in 1828 by Colbran. It was a weekly and was published on Thursdays at a price of 1d (1/240th of today's £). For a time, it was also known as the *Gazette and Fashionable Visitor*. Somewhat unusually, it declared itself to be not Independent, but Neutral. It was taken over by *The Courier* in 1892 and continued until 1939.

The *Tunbridge Wells Advertiser*, first published in 1881, was a weekly published on Fridays by the Tunbridge Wells Advertiser Co. of Grove Hill Road. It declared itself to be a Liberal paper.

The *Kent & Sussex Courier*, published on Fridays, was founded in 1872 with the financial support of the then 5th Earl (later 1st Marquess) of Abergavenny and as can be expected with such a backer, was a Conservative paper. It was a broadsheet newspaper, as were all newspapers before the arrival of the tabloid format. It was nearly always 8 pages in size and like most other newspapers, its format was standardised. The front page was always advertising, 1-2 other pages were also entirely advertising and the remaining pages carried advertising generally on the LH and RH borders, so 50-60% of the newspaper was advertising. It was a weekly newspaper but it did have two editions – on Friday morning and Friday afternoon, the latter being essentially an update on the Friday morning edition.

Reporting was very detailed in those days, was often a verbatim (short-hand) record of what was actually said at a Town Council Meeting, or the Magistrates' Court, or was a transcript of Minutes of a meeting, or an Annual Report. There was virtually no 'investigative' or 'on the spot' reporting – the *Courier* seems to have printed what it was given by others, probably without question. There was much reporting of the various Town Councils and the many Courts – the Tunbridge Wells County Bench, the Tunbridge Wells Borough Bench, the Tonbridge Petty Sessions, the Sevenoaks Petty Sessions, the Hurst Green Petty Sessions, the Cranbrook Police Court, and the Tunbridge Wells Bankruptcy Court – as well as regular reporting on the meetings of many local associations such as the Tunbridge Wells Tradesmen's Association, the Kent Farmers' Union, the Kent Hop Trade Association, the Kent Sheep Breeders' Association, the Kent County Temperance Crusade, which indicates the then current importance of these organisations to the business, if not the life, of the town. In the modern idiom, the newspaper was in many respects more announcements than reporting.

Postal and Communication Services

Since the introduction of the Penny Post by Rowland Hill in 1840, postal services had boomed, particularly because it was not only a monopoly but there were then no alternative means of communication. Before the First World War, Tunbridge Wells benefitted from at least four postal collections and three deliveries a day. The General Post Office (GPO)/Royal Mail was still the principal means of communication and it has often been said that one could send a letter locally in the morning through the postal services and receive a reply the same day by the same means. This was because opening hours were long and the collection and delivery frequent. The Tunbridge Wells Head Post Office, which moved from The Pantiles to much larger premises in Vale Road in 1895[18], was open from 7am to 10pm on weekdays and also 8-10am and 5-6pm on Sundays; and the 13 Sub-Post Offices spread around the town were open from 8am to 8pm on weekdays (with two of them at Calverley and Mount Ephraim open until 10pm) although none of the Sub-Post Offices were open on a Sunday.

Two other means of personal communication would develop in the late 19th century – telegrams and telephones. There had been a GPO Telegraph service, which sent and received telegrams, since 1870 and this was available at the Head Office 7 days a week and three Sub-Post Offices 6 days a week. The second means was the telephone which was first introduced in 1878, but which was relatively slow to take off and had not yet become the national and nationalised service which it later became[19].

Retailing and Shops

Shopping in Tunbridge Wells before the First World War was a very local affair. Few national chains of shops existed, and shops were nearly all owned and managed by local people. Shops were open for 5½ days a week – closed on Sundays and for the second half of the day on the statutory Early Closing Day, which in Tunbridge Wells was Wednesday. The two principal shopping streets were the High Street for the lower Pantiles end of the town and Calverley Road, at that time not pedestrianised, for the Calverley New Town end.

---

[18] Converted in 2001 into a development of 32 flats, called Post Office Square.

[19] The telephone service was initially run by private and mainly local companies, although national telephone companies soon formed. Indeed Tunbridge Wells Borough Council, displaying the entrepreneurial spirit of its early days of existence, was to be the first municipality in the United Kingdom to set up and run its own telephone service in 1901, but it ran into problems with competing companies and ratepayer opposition and had to dispose of it. All telephone services were effectively nationalised in 1912, when the National Telephone Company was taken over by the GPO.

Shops were also entirely counter shops – the idea of self-service shops was still many decades away – and each shop dealt only in one type of product. So there were few or no shops selling different categories of products. Even food shops, which are today 'one-stop shops', were still singular in the type of products they handled and grocers, bakers, butchers, fishmongers, greengrocers and dairies were quite separate shops and businesses.

However there were the very first signs of multiples and multi-category shops appearing and Tunbridge Wells was the home of one of the major founders of these. *Home & Colonial Stores* were a chain of grocers founded by Julius Drewe in 1883 and by 1903 it had 500 shops in Britain. When Julius Drewe married in 1890, he set up home in Culverden Castle, a mock castle built in the early 19th. century at Tunbridge Wells.[20]

Three similar companies which were direct competitors to Home & Colonial, were the International Tea Co., generally known as *International Stores*, which had been founded in 1878 and had two stores in Calverley Road and the High Street; *Maypole Dairy* which had a shop at 34 Calverley Road; and *Sainsbury's* in the Opera House Buildings. It is worth recording that the 1911 Kelly's Directory also lists the Marks & Spencer *bazaar* at 38 Calverley Road, next door to what would become the Kosmos Kinema in 1914.

The most dominant food retailer in Tunbridge Wells at this time was the Co-op – the chain of retail shops owned at least in theory by its customers, who were essentially the working classes[21]. In 1911 the Coop had eight branches in Tunbridge Wells and occupied three premises in Camden Road, two in Kensington St, and one each in Lower Green Road Rusthall, Silverdale Road and Tunnel Road.

In the context of the fragmented structure of the supply of food and drink, it is also worth recording[22] that there were then 16 Cowsheds, 10 Dairies and 51 shops selling milk; six Slaughter Houses, of which five were built before 1847; and 42 Bakeries, of which eleven were underground (presumably in basements).

Among the larger shops in Tunbridge Wells before the War were *R.W.Weekes*, a department store founded in 1854 and situated at 1-8

---

[20] He lived there nine years and then moved 'up the ladder' to Wadhurst Castle, six miles away and then subsequently to Castle Drogo on the edge of Dartmoor which he had designed and built by Sir Edwin Luytens.
[21] The Cooperative Movement had been founded in Rochdale in 1844 and had spread throughout Britain.
[22] Source: Medical Officer of Health's Report for 1914.

Mount Pleasant Road and 1-5 Grove Hill Road, opposite the Central Station[23], and also at 17-18 Vale Road and 99 & 101 Goods Station Road; *Waymark*, a family draper, founded in 1878 and situated on the corner which was 64-70 Mt. Pleasant Road and 2-4 Calverley Road, at what is now called Fiveways, but which was then familiarly known as Waymark's Corner; *S.E.Hayward*, ironmongers, who had six premises in Goods Station Road and another in Mount Pleasant Road; and *Sibthorpe's*, a milliner and costumier, at 10-12 Calverley Road.

The 1911 Kelly's Directory also lists 10 Laundries, 8 bespoke Tailors and 7 Undertakers in Tunbridge Wells.

Sports Clubs
Tunbridge Wells had a large number of Sports Clubs before the First World War, but they were essentially clubs for men:

Bowls: 2: Tunbridge Wells Bowling Club and Tunbridge Wells Grove Bowling Club. There were also public Bowling Greens at the Grosvenor Ground and on Rusthall Common.
Cricket: 3: Blue Mantle; Linden Park; and Tunbridge Wells.
Football: 1: Tunbridge Wells Football Club.
Golf: 3: The Tunbridge Wells Golf Club (9 holes); Nevill Golf Club (9 holes); and The Culverden Golf Club (18 holes).
Hockey: 1: Tunbridge Wells Ladies' Hockey Club.
Lawn Tennis   The Tunbridge Wells Cricket & Athletic Club.
& Croquet: 2: Tunbridge Wells Lawn Tennis & Croquet Club (Nevill Ground).
Swimming: 2 baths: one outdoor at Grosvenor Recreation Ground; one indoor at Monson Road.

Local Militia. Britain has not had territorial ambitions in Europe for over 600 years and as an island has always seen the Royal Navy as its first line of defence from foreign invasion. So, unlike Europe (and particularly France, Germany, Austria and Russia) which had had a system of compulsory Army conscription since the late 18th century, Britain did not have a system of military conscription until 1916. However Britain has always had a strong tradition of having military volunteers whose purpose was defence, not attack, and this stretches back to the time of the Napoleonic Wars, or even earlier. The volunteer system received a considerable boost about the time of the Boer War (1899-1902).

Often, regular regiments had volunteer battalions with regimental Companies being allocated to specific towns. In the case of Tunbridge Wells, these were the D and E Companies of the 1st Volunteer (later 4th)

---

[23] It is still on the same site, but was taken over by Hoopers in 1982.

Battalion, the Queen's Own Royal West Kent Regiment and they were headquartered at the Drill Hall in Victoria Road[24]. A second element in local militia was a number of volunteer yeomanry (i.e. cavalry) regiments, which were of their nature, essentially rural rather than urban units. The Imperial Sussex Yeomanry was raised by the Marquess of Abergavenny during the Boer War and a platoon was stationed at Eridge. There was also a volunteer squadron of the West Kent Yeomanry who drilled in the Corn Exchange in the Pantiles.

'C' Company, 1st. Mid-Kent Fencibles at Eridge Castle, May 1916

Tunbridge Wells also had "A" Company, 1st Battalion, Mid-Kent Regiment of Fencibles. The Fencibles (a name derived from Defencibles) had existed since the 18th century and were volunteer, not regular, soldiers, but generally commanded by Regular Army officers. Their only commitment was to defend England and they had no liability for overseas service.

Their role had been taken over by the Territorial Army (TA) which had been formed in 1908, but it would seem from the *Courier* reports that, despite this, there still existed 1st Bttn. Mid-Kent Volunteer Fencibles which had both Tunbridge Wells and Southborough Companies. It was still in existence in March 1916 when it would be inspected, all 450-men strong, on Mount Ephraim by the Mayor of Tunbridge Wells.

It is worth noting that while membership of the TA required no commitment or obligation to fight overseas, nonetheless many of them would be sent to Flanders in 1914 as part of the British Expeditionary Force (BEF).

---

[24] Now demolished and under the Royal Victoria Place shopping precinct.

CHRONOLOGY OF EVENTS 1914

The Great War (World War I) started as *essentially* a conflict between:

The Triple **Alliance** (Germany, Austria-Hungary and Italy) which had existed since 1882: however Italy was to withdraw and declare its neutrality early in August 1914;

and the Triple **Entente** (Russia, France and Britain), a relationship whose foundations were not nearly so long, or so deeply, rooted.

The conflict was based on deep-seated national ambitions, historical resentment and ethnic rivalries, and overweening arrogance, overconfidence and sheer bluff. No one thought that it would escalate as much or last as long as it did, but they had not understood that the nature of war, and particularly of its weapons and armaments, had changed irrevocably in the previous 30 years.

The assassination of the Archduke Franz Ferdinand was just the trigger, rather than the cause of the conflict.

1914

28th June	Archduke Franz Ferdinand, the heir to the Austro-Hungarian Empire, and his morganatic wife assassinated at Sarajevo, Serbia.
5th July	Kaiser Wilhelm II offers full support - a 'blank cheque' – to Austria-Hungary.
20-23rd July	French President Poincaré makes State Visit to St. Petersburg, Russia.
23rd July	Austria-Hungary issues ultimatum to Serbia.
28th July	Austria-Hungary declares war on Serbia. Russia orders 'partial' mobilisation of troops.
29th July	Austrian artillery bombards Belgrade, capital of Serbia. British Foreign Secretary Grey warns Germany that Britain cannot remain neutral in the event of war and proposes mediation.
30th July	Both Russia and Austria order general mobilisation of troops Germany issues ultimata to both Russia and France.
1st August	Germany orders general mobilisation of troops and declares war on Russia. France orders general mobilisation of troops.
2nd August	Germany issues ultimatum to Belgium, demanding unopposed passage through Belgium to the French border for German troops.

3rd August	Germany declares war on France. Italy declares its neutrality. August Bank Holiday Monday in the United Kingdom.
4th August	German troops cross the Belgian frontier. Britain issues ultimatum which expired unanswered at midnight (11 pm. London time).
7th August	Liege occupied by German forces.
16th August	Last forts of Liege captured.
17th August	Belgian Government transferred from Brussels to Antwerp.
20th August	Brussels captured by Germans.
23rd August	British Expeditionary Force (BEF) under command of Field-Marshal French fights its first action at Mons.
25th August	Namur captured by Germans.
26th August	BEF fight at Le Cateau. Russian army defeated at Tannenburg and the Masurian Lakes. Leuven (Louvain) sacked by German troops.
28th August	Royal Navy win Battle of Heligoland Bight.
6th September	Battle of the Marne starts.
28th September	Mechelin (Malines) captured by Germans.
2nd October	Dendermonde (Termonde) captured by Germans.
7th October	Belgian Government transferred from Antwerp to Ostend
9th October	Antwerp captured by Germans.
12th October	Flanders campaign begins, leading to First Battle of Ypres from 20th October. Ghent occupied by Germans.
13th October	Belgian Government set up at Le Havre.
14th October	Bruges occupied by Germans.
15th October	Zeebrugge and Ostend occupied by Germans.
1st November	Russia declares war on the Ottoman Empire.
6th November	France and the United Kingdom declare war on the Ottoman Empire.
16th December	Shelling of Scarborough, Hartlepool and Whitby by German Navy – 137 dead, 592 wounded.

CHAPTER 2
1914 – THE EARLY DAYS
by Stephen Bates

For all anyone knew, the summer season of 1914 in Tunbridge Wells was passing much as it did every year. The town was a tourist destination (and saw itself very much as that) and the weather was perfect: long, hot and sunny days and a third less rainfall than usual. So the priorities locally on the late June weekend that a Hapsburg archduke and his wife were assassinated more than a thousand miles away in the Balkans, were entirely concerned with pleasure.

It had been Tunbridge Wells Cricket Week and the Blue Mantles had been playing the Devon Dumplings at the Nevill Ground. The local Suffragists – the non-militant arm of the votes for women movement – had held a garden party and the staff outing of the Autocar Services Company to Brighton that Saturday had also deserved a lengthy report in the *Courier*. The Skinners' School sports day also had a long column, complete with full results and congratulations for T. Armstrong who had run the quarter mile in 55 seconds, though that was somewhat undermined by the newspaper's report that the time keeper's stop watch had failed, so it was impossible to time any remaining events accurately. The National Federation of Grocers had held their Annual Conference in the Great Hall that week, with a garden party at the Spa Hotel at which they had been entertained by the band of the Duke of Cornwall's Light Infantry and "a clever London company called the Hilarities" – that all took up five columns of type - and Ginnetts' Royal Circus on the Common was advertising that it would be firing its beautiful cannon queen from a roaring cannon at every performance: *"the most daring act ever presented…an amazing aggregation of English and Continental artistes."*

As part of its promotional drive, the town had just entertained a group of German, French and Belgian newspaper editors to advertise its attractions as a European tourism destination. There had been a banquet for them and a motor tour of the area, a speech of welcome by the mayor and, best of all, *"the weather quite rivalled the Midi."* A band had serenaded them with the Marseillaise to make them feel at home. When even Prime Minister Asquith was telling friends there would be no war and, if there was, there was no reason for Britain to get involved, why should anyone else worry?

The first distant rumblings of potential conflict took a month to penetrate the local paper's tightly-packed weekly columns and they came quite suddenly. The first intimation was on Thursday 30th July, just as the band of the Royal Irish Rifles was about to strike up for its usual morning performance in the Pantiles. The bandmaster was handed a telegram from the regimental adjutant, telling them to return to barracks immediately and the band at once packed its instruments and headed for the railway station.

Even then, there was uncertainty about their ultimate destination. Ireland was seething and the *Courier* reported: *"whether the order had most to do with the Irish crisis, or the European situation is unknown"*. The band of the Lincolnshire Regiment, due to perform the following week, also cancelled. The council's Entertainments Committee struggled to find a replacement at such short notice, but fortunately secured the services of the celebrated orchestra known as Batty and his Band to fill the gap. The Royal Irish Rifles band was not the only one taken by surprise at the imminence of war: Siegfried Sassoon, the future poet (who would win the Military Cross) and whose family lived at Mayfield, was playing cricket in Tunbridge Wells when the news of the declaration of war percolated through.

By now, army officers on leave and territorial troops were being recalled. The MP for Rye, Colonel Courthope a week earlier had been presenting his Bill in the Commons for the reform of the hops agricultural industry. Now he was in command of the Wadhurst Company of the Royal West Kent Regiment, which had taken the train from Tunbridge Wells to Dover. The 3rd Battalion of the Regiment was also being recalled. The 5th West Kents – the Cyclists' Battalion – who had been undertaking their annual training at Broadstairs were ordered to remain there and the paper listed young officers from local families rejoining their regiments. Eleven members of the Post Office were called up, though local shops such as

Messrs. Philpott and Sons of Mount Pleasant, were reassuring customers that there would be no reduction in their staff, or any other alteration of their business arrangements: *"as usual during August, the remaining summer garments will be cleared at drastic reductions and great bargains may be obtained in dainty and exclusive things suitable to finish out the season. Fortunately, the first consignment of our Paris purchases have come safely to hand..."*. At Bayham Abbey the Marquis and Marchioness Camden's garden party had been favoured with brilliant weather and a large and distinguished company: *"strolls through the grounds were indulged in, with considerable pleasure"* – this, half a century before the abbey ruins would be one of the locations for the film version of *"Oh What A Lovely War!"*

But now the talk of war was becoming serious: *"a dark shadow hangs heavily over us,"* the *Courier's* opinion column stated on 31st July, *"its oppressive adumbration reaches even to peaceful Tunbridge Wells where the holiday season has been temporarily disturbed by the cancelling of leave to local naval and military men and the sudden recall of the military band...Trifling as such an incident may be in itself, it startles us out of our insular complacency and brings home to us what might otherwise be but a distant echo of the dimly-realised Armageddon for which Europe is silently and swiftly arming. Another disagreeable reminder is the impending rise in food prices which a nation choosing to live on foreign rather than home-grown supplies must inevitably suffer...oppressive taxation in time of peace...leaves no margin of financial buoyancy in periods of stress. That the European conflagration may yet be averted is the fervent prayer uppermost in all hearts."*

No doubting where the *Courier* stood politically: against the Liberal government. In the same issue an advertisement placed by London and Raiswell, the Kent County Stores, with branches in Mount Pleasant and Grove Hill Road, warned: *"Panics, which we should all endeavour to minimise, involving the hoarding of food and gold, are what most certainly create the exorbitant prices of such necessities in times of stress...(We) feel convinced if customers will order in ordinary quantities, there will be no need for immediate alarm."*

Knots of excited people were daily gathering outside the Town Hall to read the Royal Proclamations being posted there and local troops were beginning to muster. Three days after war was declared on 4th August, the *Courier* was rallying to the flag in that week's editorial: *"There will be many sensational rumours circulating over the telegraph wires which have little or no foundation and it must be a cardinal point for everyone to avoid any tendency to panic, and loyally support the government and generously respond to any appeal which local authorities may have to make, either on behalf of the distressed poor or our gallant sailors and soldiers."*

As a first step, Sir David Salomons, Bt., whose son was already serving with the Southborough contingent of the Kent Fortress Engineers, announced that he would equip at his own expense 100 volunteers. The paper added: "*We earnestly trust that the young men of this district will not permit Sir David's patriotic offer to be made in vain*" – and indeed the men were recruited within a week.

Meanwhile, local people were scurrying home from holiday, some experiencing problems crossing Europe. Mr. Wynford-Dewhurst, the "*well-known Impressionist artist*", had had an exciting journey across France, though fortunately, as he told the paper, English people there had been given preference in obtaining seats on the trains. Dr. and Mrs. Pigott of Calverley Park Gardens were stranded at Carlsbad and Dr. Wilson of Church Road and his wife and lady friend had struggled to get back from Lucerne. Even those holidaying elsewhere in England had problems as trains were requisitioned for troops: Mrs. Montague Lucy, wife of the Liberal agent for Tonbridge, had found herself marooned in Felixstowe: "*a unique and none too pleasant experience…she is practically stranded and cannot get back. The town is to all intents and purposes under martial law, inhabitants warned they must not be out between 8pm and 4am under peril of being shot. Mrs Lucy will not be sorry when she is able to get back to Tunbridge Wells.*"

Such restrictions were not imposed in west Kent, where shows continued at the Opera House in Tunbridge Wells, though the meeting of the Crowhurst Otter Hounds that Saturday was cancelled because the South East Railway could not accept civilian traffic. There was always a silver lining too: '*the town*', the paper reported, "*has lately been invaded by a small army of holiday folk from the seaside towns, particularly of the Kent coast. This fact augurs well for…the condition of the town during the war.*" It was promised that there would be reduced tariffs at local hotels and guest houses for officers and their wives (but no mention is made of this for other ranks): "*the town should be a pleasant and peaceful resort for many who desire to get away from the stress of war. Many would find…a cheerful place of residence over the next few months…easy access, rail services little interfered with, the band season could be extended…*"

Class was an important consideration. The congregation of St. Augustine's Catholic Church was asked to sponsor Belgian refugees and were asked "*to state the number of rooms available, the class of person desired, whether food, or lodging, or both, will be given and for how long and whether payment is desired.*"

For the time being, passenger rail services were blocked by troop movements. The Territorial – part-time volunteer – troops of 4th Battalion of the Royal West Kents, having taken nearly 24 hours longer than scheduled to return from their annual training exercise because of rail congestion, arrived back in Tunbridge Wells at 6am on the day war was declared, only to be told to reassemble six hours later at the drill hall in Victoria Road. The 274 men who were mustered under Captains Cheale and Kelsey, were surrounded by a dense crowd: there were *"many affecting farewells outside the fateful red brick building and all up Camden Road, for it was fully expected the Rifles would march to the station at once. Inside, all was bustle and preparation. Kits had to be inspected, rifles and other accoutrements cleaned, while most of the men had little luxuries such as bananas and sandwiches brought by fond relatives to pack away in their kitbags."*

The men were addressed by the Mayor, Councillor Emson; the Town Clerk W.C.Cripps; the Assistant Town Clerk, the Borough Accountant and several others. *"The Mayor told them they were assembled in connection with one of the greatest crises that had ever been known in the world's history…the dogs of war had been let loose all over Europe, due to the aggression of one country. Honour and the existence of the country was at stake. Few of them had seen war and its horrors, but in Tunbridge Wells the inhabitants could rely on each of them doing his duty and obeying every order. They could and would maintain the honour of the town and they could rely on everything being done to ensure their dependants did not suffer through an absence of bread-winners. The Mayor was essentially a man of peace ,but if ever they had fought a righteous war, it was this: 'Place your faith in God and fight for all you are worth,"* (Cheers and applause.)

Such fine words about looking after the families while the men were away were probably lost on one soldier's wife in the town who applied for hardship assistance that September, only to be told by an officious woman visitor that she should sell her house and go into service and that it would not be appropriate for her to take in a lodger during her husband's absence. Doubtless the anonymous visitor was herself affluent as she was described as a lady by the *Courier*, which added charitably: *"the incident arose from well-meant but perhaps excessive zeal."*

In the event, the 4th Battalion did not leave for Dover until the following evening. By then the Yeomanry had also departed a few hours earlier for Maidstone, also from the South East Station, marching from the Corn Exchange drill hall, carrying their kitbags and greeted with salvos of cheering from the large crowd.

1st. Bttn, Mid-Kent Volunteers marching up Mount Pleasant, on leaving Tunbridge Wells 6 August 1914

These, of course, were all men drawn from civilian life, with jobs and families at home. The *Courier's* report was affecting: "*flags were waved and hats flung into the air…one would have to go back to Mafeking night to find a parallel.*" By now it was raining, but the crowd around Vale Road and half way up Mount Pleasant was singing patriotic songs:

"*All classes were mingled. One little chap perched on his father's shoulders in Vale Road pressed a little flag upon one of the Terriers, urging him to take it for luck – which he did. Men and women in motorcars shook the troops by the hand and slapped them on the backs. Every window in the vicinity was full. When the troops arrived in the station yard, there was a lull and a little group of men started the National Anthem. Immediately all the men bared their heads, soldiers stood to attention and every man and woman, civilians and soldiers, joined in lustily but solemnly.*" The paper noted a group of weeping women, "*their faces a pathetic mixture of pride and pain.*" But "it was a note of destiny for the men had crossed the Rubicon and were irrevocably faced with a great responsibility and a momentous future, the outcome of which they could not fathom."

Four hundred local men marched out of town that night. That weekend, the Rev. C.H. Bellamy preached at Holy Trinity Church on the sacrifices of valuable life: "*thousands of women would be made widows and children fatherless: 'rebuke the company of spearmen and scatter thou the people who rejoice in war'.*" Prayer, he said, was the answer.

Within weeks however, any early euphoria about volunteering seems to have slackened and the paper as well as the town's leading citizens were berating local men for failing to enlist as enthusiastically as those in other local towns. By the second week in September 562 men had joined the Royal West Kents and 49 the Royal Sussex Regiment and firms were reporting a loss of staff: the Tonbridge waterworks had lost 60% of its staff, 12 had joined up from the Powder Mills, eight from Ives' cricket ball manufacturers (and Mr T. Ives Jnr. had become captain of the town fire brigade), five printers had left the *Courier* and 23 had gone from the Tunbridge Wells Gas Company, while the Baltic Saw Mills offered to pay 25% of the usual wage of any of its men who enlisted; and to keep their jobs open for when they came home.

An evening open air recruitment meeting, "illuminated by electric light", at Five Ways in the second week of September, at which an elderly veteran of the Crimean War waved the Union flag and a Mr Ard sang "Soldiers of the King" as a solo, produced *"a good many young fellows handing in their names"*. It was addressed by Councillor Dennis, whose son Claude was among those who had already enlisted. All this effort was not enough for some, most notably Sir Arthur Conan Doyle who demanded that non-volunteers should be publicly shamed – an open invitation to the nascent white feather movement: *"No day should pass which did not remind him he was a shirker. This healthy public sentiment, fearlessly expressed, will do more than public meetings. There may be some cases of injustice, but the times are hard and this must be disregarded."*

It was not only men who were being recruited. Horses were also required in large numbers and the local gentry were ostentatiously emptying their stables: 40 horses were sent by train to Tonbridge for onward shipment in the first week of the war and Mr W. Cazalet of Fairlawne was said to have "sacrificed" a dozen mounts of his own, including a hunter valued at £250.

And, as local men joined up, so the town began to fill up with encampments of troops from other parts of the country, training and preparing for eventual embarkation. The first to arrive, in early September was a detachment of 350 territorial Royal Engineers from Birmingham who set up rows of bell tents and a field kitchen on the Common. They were telegraph engineers and they established their headquarters in the cricket pavilion. This was a novel experience for a tourist town which did not normally have a local garrison like most county towns. The sight of the troops and their facilities fascinated the locals: *"the cooking of rations and the boiling of big cauldrons of tea over a wood fire afforded endless interest and plentiful supplies of lettuce and jam came in for much attention."*

Camping on the Common 1914 – Emmanuel Church spire in background

Visitors plied the rows of horses the troops had brought with them with apples and then, perhaps, on Sunday afternoon, moved on to the cricket ground where a public meeting opposing the war was being held by local socialists. It was, said the Courier complacently, a sight which could probably not been seen anywhere else than in such a freedom-loving country: "*Socialists were ...delivering anti-war speeches followed by good-humoured argument and interruption. The bulk of people were much too interested in the soldiery: the meeting an instance of English sang-froid which is always a source of wonder to foreign visitors.*" The reporter was particularly tickled that the orator, a man named Blatchford, was being heckled by an argumentative German waiter who engaged him in "*futile dialectics...inconsequent futilities,*" while the strains of a band playing Tipperary echoed across the Common.

The presence of Germans in Tunbridge Wells did not seem particularly troubling at this stage, though those of military age would soon be rounded up and moved to a camp further west in Sussex. In late August there were said to be 122 Germans and Austrians living locally, many of them long-established as waiters in the town's hotels and restaurants. *The Courier* advised: "*It may be pointed out that there are residents of German extraction who have resided here and traded honourably as fellow citizens and fully discharged their civic obligations. There is no reason why they should be regarded with suspicion: they are in fact deserving of sympathetic consideration for their invidious position...Ample precautions are being taken against possible espionage but in a quiet town like Tunbridge Wells there is really no scope for the activities of German spies."*

That did not however stop the paper reporting suspicious – and groundless – rumours such as telegraph wires being cut between Frant and Mark Cross, immediately denied by the Post Office which said all its equipment was working normally. One anonymous local German businessman – was this the jeweller Reich? – was said to have proclaimed defensively that he had fought for Britain in the Boer War. If it was him, it did not prevent his shop's windows being smashed one Saturday night in October by Albert Lyford of Quarry Road, drunk and egged on by the "hotter-headed section" of a large crowd. When Lyford was remanded in custody for a week by the magistrates on the following Monday, Mr Reich employed a solicitor, Mr Robert Vaughan Gower[1] to tell the court that he wished to clear up any misunderstanding concerning his client's nationality: *"Although of German extraction, he has resided in England all his life and has long been naturalised. By making liberal subscriptions to various patriotic objects he has shown that his sympathies are thoroughly English."* The assertion did not help Reich as the war dragged on.

The presence of the troops on the Common had a notable effect on one section of the local population. The camp became what the paper lubriciously described as *"a great centre of feminine interest"*, which immediately caused consternation among some members of the community: the town's reputation for stuffiness was already long-established. The Church of England Mens' Society proposed that women should be kept indoors after 8.30pm while troops were in town and that pubs should be closed early to encourage a curfew. The Town Council did not think that was yet necessary (though pubs were closed at 10pm) but was shocked at the notion that women police constables should be recruited to patrol the streets. On 29th September, Colonel C. Pulley of Langton expressed his fears in a letter to the *Courier*: *"The influx is not an unmixed blessing. Complaints are heard as to the undesirable state of things prevailing on the Common and in the vicinity of the camp on the Lower Cricket Ground. I would suggest that parents and guardians absolutely forbid their girls from being out at night after a reasonable hour. The local constabulary should have orders to move on known or suspected immoral characters, many of whom I understand have come into the town in the wake of the troops. Given a number of healthy youngsters, the admiration of the girls with not overmuch to do and plant them down in the*

---

[1] Who had been a Cllr. for East Ward since 1910 and would be the Mayor in 1918,

middle of a town and it follows a tight hand is necessary if trouble is to be avoided. Human nature is much the same the world over and the khaki jacket may not always enwrap a saint."

Perhaps the Colonel knew whereof he spoke. Had prostitutes descended on the town? Who knows? Within a few weeks, there would be more troops and they too would attract attention, as the *Courier* archly reported in late October: *"The military are quite an attraction to the feminine portion of the community and the 'glad eye' is used with great effect when the shades of night are falling fast! In darkened London the invitation conveyed in the manipulation of a lady's eye would pass unnoticed but here in Tunbridge Wells the Zeppelin fear has not yet taken root and there is plenty of light for a walk and a talk...the girls are only too willing to do both."* No blackout was considered necessary in the town.

In mid-October, about 5,000 Territorials from the North of England and Scotland arrived in nine troop trains. Mainly they were from the West Lancashire division and they included, exotically, soldiers in kilts from the Liverpool Scottish Regiment. These were almost alien, incomprehensible figures: *"awaited with an interest that almost amounted to anxiety"*. The *Courier* warned nervously: *"The duration of their stay is unknown. Never in the history of the borough has the military proportion been so heavy and the interest and excitement aroused by the visit was therefore natural...if there was an absence of any demonstrative enthusiasm as soldiers passed through the streets they have already been assured in many ways of a really warm-hearted welcome."*

The Northerners seemed *"a particularly sturdy lot of men, very fit and well, though obviously tired...soldiers, soldiers everywhere. Tunbridge Wells is becoming accustomed to continual marching through the streets, incessantly on the move, undergoing strenuous training. Military regulations preclude detailed references to the movements of the men, but useful training (is occurring) on the rifle ranges and at drill."* The paper need not have worried: this was an elite Territorial regiment, containing several rugby internationals and Presbyterian church elders in its ranks.

The Liverpool Scottish in Tunbridge Wells

But where to put them all as the town's population expanded by a quarter overnight? Tents on the Common were no longer a feasible option as the autumn drew on and they were struck at the end of October, leaving the Lower Common a morass. Instead, the town's Chief Constable, Prior, in charge of billeting the arrivals, began requisitioning church halls, public rooms such as the Great Hall and a large number of empty private villas. He found room for 250 at the skating rink, 150 in Byng Hall at Skinners' School, 225 at the Crabb Memorial Institute, 300 in the Great Hall, 120 in the St. James's parish room and 80 at St. Barnabas. Sixty officers and 75 men were quartered at Beechwood on the Pembury Road and 30 officers and 30 men at the Dell in Ferndale. Houses were taken over in Molyneux Park, Boyne Park, Earl's Road, Court Road, Oakdale, Beulah, Queen's and Mount Sion, Grove Hill, Linden Park and Linden Gardens, Upper Grosvenor Road, Lime Hill, Warwick Park and Clanricarde Gardens. The field ambulance of the Lancashire Brigade set up its headquarters in the *Hollies* on Frant Road. "*There are now few if any empty houses in Tunbridge Wells,*" the *Courier* reported.

Rates of pay to private landlords were initially 3s/4½d (17p) per man per day: pro rata: 9d for a bed, 7½d for breakfast, 1s/7½d for dinner, 4½d for supper. "*Proprietors who have men quartered on them certainly have little to complain of,*" sniffed the *Courier*, it was considerably more than the average amount paid by single male boarders in small houses and well within the range of many boarding house tariffs: "*the payment of officers is, of course, on a much higher scale.*" The Army had started by renting three empty houses on Broadwater Down, Upper Grosvenor Road and Mount Sion for the Royal Engineers' officers, but now the influx meant that the payment rates were cut to 1s/9d (8p).

To feed the new troops, the Army Service Corps rumbled into action and set up food kitchens for the "*expeditious provision of wholesome meals*". Perhaps one reason for the cut in boarding rates was that meals were now provided centrally. Large gas cookers were installed in parish rooms by the gas company and lorries delivered carcasses of meat, sacks of potatoes and vegetables and trays of loaves (baked by Parker and Hammick of the Pantiles) each day to warehouses in Goods Station Road. Each man was entitled to 1 lb. of meat and 1½ lbs. pounds of bread a day, 2 oz. of bacon, 2 oz. of sugar, 1 oz. of jam, 1 oz. of cheese, ½oz. of tea and "*a suitable quantity of salt, pepper and mustard*". There were, it was said, very few complaints heard.

G. R.

Army Form B. 218M.

HIS MAJESTY'S ARMY.

10th November, 1914.

This Leaflet is intended to take the place of any issued before this date.

WEEKLY RATES OF PAY OF PRIVATE SOLDIERS IN THE REGULAR ARMY AND SPECIAL RESERVE.

ARMS DRAWING PROFICIENCY PAY.

	On Enlistment.	After two years' service.	PERIODS OF SERVICE. For the War only, or	
			With Colours.	With Reserve.
Household Cavalry	12/3	14/- to 15/9	8 yrs.	4 yrs.
Cavalry of the Line	8/2	9/11 ,, 11/8	7 ,,	5 ,,
Horse Artillery—				
Gunner	9/4	11/1 ,, 12/10	6 ,,	6 ,,
Driver	8/9	10/6 ,, 12/3	6 ,,	6 ,,
Royal Field Artillery	8/5½	10/2½ ,, 11/11½	3 ,,	9 ,,
Royal Garrison Artillery	8/5½	10/2½ ,, 11/11½	8 ,,	4 ,,
Foot Guards	7/7	9/4 ,, 11/1	3 ,,	9 ,,
Infantry of the Line	7/-	8/9 ,, 10/6	7 ,,	5 ,,

ARMS DRAWING ENGINEER OR CORPS PAY.

	On Enlistment.	On completion of recruit training if qualified for corps duties.	Thereafter according to qualifications.	With Colours.	With Reserve.
Royal Engineers—					
Sapper	11/8	15/2	17/6 to 22/2	3 yrs. 6 ,,	9 yrs. 6 ,,
Pioneer	8/2	11/8	11/8	6 ,,	6 ,,
Driver	8/2	10/6	10/6 to 11/8	2 ,,	10 ,,
Royal Flying Corps		Special Rates.		4 ,,	4 ,,
Army Service Corps—					
Supply Branch, Private	8/2	9/11	11/8 ,, 16/4	3 ,,	9 ,,
Horse Transport Driver	8/2	9/11	11/8	2 ,,	10 ,,
Mechanical Transport Section—Artificer	8/2	9/11	11/8 to 17/6	7 ,,	5 ,,
Driver	8/2	9/11	11/8 ,, 16/4		
Royal Army Med.	8/2	10/6	11/8 ,, 12/10	3 ,,	9 ,,
Army Ordnance Corps	8/2	9/11	11/8 ,, 16/4	6 ,,	6 ,,

Pay increases considerably on promotion.

[No. 1.]

The northerners were apparently impressed by the town: "*It makes a change anyway,*" one told a reporter in what sounds suspiciously like journalistic prose. "*Our experience will be one to remember all our lives. I wouldn't be back at my ordinary job for anything. I never realised until now how monotonous daily toil in a factory is.*" They were said to be charmed by the healthy climate and the beauty of the neighbourhood. Keeping the troops entertained also required some ingenuity. The Corporation Baths Committee invited them to use the municipal baths in Monson Road and detachments marched there every day for a swim. The YMCA in Mount Ephraim set up a recreation marquee with space for reading and writing and sing-songs and the Rev. W.H. Parsons, the vicar of St. John's, loaned a piano to the troops at the Skating Rink just down the road. Charity lantern slide lectures were planned and, at a smoking concert in the Great Hall, Mr T.H. Sleddall, a well-known local tenor was loudly applauded for his spirited solos, while the Rev. Hockey's Albert Chevalier monologues created gales of laughter.

Occasionally too there were propaganda talks, such as that given by Sir John Matthews, the chief of Kent's Boy Scouts[2], who greeted "*the lads from the North*" and told them how anxious he knew they were to get to the Front: "*It was a grand business they were now involved in, the Kaiser would get it in the neck – the Germans had swelled heads and were jealous of the British Empire. Each scout regretted being now too young to fight, but one day might get the opportunity. If there was anyone today that elderly men and boys envied, it was the soldiers of the King in whose hands rested the fate of the world. It was a grand thing that they were out for: honour would prevail as it always did.*"

The Liverpool Scottish on Church Parade in London Road by the Pantiles.

On Sundays, the troops paraded for church services. The Liverpool Presbyterian troops, 700 strong, fell in at the Dell in Ferndale and marched in their kilts to a service at the Pump Room, "*providing Tunbridge Wells with a unique Sabbath scene*", while the Anglicans marched to Christ

---

[2] Incidentally he was also Chairman of the Bench and husband of Lady Matthews whose Diary is extensively quoted in this book. (See Appendix 1 for more biographical detail)

Church, King Charles the Martyr and St James's and the soldiers *"who are of the Roman Catholic persuasion"* attended St. Augustine's.

The Courier marvelled: *"The boys in khaki are here, there and everywhere and even the most captious of critics could not say that the Wells is a dull place now. The Territorials have certainly livened things up and their presence should at least be a help to the tradesmen of the town. Empty houses now teem with life and erstwhile tenantless rooms resound to the good humoured chaff of the lads in khaki. Sentries with fixed bayonets are to be seen on almost every street of private houses and everywhere is heard the sharp staccato commands of officers, the sound of brazen bugles and the steady tramp, tramp of troops on the march. Huge Army Service Corps lorries daily traverse the town, laden with necessities for the troops and hay and fodder for the horses. The men are very cheerful on the march and are improvising all kinds of bands from paper and comb to full-blown mouth organs and tin whistles."* Tipperary was a favourite, but the Liverpool regiment favoured the Marseillaise.

By now the war was getting serious and casualty figures were beginning to be noted in the paper. The regular soldiers of the 1st Bttn. of the Royal West Kents, who had been in barracks in Dublin, were sent nine days after the declaration of war to the front around the Belgian border town of Mons. With the Royal Sussex Regiment and the East Surreys, they were among the first British troops to find themselves fighting the invading Germans of von Kluck's First Army north of the town on 23rd August as the two armies blundered into each other. Soon they would be in retreat, back into France, though readers in Tunbridge Wells would not have realised that.

The first accounts the local paper published were upbeat, taken from the letters sent home to relatives by the men at the front: *"an immense mass of German troops hurled themselves at the British,"* wrote W. Keats of the 1st Bttn. *"It was like shooting rabbits: you couldn't help hitting them...we must have done a mighty lot of execution. As to the rifle fire, they couldn't hit a haystack."* Then he added: *"The brave fellows of the West Kents want to know when their chums are coming out to reinforce them."* The German fire was not that inaccurate: Private Fred Norris, in happier times the goalkeeper of Southborough FC, was soon on his way home, having been shot in the hand, leg and back during an ambush: *"I wish to be remembered to all my old fellow footballers,"* he wrote to his wife. Proof of how rapidly the war was becoming a global conflict came with a brief report of the death of Petty Officer Fred Coomber, who was 34 and from Rusthall, who died of wounds received in Nyasaland, on the frontline of the imperial struggle in southern Africa, on 12th September.

By then there was news of fatal casualties from France such as Private Arthur Whiteham, of Frances Terrace, Victoria Road, a reservist whose nine years and three months' service had ended a week before the declaration of war, when he had been employed as a carman by the Co-op. Whiteham had rejoined the regulars immediately and been wounded at the battle of the Aisne. Before he died he sent a last letter to his wife of five years and baby daughter: *"Dear Wife, I am wounded and do not hope to live."*

The General Hospital set aside 50 beds for the wounded – this left just 40 for general patients - but these were soon taken up by injured Belgian troops and space for more was found at the Eye and Ear Hospital and then at West Hall, followed by the VAD Red Cross Hospital in Chilston Road. It was said that there were already shortages of medicines and drugs, because many were manufactured by German companies.

There were some things that could be found however: the Tunbridge Wells branch of the Royal Surgical Aid Society managed to find sufficient false teeth for 17 recruits, otherwise they would have been unable to volunteer. For those still on their feet and in uniform, the *Courier* launched its "A Bit of Orlright" fund – to provide cigarettes and tobacco to the troops. Illustrated with a cartoon of a smiling soldier opening a packet, the newspaper's promotion declared: *"Every 6d sends your personal gift and greeting to a soldier at the Front"* and promised to list all individual donors, presenting their sixpences at its office. The sum, it announced, would provide half a pound of excellent smoking mixture with the donor's name and address on the packet and five cigarettes from the newspaper. The Rev. A. W. Oliver of King Charles's Vicarage immediately donated two guineas.

The Courier Tobacco Fund, which was part of a national scheme, became a regular weekly feature and the amounts raised were announced every month. Cigarettes were then relatively cheap at about 6d. (2½ p.) for twenty (the price did vary slightly by brand), so £1 would buy 800 cigarettes and any knowledge or understanding of the health risks attached to doing so, was still about 45-50 years ahead in the future.

By Christmas, while the Western Front had settled into stasis, Tunbridge Wells had become used to 'its' troops. Many of them were given leave over the holiday period and went off blithely to the station *"their marching songs had an even more jovial ring than usual."* But for the more than 2,500 who remained, there were calls for the residents to provide hospitality and entertainment, including Christmas lunches.

The Town rose to the challenge of entertaining its remaining uninvited military guests. Under the leadership (and funding) of Mr. & Mrs. D.

The Liverpool Scottish 'standing at ease'

Elliott Alves, some hundreds of volunteers organised a Christmas Dinner (as it was then known) in a variety of venues for these 2,500+. The Crabb Institute laid on 250 dinners for the 9th King's Liverpool Regiment; the vicar of St. James's provided for 450 men of the 5th Welsh Regiment and St. Barnabas had 100 – "the excellent catering of Mr Wiseman of Auckland Road is worthy of special mention". The residents of Lansdowne Road entertained the 50 NCOs and privates quartered in their street to dinner at the Mikado Café in Vale Road and more than 150 other troops were looked after in private houses.

The Liverpool Scottish detachment had moved on after a few weeks in November, though another battalion of the regiment would arrive the following year. They had boarded a troop train to Southampton for embarkation to the Western Front in France, where many of them would be killed during an offensive in the Spring.

By this December, some units of the Lancashire Brigade had been superseded by Welsh soldiers – "Terriers from Glamorgan" who were presumably too far from home to be given leave – and they were indeed spread around various halls and residences *"in a manner worthy of the best traditions of the town...no soldiers went without the opportunity to enjoy Yuletide hospitality."*

In the evening there were shows provided by the troops, such as Trooper H. S. Winters of the Middlesex Yeomanry *"who presided at the piano"* and by local entertainers. And, for the duration of the holiday period, Belgian refugees were admitted free to the Picture Palace in Camden Road – but only for performances between 3pm and 5pm.

By then, everyone knew that the war would certainly not be over by Christmas.

Patriotic postcards sold well

Soldiers 'at ease' at the Pantiles

The Buffs marching down Sandrock Road

CHRONOLOGY OF EVENTS 1915-1917

1915

15th	January	First large-scale use of gas by Germans against Russian Army.
19th	January	First Zeppelin raid on Great Britain.
25th	April	Allied forces land at Gallipoli, at Anzac Cove and Cape Helles.
7th	May	The British liner *Lusitania* sunk by a German U-boat off the coast of Ireland, with loss of 1,198, including 128 American citizens.
23rd	May	Italy declares war on Austria-Hungary.
15th	August	Germans capture Warsaw.
27th	August	Italy declares war on Germany. Romania enters the war on the Entente's side, but is defeated by Austro-Hungarian army in a few weeks.
8th	October	Sinking of HMS Hythe in a collision in the Dardenelles, with a loss of 155 men, mainly 1/3rd Field Co., Royal Engineers from Kent and particularly Tunbridge Wells.
19th	December	Field-Marshal Haig replaces Field-Marshal French as commander of the British Expeditionary Force.

1916

9th	January	The Gallipoli Campaign ends in an Allied defeat and an Ottoman victory.
17th	January	Conscription introduced in the United Kingdom by the Military Service Act.
21st	February	The Battle of Verdun begins.
23rd	April	Easter Rising by Irish rebels against the United Kingdom.
31st	May	Battle of Jutland – a draw, but German Navy never again engaged in a major surface battle.
5th	June	Kitchener, on a diplomatic mission to Russia, drowns in the sinking of HMS Hampshire, along with his staff & 643 crew.
1st	July	Start of the Battle of the Somme.
29th	August	Hindenburg replaces Falkenhayn as German Chief of Staff.
15th	September	First use of tanks *en masse* at the battle of the Somme
18th	November	The Battle of the Somme ends with enormous casualties and no winners.
5-7th	December	Asquith resigns and is succeeded by Lloyd George as Prime Minister.
9th	December	British forces capture Jerusalem from the Turks.
29th	December	Grigori Rasputin, Russia's éminence grise, is assassinated.

1917

16th January	German Foreign Secretary Zimmermann sent a coded telegram to his Ambassador in Mexico, instructing him to propose to the Mexican government an alliance against the United States. Decoded by British Intelligence, it played a significant part in the USA's decision to enter the War on the Allied side.
1st February	Germany resumed unrestricted submarine warfare.
February	The February Revolution established a *Provisional* Government in Russia.
23rd Feb-5th Apr	German army withdrew behind the fortified Hindenbur Line which it had built.
2nd March	Czar Nicholas II abdicates – *Provisional* Government takes control.
6th April	The United States of America declared war on Germany.
13th June	First successful bomber raid on London carried out by Gotha G.IV planes.
25th June	First American troops land in France.
6th July	Arab insurgents against Turkey, led by Lawrence of Arabia, seize the Jordanian port of Aqaba.
31st July	The Third Battle of Ypres (aka the Battle of Passchendaele) begins (July-November 1917).
24th October-19th November	Battle of Caporetto – Italian Army heavily defeated by the Austrians.
25th October	(according to Russian Julian Calendar, but in the Western Gregorian Calendar, it was 7th November). The October Revolution – capture of the Winter Palace in St. Petersburg by the Bolsheviks, ends the control of the Russian Provisional Government over Russia.
20th November	British tanks win a major victory at Cambrai.
21st November	Francis Joseph I, Emperor of Austria and King of Hungary dies - succeeded by Emperor Charles I.
5th December	Armistice between Germany and <u>*Soviet*</u> Russia signed.

CHAPTER 3
1915 - THE END OF THE BEGINNING
by Roger Kasper

New Year came and January 1st was marked with an edition of the *Kent and Sussex Courier* – which reported on how Christmas Day church services were packed, with *"a large number of soldiers in the khaki uniform"* serving as a reminder to worshippers of the *"terrible state of Europe to-day."*

A wealthy Tunbridge Wells couple, Mr. and Mrs. D. Elliott Alves, had organised a Christmas dinner for more than 2,500 troops stationed in the town and entry to the pantomime 'Babes In the Wood' was free for sailors and soldiers. Many Belgium refugees and soldiers were entertained in the General Hospital – victims of *"the mad war lust of Germany."*

A large crowd gathered on the Lower Common cricket ground on Christmas Day to watch a military sports meeting. Events included the 400 yards flat race, putting the shot, kicking the football, inter-company cock fighting, Victoria Cross race and the company tug of war.

Soldiers were given a New Year party at the Emmanuel Church Lecture Hall about which Lt. Armstrong said *'the men would often recall with pleasure such evenings...when they might be under very different conditions in the trenches.'* Yet this kindness was in stark contrast to the experience of a correspondent to the Christian Commonwealth Fellowship who found *"the natives of Tunbridge Wells the coldest, most unsociable folk I have ever met, though travelling all my life."*

Regular requests from soldiers were printed in the paper. After an appeal for a gramophone for the crew on HMS Crescent, Mrs Payne of Broadwater Down, sent records and crew member G.H. Bell wrote in thanks: *"The lads gathered around for a musical treat. We had the inevitable wag, an Irish wit, who greeted the Caruso record with puns on the singer's name. Such a vile punster was duly invested with the noble order of the boot and is now busy hatching other puns."*

T.W.Godly of Hollambys, Speldhurst appealed for cricket bats, balls and an old bag to send out to his son Cpl. P.C.Godly. *"Where we are at present, it is possible to play,"* said Cpl. Godly. *"I am sure there are plenty who would like to help those at the Front enjoy themselves when they have a spare hour."* There was also an appeal for mouth organs. *"It would pass the winter nights away,"* wrote Pte. F. Young of 1st Royal West Kent.

On Christmas Day, Sgt. R. P. Page (late of the 2nd Queen's Own Royal West Regiment, now of the Norfolks) married Lilian Nordish at St

Matthew's, Southborough. In the evening, *"the happy couple left for Folkestone where the honeymoon is being spent. The bridegroom leaves for the Front early in the New Year."* There were many similar hurried weddings.

There were also Christmas miracles. Pte. E. Russell came back from the dead. In October, the War Office had informed his family that he had been killed at Mons. At Christmas came a postcard which read: *"I am all right. Prisoner of war. Kindly send me tobacco, cigarettes and food."*

Cpl. Shipway of the South Wales Borderers was saved by a pocket book in his tunic which took the force of a bullet. He was being nursed in the town's Eye and Ear Hospital. Pte. John Thomas Giles of Percy Cottages had a 'narrow squeak' when a bullet struck a large tobacco tin in his left breast pocket. The bullet made *'a groove in the thick lid of the box. Giles now keeps the tin as an interesting souvenir of his lucky escape from death.'*

Pte. Robert Goodwin of Forge Road, Southborough lost a finger in a sniper attack – but the biscuit tin he was carrying to protect his head was later found with half a dozen bullets embedded in it.

For others, the news was not so miraculous. On Boxing Day, the family of Pte. Reginald Thomas William Southerden of The Common, Southborough, received the news that he had been killed in action on September 4th in Cambrai. He was 23. His last words to his uncle, while on leave in July, had been: *"Look out for my name in the list for the VC, uncle."* The Courier reported: *"But he was only destined to have the little wooden cross on his grave at Cambrai."*

Plenty of news was coming home from the Front and some of it, in retrospect, was inaccurate if not positively misleading. There was a great deal of paranoia in the early part of the War and it is understandable that rumour outraced reality. There were indeed a number of atrocities committed by the Germans in their invasion of Belgium, but their number and nature became exaggerated to the extent that returning troops often claimed to have witnessed the events themselves. Pte. Summers of Belgrave Road, Tunbridge Wells, home with frostbite, gave the *Courier* his 'thrilling war diary.' He told of drunken German soldiers rampaging through Belgium, mutilating women and children. A local artillery officer told the story of a sniper who had been caught by the Germans, stripped naked and crucified to a door. A Southborough soldier related a similar story of a girl found in a cottage crucified. *"The Germans within reach met with very short shrift indeed"*, he said.

Pte. Rowswell from Sheffield Road, Southborough, was recovering from a shoulder wound when he had *'a little chat'* with the *Courier,* revealing that the Germans were starving and giving themselves up.

Dvr. S. Westover of Woodbury Park Road, a member of the Royal Engineers Pontoon Section, recounted events from the *'hell'* of the retreat from Mons. But, a week later, (in the January 15th edition of the Courier) he was writing of a monumental event on the Western Front – the Christmas Truce of 1914.

In a letter to his mother, given to the paper, he wrote: *"We had a truce with the enemy on Christmas Day, but what was most remarkable was that we were exchanging pipes and cigarettes with them as souvenirs. Not only that, but we helped them bury their dead and spoke quite freely with them. Of course, the "truce" is now over but not much fighting has occurred yet. "The German soldiers are sadly misinformed. They believe Russia is beaten and England invaded and they are only waiting here for the troops to come back from Poland. Poor devils! If they only knew the truth they would soon chuck their hand in."*

And Pte. N. Robinson, 3rd Rifle Brigade and an old boy of St John's School wrote to his headmaster, W. J. Wheatley: *"We had a sort of mutual truce between us and the Germans on Christmas Day. We visited each other and conversed as if nothing had happened. I went over their barbed wire entanglements and three Germans came and shook hands with me and wished me a Merry Christmas. I must say it was quite a treat as they loaded me with cigars and other things."*

L/Cpl. Copsey of St Johns Road, Tunbridge Wells wrote to his parents: *"Christmas Day went down very well, under the circumstances, and I think every man enjoyed himself, ending up with a fine game of football. At the end of the match we all had a sing song."* But Pte. Beesby RFA, writing to his brother at Tunbridge Wells was somewhat more serious: *"We came here to fight for our country and not for the benefit of our health or for a picnic."*

Pte. Sidney Smith (*Courier* March 12th) of North Farm Road, High Brooms, was recovering at home after being stuck in a trench for eight days solid, and was now suffering from frostbitten feet. Interestingly, he discredited stories of the Christmas truce saying he saw *"no such incidents of fraternising between British and German soldiers as have been so frequently described."*

Snow at the end of January was greeted with glee by soldiers, who took to tobogganing on the Common. One said: *"We are going to the Front in a fortnight and intend to make the best of the time left with us in Tunbridge Wells."*

In the Letters From the Front section in the paper, H. Jeffrey of the Rifle Brigade but previously employed at the Tunbridge Wells High Street Dairy, wrote to his friend Mr T. Francis, of the awful condition of the ground on the Western Front.

"We had a dust up with the Germans on December 19th and gave them something to go on with," he wrote. *"I am very sorry to see Tunbridge Wells is so backward in recruiting. I always thought that the Wells would be the first in the field. I do hope some of the young fellows will buck up and let us know out here that they are coming to help win the fight."*

L/Cpl. Willie Holding, 44, a former Tunbridge Wells postman of Sunnyvale Terrace, was killed on his first day in the trenches. The father of one son, he had written to his wife a week before his December 17th death to say: *"I would not come home if I could. Our men are highly amused at the shelling and only laugh at the report of the big guns. I pity the poor, delicate young men at home who won't enlist. They are missing a splendid experience that would make men of them."*

Recruitment would dominate the mood of Tunbridge Wells in 1915, ending with a mad rush to sign up under the Lord Derby Scheme where men aged 18 to 40 could either enlist voluntarily, or 'attest' with an obligation to come, if called upon later. Many enlisted at once, but most attested their willingness to join when called upon. It was said that married men would only be called up once the supply of single men had been exhausted, but this did not prove to be the case later. Those who attested were issued with an armband which they could wear in public, to show they had demonstrated their willingness to serve. In anticipation of the introduction of compulsory conscription, the War Office announced that voluntary enlistment would soon cease and that the last day of registration would be December 15th 1915.

The Tunbridge Wells Volunteer Training Corps got official status when the War Office recognised the national movement – and the Tunbridge Wells Mayor, Cllr. Charles Emson, supported it. The group was set up for those aged over 38 or not able to join the Army, to serve their country at home. Mr A. E. Hobbs was largely responsible for forming the local branch. The *Courier* said: *"The Germans had shown they would not respect any of the conventions of civilised warfare and they would commit even greater atrocities in England than in Belgium, if they had the chance. It was therefore the duty of all men to prepare to fight the Germans to the utmost should they ever land."*

It was hoped 500 men would sign up to the Corps which would perform its drills at the ice-skating rink and subsequently, after having to vacate the skating rink, in the Skinners' School Gymnasium.

An enthusiastic meeting was held in Southborough, aiming to get more men to join the Volunteer Training Corps. It was hoped 200 from Southborough and High Brooms, with another 30-40 from Pembury, would be willing to join the South West Kent Battalion of the Mid-Kent Regiment of the Kent Volunteer Fensibles.

A Tunbridge Wells officer, F. Raymond Curry of the Royal Dublin Fusiliers was home on sick leave and wrote about the scene in his home town. He noted *'the apathy and ignorance shown by so many people'* and raged: "*Nothing is more discouraging to our troops at the Front than to read of labour troubles and 'strikes' at home and of the many signs of slackness and selfishness. Germany will be beaten in the end but that is a long way off yet and before we reach our goal, there will be many more sacrifices to make and many lives must be laid down.*"

The Liverpool Scottish at ease in Tunbridge Wells

Delightful weather in May greeted the town's second "Recruiting Week." The bands of the Liverpool Scottish and the 4th South Lancashire Battalions played patriotic music on the Common and the first parade was made by the Women's Volunteer Reserve. Alderman J. B. Snell who chaired the meeting asked: "*Why are young men at this meeting and not beside their brothers carrying on the fight. Those who could not go, should join the Volunteer Fencibles*".

Captain Duncan Campbell of the Black Watch urged men forward. "*Babies had been picked up on German bayonets and carried through the streets as a warning to the Belgian population not to raise a hand against the almighty German War Lord.*" (to cries of 'shame' from his audience).

Recruitment was always at the forefront with the *Courier* running a weekly column detailing the number of men signing up to different regiments.

A meeting on the war was held in early February in the Great Hall with *'the object of stimulating recruiting in Tunbridge Wells'*, with speeches by Lord Airedale (the half-brother of Lady Matthews) and Labour MP John Hodge. Some 1,300 Tunbridge Wells men had enlisted, it was revealed to applause. Mr Hodge said: "Tunbridge Wells had done well, but it could do better. The men at the Front were asking their pals here, 'What are you doing? When are you coming to help us?' It was up to the young men to raise the cry, 'We are coming.' (to cheers from the audience).

But the *Courier* also had time for the lighter side of life, reporting on 'an amusing recruiting poster' in a travel agents which read: *"To Berlin. A trip to Germany is arranged for the Spring, open to a few sportsmen. All hotel expenses and railway fares paid. Good shooting. Rifles and ammunition supplied free. Cheap trips up the Rhine. Apply at once as only a limited number (about a million) required.'*

The December 1915 rush to enlist was 'phenomenal', as men signed up under the Lord Derby Scheme. In the stampede, some 2,000 signed up but 200 were rejected *"for various reasons." "Whether the Government will now allow the remaining slackers and shirkers to have the laugh of them remains to be seen."*

The Mayor, Cllr. Charles Emson, wrote to the *Courier* appealing for funds to help with the Belgian refugees. Some 110 were being looked after and four houses had been furnished, with money raised from an appeal through the paper in October. One resident had offered £1 a month for the year, provided 99 others match-funded.

The annual meeting of the Tunbridge Wells Licensed Victuallers Association was held at the Duke of York on The Pantiles and discussed the thorny subject of early closing. The clergy and the teetotal party were bringing pressure to close pubs at 9 pm.

Frederick William Freeman, landlord of the Bridge Hotel, admitted selling alcohol between 9 and 10 pm, breaking the November 1914 Intoxicating Liquor (Temporary Restriction) Act. He was the first to be prosecuted in the town.

R L Gwynne wrote about clubs applying for extensions, claiming they would perish. He said: *"Surely we English are willing to lose profits and dividends if we can help our gallant lads to a greater readiness for the fight."*

Street Lighting and Blackout

At the end of January 1915, the lights went out over the town – with blackouts from 5pm to 7.30am brought in. In April, Southborough Council called for street lamps to be put out until August 15th. *"The country was at war and people ought to put up with a little inconvenience."*

By September, people were irate that *"in our darkened streets, few people have been sufficiently educated to keep to the right."*

A 'Puzzled Ratepayer' wrote of his surprise that his demand was higher, not lower, this year, despite no street lighting since May. *"Is the unhappy ratepayer not only to pay more highly for everything he gets, but also to pay for what he does not get, viz public lighting."*

In court, 18 summonses about blackout were issued in November: among them Joseph Charles Robinson of Queen's Road, who was fined £1. He told the police: *"That's a bit rough when my son has (just) come home from the Front. The light from the window could not possibly be visible to Zeppelins."* (This was just after Tunbridge Wells's only Zeppelin raid.) Lights out was causing vexation for a writer to the *Courier* who was worried at the number of *"quite young girls in the streets late at night, after the shops are closed and apparently not under parental control."*

Girls came particularly under the spotlight of public opinion. Mr A. Taylor-Jones of Wybourne Grange thought they should be doing their patriotic duty too, and volunteer to help at the Red Cross Hospitals in the area. *"I believe I shall be voicing the majority of right-thinkers when I state that it is the bounden duty of all girls and women who have the time to spare for golf, hockey etc. to come forward and do their duty as our boys have done. Why should our girls be spared? I will not enlarge on the subject, but trust the good sense of the 'slackers' will enable them to lose no further time in coming forward to fulfil their obvious duty."*

The Women's War Emergency Corps in Monson Road was doing its bit. Under the direction of Miss B. Molesworth, it had started basketry classes to supply baskets which usually were imported from Germany. A unit of the Women's Volunteer Reserve (which was the first para-military women's unit and preceded the Women's Auxiliary Army Corps [WAAC]) was formed and the Mayor, Cllr. Emson said that if it had done nothing else, it had gained solidarity for the nation which was now unquestionably of one mind. Its Honorary Colonel, Mrs Evelina Haverfield, provoked laughter at a meeting when she said the women were to wear no make-up on the face. *"They were seeking to remove all feeling of sex antagonism and to show that women and men were comrades and ought not to be always wanting to contend with one another."*

An effect of the formation of the Women's Volunteer Reserve *"would be be to effect a revolutionary change in women's clothing. They would not see so many ridiculous and preposterous fashions in the drapers' shops."*

Lady Matthews added the Corps would give shopgirls something to do on a Saturday afternoon. *"We would not have had so much trouble with the girls in the town since the coming of the soldiers, if the girls had had some raison d'etre for their existence. The Volunteer Reserve would give them something to usefully occupy their time."*

The Women's Volunteer Reserve was flourishing *"to almost an embarrassing degree"* with 130 signed up. It needed to find a place big enough to perform drills.

A girls' war club for members of the National Union of Women Workers was opened at 13 Quarry Road with billiards, bagatelle and other games provided. It was intended *"as a place to which girls can take their soldier friends to spend the evening in innocent recreation."*

Women were being encouraged to do their bit. In a letter to the *Courier*, D G S wrote a poem:

> *"If you cannot nurse, you can scrub or cook,*
> *for Tommy needs feeding up,*
> *If you can't do these, then why, if you please,*
> *don't you do the washing up?"*

The danger of a tight skirt was made plain when Nellie Martin, 19, of Rusthall died, after climbing out of a moving car opposite the Opera House. *"Miss Martin was wearing a tight skirt and new boots and the road being newly tarred caused her to fall,"* her inquest heard.

And a woman, who had taken advantage of the numbers of soldiers who had flooded into town, was in court, charged with improper behaviour in Mount Sion Road. Evidence was given that said Clara Alice Coomber had for several years lived an immoral life, but her *'indecency had been most frequent since the soldiers had been in town and had taken place, in numerous instances, right in front of the windows of private homes'*. She was fined £1.

Colonel Pulley from Langton Green was worried about war babies, blaming lack of parental control. *"Our girls are seemingly allowed licence to do as they please. Cases have been brought to my notice where the mother has actually encouraged the daughter to have what she called 'a good time…We are not slow to pick holes in the morals of our continental neighbours; is it time we looked to our own?!"*

Dorothy May Hazelden, aged 17, of Bedford House, Mount Sion, drowned herself in the River Medway after receiving a letter from a soldier, W. Spencer of the 2nd Battalion South Lancashires, which read: *"I leave*

Southampton tonight for France. I have only one wish and that is that you will meet with someone that will love you with a true love and make you happy all your life. I am going with a sad heart but with a good spirit, but if I have to die, I will think of you to the last second as one of my best friends."* The inquest into her death heard she was *"in a certain condition."*

The Salvation Army had to deal with several similar local cases. In one case, a girl *"in a good situation"* became attached to a Territorial who claimed to be single. He got her pregnant and she asked him to marry her and *"save her unborn child from disgrace."* She paid for a Register Office wedding – only for him to admit he was married. She entered the Maternity Home at Clapton.

Residents in Tunbridge Wells wrestled with the dilemma of keeping life as normal as possible at home while so many were serving at the Front. The annual Agricultural Show was abandoned, as organisers predicted it would end in finanacial disaster through lack of attendance. County Cricket Week went the same way, but the Linden Cricket Club, some 40 years old, vowed to carry on playing cricket during the summer despite the conflict. Members were aware of public opinion against it. *"People who saw them playing and did not know the circumstances would make insulting remarks,"* said a report quoting the captain, Mr W. F. Rathbone. *"But if members could not go out to the war to fight, he saw no reason why they should not play cricket."*

When the Town Council met for the first time in 1915, more argument was given over to the grant of £750 on the Corporation Band Season for The Pantiles and the Grove, than on the effects of the war. The Tunbridge Wells Tradesmen's Association criticised the council for reducing its grant to the Borough band from £750 to £500 – as it expected an upsurge in summer visitors, as tourists were too scared to go to the east coast of Kent. The Mayor said Tunbridge Wells was one of the safest parts of the country and in reply to a request for guidance as to what to do in the event of an air raid by Zeppelins, said: *"Crowds should disperse, everyone take shelter, those in houses should go into cellars or lower rooms. Children should remain in school."*

Days after news of the sinking in May of the RMS Lusitania , the British liner which was torpedoed by a German U-boat off the SW coast of Ireland, Tunbridge Wells experienced a few mild *"thrills"* when there was an anti-German demonstration took place in Grosvenor Road outside the hairdresser's run by Joseph Urban, who was German-born. The *"small riot"* started on a Friday night with a few individuals, whose presence drew *"a small army of police constables"* to disperse the crowd that then gathered. The next night, more than 1,000 people were at Five Ways and the army had to be brought in, to help police deal with the crowd, with pockets of demonstrators breaking off to Goods Station Road and the road *"between the Catholic Church and the hospital. (Grosvenor Road)"*. 95% were peaceful, but a few *"fiery spirits"* tried to incite the crowd by shouting out about the Lusitania.

Mr Urban's window was smashed, incurring a bill for the Council of £10 5s 6d. Mr Urban wrote to the *Courier* which, in a rare move, published his letter on the front page, normally reserved for display advertisements. In it, he condemned the Lusitania sinking and wrote: *"I have lived in England for the greater portion of my life, viz. for nearly 20 years, during 15 years of which I have been engaged in business in Tunbridge Wells, married an English woman, the whole of my staff is English and I have not, for many years, employed a German."* He revealed that several months earlier, he had renounced his German nationality and applied to become a British subject. The letter seemed to do the trick – there were no further reports of demonstrations against him in the 1915 editions of the *Courier*.

Food prices were rising and Labour MP Tom Richardson spoke to the Tunbridge Wells Co-operative Society: *"The leap in prices of coal and food was due not to the law of supply and demand but almost entirely to vested interests,"* he said. *"The same forces that were at work in times of peace were at work in time of war and the sooner the middle classes awoke to a realisation of that fact, the better it would be for the country."*

Some tried to take advantage of the situation. Barrow boys set up stalls outside barracks. George Woodman was summoned for obstructing the highway on March 14th. He was one of many offering pastries, unripe fruit and ice creams. There were also numerous court appearance of traders selling watered-down milk.

But it was the Tunbridge Wells Army Meat Scandal which dominated press reports for several months, ending with Sgt. George Shepherd and Cpl. Percy Smith, along with Tom Lawes, a local *"cartage contractor"*, being fined for stealing and receiving army meat. There were numerous court hearings, which were packed with the public *'gorging themselves'* on the case.

The Director of Public Prosecutions took action against Calverley Meat Market butcher John Herbert Semple – accused of receiving nine hinds of beef - and Edward Dickenson, a partner of Dickenson and Farmer, Butchers of St John's Road, for receiving army beef. The scandal also reached the House of Commons, resulting in the War Office issuing an instruction to all General Officers Commanding (GOCs), to tighten up control and security of their food and other supplies.

THE WAR A YEAR ON

In the July 30th 1915 edition of the *Courier*, its editorial talked about the first year anniversary of the outbreak of the war and how the country and the town had coped.

"The soundness of the nation's heart stands proved to the world."

The anniversary was marked with intercession services at Holy Trinity Church on the Sunday afternoon and a patriotic meeting at the Great Hall in the evening. The Mayor and Aldermen and the Town Clerk were in their official robes and several military officers took part in a procession, formed at the Town Hall, which went to the church via Monson Road.

"The progress through the streets was watched by large crowds. The church was crowded, every available seat being occupied while dozens stood in each of the doorways. Hundreds of people had to be turned away."

In the evening, the Mayor, Cllr. Emson, said: *"The war had cemented the solidarity of our Empire (applause)."* But the *Courier* also reported: *"A lady who said she had a son at the Front asked why national service had not been made compulsory?"* The Mayor replied *"the question of national service was one for the country. If he could settle it, he would do it in five minutes."*

It was in marked contrast to the anniversary of the first arrival of wounded soldiers to Tunbridge Wells General Hospital. Dense crowds waited for hours outside the hospital on September 29, 1914 to greet the first batch of 24 wounded men. On the 1915 anniversary, 60 wounded men were delivered but *"their advent passed comparatively unnoticed."*

In September 1915, the Medical Officer of Health reported that the health of Tunbridge Wells had been *'very satisfactory'* in 1914. Deaths and births had been very evenly balanced - 504 deaths, 57% of them over the age of 60, which is somewhat low by today's figures; and 505 births, 263 (52%) of them being boys which is slightly above.

The National Register showed there were 20,000 women in the town, compared to 15,000 men – and that included the *"large number of visitors staying in the town."* (These figures refer to 1914 or even earlier, before a large number of troops arrived.)

More than £500 was raised for a 50-bed Red Cross Voluntary Aid Hospital in Rusthall where wounded soldiers would be treated in the open air by a *'number of ladies in the parish who...have been trained as Voluntary Aid Detachment nurses'*. Tents were to be erected on the lawn of the 12-acre Rust Hall, Langton Road, for the treatment of special cases, including wounded soldiers with bullet wounds through their necks. It was thought open-air treatment was the best for them. *"The people of Rusthall are helping to pay off a national debt,"* said the *Courier*.

About 250 soldiers had been treated at the General Hospital, its annual meeting in March 1916 was told. It had also received royal approval – the King and Queen had sent representatives to give souvenirs to every soldier. *"To their astonishment, the Hospital Committee also received from Sandringham a magnificent lot of pheasants and hares."*

The Tunbridge Wells Tradesmen's Association objected in March 1916 to a Kent County Council plan to open a tuberculosis hospital in the town. Mr T. H. Sleddall said: *"Was Tunbridge Wells a health resort, or was it going to be a place of reception of persons suffering from tuberculosis?"* which would scare people away from the town. The hospital should be five or six miles out of town. Alderman R Vaughan Gower added: *"Residents did not wish to have it noised throughout the length and breadth of the land that there was a tuberculosis sanatorium at Tunbridge Wells."* Councillor A. A. Foster prophesised the sanatorium would have *"a ruinous effect on the trade of the town"* and the plan was opposed.

An Army Veterinary Hospital had been set up in the town to treat the many horses wounded at the Front. Referring to a particularly intelligent horse-patient, Lt. Bell, the Officer Surgeon-in-Charge of the Army Veterinary Hospital at Tunbridge Wells said *"He knows as much as a man and more than some men."* Among his 200 patients were those being treated for mange, ringworm, diseases of the head and foot, and abscesses. One horse had a broken jaw bone, another paralysis of the nostrils and lips, so it breathed and ate with difficulty. In contrast to this care, the *Courier* reported that an animal cruelty case had come before the magistrates when Romanian James Lanzoni was prosecuted for ill-treating a bear by making it perform *'when it was exhausted'* in Standen Street.

In September 1915, some 80,000 hop pickers, as they traditionally did, headed to Kent. However this year, they were threatening to strike because of increased food costs, the lack of work, and the illusory threat that Belgian refugees would threaten to undercut their wages. The *Courier* said: *"The hop picker in war time has in many parts of Kent proved that for selfish disregard of the national crisis, he is a good second to the Welsh coal miner."* The crop was the shortest for 20 years.

On 12th October, Lady Matthews reported the introduction of a new restriction popularly called the 'Treatotal Order' which was obviously an extension of DORA and forbad 'treating' i.e. buying drinks for one's friends. She said that the immediate result was *'a diminution in convictions for drunkenness'*.

In October 1915, there also occurred the two events which probably had the most impact on Tunbridge Wells during the Great War - the bombing of the town, by what was probably a lone Zeppelin; and the accidental sinking of HMS Hythe, with the loss of 129 local men.

The Zeppelin Raid

The first event occurred at 10.45 pm on Wednesday 13th October, and was the only event which involved enemy action against Tunbridge Wells during the whole of the War. The following day, Lady Matthews wrote in her Diary " *War has come to our doors at length. Last night at 10.45pm a violent explosion occurred close by, followed immediately by two more. There was a faint burring, purring sound* (obviously this was the sound of the engines), *but nothing further. I was still up & dressed, & so was J.* (her husband). *The children slept peacefully on; the rest of the house, very trim and neat in dressing gowns, came down from their rooms & we waited & did not go to the cellars because all noise had ceased. J. went out & discovered that it was indeed a Zeppelin & that bombs had been seen to drop somewhere not far off. The household was all in bed again soon after 11, & spent a quiet night, though one of the maids preferred sleeping on the floor with the others, to remaining in a room by herself."*

The following day it was established that three bombs had been dropped by a Zeppelin airship on Calverley Park; that they landed on open ground; one house had been slightly damaged, and many windows had been broken as far away as Crescent Road, but that no one had been killed or even slightly injured.

However because of censorship, the local papers were not allowed to report anything about it and the only reason why anything is known today about the incident, apart from some rather vague 100-year-old word-of-mouth mythology, is because Lady Matthews recorded the detail in her Diary. She also recorded that the *'Zeppelin**s**'* went on to London where eight were killed and 34 injured (she later revised this to 55. all but 9 in London) and also said that 11 incendiary bombs were dropped on the *'fields and hedges of Frant'*. *'It is truly a miracle'* she said that Tunbridge Wells suffered so little.

A 'humourous' postcard of the period

In one respect, her reporting is possibly inaccurate. Tunbridge Wells, despite the number of troops in the town (a fact which it is unlikely that the Germans would ever have known), would not have been a strategic bombing target for the Germans. It is far more probable that the bombs were dropped by a lone Zeppelin (possibly just a little off-course) *returning* from bombing London, which ditched its remaining bomb-load on what, even with black-out, it could see was a built-up area.

The Sinking of HMS Hythe
The sinking of HMS Hythe was the largest single disaster to befall Tunbridge Wells during the whole of the War, let alone 1915. Collectively, Tunbridge Wells would lose more men at the Battle of the Somme in 1916, but their loss was spread over a six-month period. The Hythe tragedy was compounded by the fact that these men died by accident, and not as a result of enemy action.

On October 28th 1915 at about 8pm, the former Dover-Calais ferry steamer HMS Hythe was about to land the troops it was carrying at Cape Helles, Gallipoli, when it was in a collision with a much larger and empty troopship, HMS Sarnia, with such force that the Hythe was carved in two and stopped dead in the water. It was pitch-black, lights on both vessels had been dowsed and both had been travelling at about 12 knots. The Hythe sank rapidly in 10-15 minutes, taking with it 155 of the 275 men on board. Some 129 of the 155 were Fortress Royal Engineers from 1st/3rd Kent Field Company, Royal Engineers, who came mainly from Southborough, Tunbridge Wells and Speldhurst.

Royal Engineers 1/3 Kent Field Co.

1/3 Company, led by Capt. Salomons (mounted), marching down Southborough High St., on their way to embarkation.

They had been recruited by Captain David Salomons, of the philanthropist Salomons family whose home was at Broomhill (now Salomons). Among the recruits were bricklayers, plasterers, clerks, masons, electricians, painters, plumbers, blacksmiths and tailors – men from all walks of life. Weeks earlier, the soldiers had been cheered off by family and friends as they left Kent by rail for Devonport, Plymouth.

Capt. 'Reggie' Salomons

Capt. Salomons was the only officer to die in the disaster. The rest of the officers managed to jump overboard and swim away from the ship, but most of the troops could not swim and so drowned. As the officers and those who could swim jumped overboard, the Hythe's commander, Captain Arthur Bird, ordered the ship to be abandoned. Reggie Salomons was seen with his Company-Sergeant-Major trying to launch a lifeboat. Told by Bird that it was his last chance to jump, he apparently replied: *"No. I will see my men safe first,"* and handed his lifebelt to another man who could not swim.

Many of the troops did not have life-belts and there were not enough lifeboats either.

"When the news arrived in Southborough it seemed that every family was concerned either through relationship or by acquaintance with the men

lost," wrote Frank Stevens in his book *Southborough Sappers of the Kent (Fortress) Royal Engineers*. "For Sir David and Lady Salomons, the death of their son and heir was a tragedy from which they never recovered."

Captain Salomons was well liked and respected by his men. He was generous and looked after his command. There are reports of him buying a round of drinks for them all on one occasion - 161 pints of beer at 4d per pint, plus two lemonades at 2d each.

The full story of the Hythe disaster did not appear in the *Courier* until the November 12th edition when the paper admitted that: *"When it was briefly announced a fortnight since, that HMS Hythe had been sunk in collision with another ship off Gallipoli, the fact was not connected locally that a month ago a detachment of the 1/3rd Kent Fortress Engineers, under the command of Captain Salomons and chiefly recruited by him, (had) sailed for an unknown destination."*

But the penny dropped as official notifications of deaths started arriving in such numbers. Mrs Pook of Hill Street, Tunbridge Wells was probably the first locally to hear the sad news – her husband Driver Richard Thomas Pook had drowned. Mr and Mrs W. Groombridge of Albion Square suffered their third bereavement of the war. Their sons, Arthur and Edward, had already been killed in action when their adopted son, Driver Sidney Betts, died. They still had another son, Pte. Frederick Charles, was at the Front. Mrs Longhurst of Edward Street, heard the news that her son, A. Smallcombe, had drowned a day after learning that his younger brother in the 2nd Buffs, who had been missing since February, had been given up as dead. Sapper R. T. H. Edser of Goods Station Road survived the Hythe – only to die in Gallipoli, when he was severely wounded by a bomb, an hour after arriving in the trenches.

Monument to the 129 dead

The Vicar, Rev. W. W. Martin, at a service in Southborough for the victims said: *"This very death roll of Southborough is more or less a penalty for our loyalty."*

Sir David Salomons, in a letter acknowledging the condolences from the Southborough Urban Council on the death of his only son, wrote: *"The event is especially sad for us since it means the family name disappears when my day is over. But I hope my daughters will take the same interest as Lady Salomons and I do now and I know my lost son would have done, had he been spared."*. Sir David would arrange and pay for a Memorial to the 129 dead, which was unveiled in 1916 by him in the HQ in Speldhurst Road and which is now in St. Matthew's Church, High Brooms.

With Christmas approaching, a campaign was launched to snatch the toy trade from the Germans. It seems astonishing that while Britain was at war with Germany, toys to the value of £1 million were still being imported from Germany and Austria – and as the *Courier* said, there was no reason why we could not make our own toys. Financial contributions to the campaign, had been received from Mrs Ross Fairfax, the Mayor of Tunbridge Wells, Lady Henry Nevill and Mr John Smith.

The year ended on a sombre note with the death of a leading Tunbridge Wells figure, the Marquess of Abergavenny who died aged 89, on 12th December 1915 at Eridge Castle, having slipped on the stairs.

1st. Marquess of Abergavenny, wearing the Abergavenny checks, for which he was famous.

William Nevill, the 1st. Marquess (and 5th. Earl, and also 13th Baron Bergavenny) had been an 'eminence grise' in both the national and local scene for many years. He rarely spoke in public or in the House of Lords, and never put pen to paper, at least publicly. Yet he was known as the 'Peermaker' following in the mold of his ancestor, Warwick 'the Kingmaker' in the 15th century, since he was instrumental as a major Conservative Party manager in creating the very successful Party administrative structure of local Conservative Associations, which ensured their control of the Commons under Disraeli and Shaftesbury; and also of ensuring an adequate majority in the Lords at the same time, by 'topping up' i.e creating a suitable number of Conservative peers.

In recognition of his services, he was raised from being the 5th Earl to become the 1st. Marquess by the Conservative Prime Minister, Disraeli, in 1876; and was made a Knight of the Garter (KG) by the succeeding Conservative Prime Minister, Lord Shaftesbury, in 1885.

In 1900, he owned 100,000 acres, mainly in Kent and Sussex including large parts of Tunbridge Wells, and it was said that one could walk from Tunbridge Wells to the English Channel, without leaving his land. He was without doubt the leading peer in the area.

The sombre tone would continue in 1916.

CHAPTER 4
THE RESPONSE OF THE BOROUGH COUNCIL TO THE WAR
by Alastair Tod

Crisis

In the summer of 1914 England was buzzing with talk of war – not in Europe, but in Ireland. For the *Courier* as late as the end of July, Ireland was a 'crisis', but Europe merely a 'situation'. Tunbridge Wells and Kent Councillor Robert Gower was Treasurer of a committee for the 'defence of Ulster and the Union', referred to by the *Courier* as 'the struggle for freedom'. The Drill Club, which had just incorporated the Rifle Club, was actively recruiting. The National Service League, which preached that all young men should have military training, was holding public meetings in the Great Hall.

Nationally there was concern about spies, but those who travelled to the Continent that summer were perhaps more aware of rivalry with Germany than a military threat. More urgent problems, apart from Ireland, seemed to be unemployment and industrial unrest, the housing shortage, drink, the women's question and the burden of income tax. For the Conservative *Courier*, the recent Marconi affair illustrated the essential dishonesty of the Liberal Government. It was the heyday of patent medicines and in the papers a certain hypochondria appears, with cases of myalgia and nervous debility merging seamlessly with troubling news from home and abroad. Those living then would have been surprised to hear their time later referred to as a 'golden afternoon'.

The Mayor, Charles Emson

From November 1913 to 1917 Tunbridge Wells Council was presided over by Charles Whitbourn Emson, a solicitor first elected to the Council at the age of twenty eight in 1909. His successor as Mayor, Robert Vaughan Gower had made his name precociously as Hon. Secretary to the Ratepayers' Association from the age of sixteen. It would fall to Mayor Emson to steer the borough through the first four years of war.[1] The Mayor then had wide powers, and as well as the now familiar duties, the Council had responsibility for water, electricity, the police, education, health (though not the General Hospital) and the veteran Alderman Delves was chairman of the Gas Company[2]. And Tunbridge Wells was about to be hit by an unforeseen hurricane.

No doubt it reflected an energetic approach to the affairs of the relatively new

---

[1] Such an extended term of office was quite usual in the First World War and was practised in most towns in Kent.
[2] The Gas Company was independent of the Council, but the Council was a major customer for street lighting; the telephone system had been taken over by the Post Office in 1912.

borough that they chose such a young mayor, and appointed a successor almost equally young[3], whose role was greatly enhanced by the demands of war. Mayor Gower, also a solicitor, was knighted after the war for his efforts to maintain the business of tradesmen while they were serving in the forces.

In the days before party politics in local government, the Mayor was an executive with the task of holding together the factions of the Council, 'ratepayers', preoccupied with the need to limit costs, and 'progressives' more concerned with promoting the town. This echoed a wider tension between those, often of moderate means, for whom the town was a respectable home, and those epitomised by the Tradesmen's Association and the Advertising Association identified with its business role and recommending it to visitors. About half the Council were Nonconformists, more inclined to take a moralistic view; in spite of pleas from the Anglican Mayor more than half were absent from his Mayoral Service in 1916. There were no Catholic or Jewish members.

The old Council Chamber, as it existed up to 1939

At the July 1914 Council meeting, the chief debate was whether to light all the faces of the new Trinity clock. There was also discussion of a long-standing item associated with the progressives, the possibility of buying land behind the Great Hall for a winter garden. After only twenty minutes, the meeting broke up with the Mayor wishing members an enjoyable holiday.

Bank Holiday fell on Monday 3rd August and the band of the Royal Irish Rifles was booked to perform in the town. According to Lady Matthews, married to the Chairman of the Bench, it was only on Friday or Saturday that the general public realised that the developing European crisis could affect Great Britain. This was when the news broke that the Irish Rifles had been recalled to barracks, just as the Territorials assembled for their annual camp at Aldershot.

The Band Committee succeeded in securing a replacement at short notice, but at the same time the Tunbridge Wells-Shoreham Air Race based at Liptraps Aerodrome[4] was cancelled. On Sunday 2nd August, a mass meeting against war was held on the Common attended by 1,000[5]; further public

---

[3] Gower was 38.
[4] Litraps Aerodrome was a meadow used for flying, on the site of Litraps Farm north of the Pembury Road and east of the Dorking Charity Farm site.
[5] The British Socialist Party worked to persuade men not to enlist and also to head off conscription; this led to the forming of a local branch of the National Council for Civil Liberties (now Liberty). In June 1917, following a conference of anti-war parties in Leeds, a Workers' and Soldiers' Council (a `soviet`) was set up in Tunbridge Wells. There seems to have been no formal action against them but their activities were disrupted by member-soldiers being posted elsewhere. A meeting of the related No Conscription Fellowship booked for the Town Hall was cancelled when its purpose was discovered (*Courier* 2.6.16).

protest meetings were held, organised by the radical Quaker Candler sisters and Alexander brothers.

When war was declared on 4th August the *Courier* reflected gloomily that this would mean an increase in taxes; more perceptively, Lady Matthews remarked it would be hard on the poor. At once manual workers began to be laid off and wages to fall. Mayor Emson appealed for 'restraint', meaning it seems economic as well as emotional, and set up a Fund 'for the assistance of those in distress', proposing to send the surplus to other towns. Lady Matthews commented that the most well-off were reluctant to contribute to the fund, because of the fear that dividends would not be paid.

She reported on a lady who 'dared not reduce the five or six courses to which the man of the house was accustomed' in the evening. However with a household of nine, she set about filling her store cupboards herself, and the *Courier* reported an appeal by the Tradesmen's Association for shoppers to limit their demands to avoid pushing prices up. Indeed even with increased prices some shops, including Sainsbury's, closed their doors, having sold out. There were stories of spies at Pembury, of trains full of Russian reinforcements[6], and the air of crisis was reinforced by the banks being closed that week for the replacement of sovereigns with paper money.

The Town Hall, then in Calverley Road

The initial response of the Council focussed on welfare, and the preservation of order. By the end of August the Mayor was proposing a public loan for housing and his Distress Committee was meeting at the Town Hall; the Mayoress had a Red Cross and Clothing Fund. There were immediate appeals for young men to join the colours.

At an emergency meeting on 2nd September the Council agreed to keep posts open for its staff who volunteered, and to make up their pay. At the same meeting they agreed *nem con* that there was 'no scope within the borough for building operations under the Housing Act 1914'. But they resolved to pursue the owners of slum houses in Hervey Court who were refusing to carry out repairs.

Arrangements for a military camp on the Common were approved by the Council on 2nd September, as were the sanitary facilities for the use of the Corn Exchange as billets, and the removal of locks from public lavatories to enable soldiers to use them. The same meeting agreed that soldiers in uniform could have free use of the public baths, and exempted houses used by or for the military from paying rates. On the 9th, Royal

---

[6] Lady Matthews 9.8.14; the famous 'snow on their boots' rumour.

Camp on the Common: Holy Trinity on skyline

Engineers arrived to pitch tents on the Lower Cricket Ground, 'joyfully assisted by boy scouts'. At the same time the Chief Constable was appealing for private houses to be made available as billets.

The following week it was reported that the Mayor was forming a committee for the reception of Belgian refugees, and chairing a conference on help for them, asking for houses to enable whole families to be housed together. The arrival of the first, 'a number of Belgian peasants', was reported on 9th October. Possibly revealing the speed at which events developed, he also appealed for food and clothing for refugees within Belgium at a time when almost none of Belgium remained in Allied hands.

There is no evidence of resentment at these waves of newcomers (though possibly this would not have been reported), but before the end of the year Mayor Emson is appealing again for houses 'for Belgians of the upper class', and for money to pay for these. Lady Matthews was concerned about upper class Belgians having to share with lower class ones. Meanwhile, with help from the railway company, the Advertising Association was advertising Tunbridge Wells for holidays, among other things as 'the safest place in the south of England'.

At a meeting of the 'Suffrage Committee' presided over by Sarah Grand, it was agreed to suspend campaigning and divert their efforts to collecting and distributing clothing for those in distress: 'the tone was grave and fine'[7]. With the approval of the Mayor, the Committee turned over their office and social club at 18 Crescent Road to the borough clothing depot, and the Mayor appealed for funds for this. With a handful of other ladies, Lady Matthews attended a recruitment meeting in the Great Hall, the first of many, forcefully addressed by the Town Clerk, W. C. Cripps; it was a fine moonlit evening, the doors of the hall stood open and Territorials with bands and flags paraded outside, made it 'an inspiring occasion'.

In October, Mayor Emson agreed to form an Emergency Committee if required and in November members of this Emergency Committee were listed as the Mayor, the Deputy Mayor, the Town Clerk, the Borough Surveyor, the Chief Constable, General E. O. Hay as an ex-officio member, representing the military, with the Deputy Town Clerk acting as the Secretary of the Committee.

---

[7] The local branch of the National Union of Women's Suffrage Societies: Matthews 17.8.14; Advertiser 14.8.14

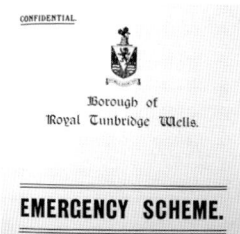

In 1915, an 18-page booklet on the Emergency Scheme was printed but not distributed. This was described as a precaution in case of invasion, but the fact that it was done indicates a level of concern. In the Scheme, the Borough would be divided into districts, each with a marshal, sub-marshal and special constable, to carry out the following:

- disable vehicles by sawing through 4 adjacent spokes;
- tree felling;
- transporting or slaughtering of animals [instructions were given how to kill the animals];
- destroying of food and forage;
- collection of rifles, guns and ammunition;
- destroying or defacement of signposts;
- destroying of property so as not to be of use to the enemy;
- evacuation of population and immigrants [refugees?];
- collection and handing over to military authorities of horses, donkeys, mules, harness, vehicles.

The Council's Electricity Generating Station by Grosvenor Bridge

In the event of evacuation of Tunbridge Wells, all motor-driven vehicles would be commandeered by the military; apparatus from the Post Office Telephone Dept would be removed; as would be tradesmen's stock required by the civil population leaving the Town.

Meanwhile the Government had enacted the Defence of the Realm Act, commonly referred to as 'DORA'. This enabled them to make regulations for 'public safety and the defence of the realm', with breaches punishable by court martial; also, to 'prevent communication with the enemy and obtaining information for that purpose', and to secure means of communication[8]. Early on the lighting of bonfires and the flying of kites were prohibited, because they might be used to signal to an enemy. The Act was amended and extended several times during the war, and a stream of regulations and circulars under the Act were issued to local authorities. The Government took control of the railways; travel concessions were cancelled and the timetable cut.

The Act itself did not provide for requisitioning. Nevertheless the Council

---

[8] *Courier* 8.8.14. Gilbert 14; the Act enabled the introduction of censorship, and somewhat oddly prohibited `discussion of military matters`.

surveyed the resources available[9] in November, and recorded the town had 250 motor cars, 107 'with driver' (presumably a chauffeur), 25 motor buses, and 4 traction engines, as well as 767 horses and ponies and a similar number of horse-drawn vehicles (305 vans; 324 carriages, waggonettes and dog-carts; 103 carts; 17 waggons and 13 timbertugs). The Medical Officer reported more than 40 'factories' and 300 workshops. With or without formal powers, in that first week Lady Matthews records horses being removed from their carts while making deliveries in the town, leaving the carts stranded. The baker's motor lorry was taken and his flour arrived from London by traction engine.

According to Lady Matthews, unlike in the Boer War, there was 'no war fever' but a grim sense of necessity, while resentment and anti-German feeling built up as stories, accurate or otherwise, spread of the behaviour of the German army in Belgium. The town and the Council reacted quickly to the new situation, responding to appeals, providing against future shortages, and seeking out those of German descent. Registration by the borough police identified 139 'aliens' of all nationalities – not many in a population of 36,000; five Germans were arrested. The outbreak of exotic tales about spies and saboteurs provoked a satirical story in the Advertiser about Germans 'acting suspiciously near banks and public buildings'.

Adjustment

With the arrival of troops hygiene, physical and moral, became a key concern. It was a challenge to reconcile the presence of large numbers of soldiers, however well disciplined, with the prevailing ethos - sabbatarian, teetotal and a little naive - of many of the town's leaders, and preserve the economic role of a resort. The Council agreed to keep the Opera House open (for live performances on weekdays only), but refused to let the Kosmos cinema open on Sundays, and a request from the Chief Constable to recruit women as special constables 'on the same basis as men` was rejected because they could not be expected to enter pubs in the course of their duties.

In due course, the proper observance of Sunday would become a key topic. Otherwise the town threw itself into providing for the needs of the troops. The completion of King Charles' Church Hall in Warwick Park was hurried on, so it could be handed over to the military as a social centre for soldiers, and the Army commandeered the Great Hall and the Corn Exchange. The Council handed over the pavilion at St John's Recreation Ground as a 'rest room'; in time it was also used for social events, such as Sunday concerts as long as these consisted of 'sacred music'.

A storm was then provoked by a Captain Screech of the Church Army alleging that a 'non-sacred' item had been performed on a Sunday. This was apparently a soldier taking over the stage, uninvited, to perform animal noises – to enthusiastic applause, according to the *Courier*. With some

---

[9] Kent Archives C/A2/6/29

hilarity, the Council decided to tell Captain Screech that he had been misinformed.

At the end of September the first wounded soldiers, British and Belgian, arrived from France, and the Tradesmen's Association appealed for blankets. In October the Mayor was appealing for houses for use by the Belgian civilians, as well as for billeting and soldiers' welfare, with the exemption from rates. There was a steady succession of claims for exemption from bodies supporting the war effort; the Kent Nursing Institute at 10 Calverley Parade was refused. Le Rendez Vous des Refugiés Belges in Rock Villa Road and the Soldiers' Club in Carlton Road were exempted.

By mid-November the town was hosting the 2nd Army HQ in Lonsdale and Clanricarde Gardens, and what was designated the South Lancashire Brigade, with signallers, parts of four regiments and a Field Ambulance, in all about 5,000 men[10]. Some 120 houses were in use by the troops, the responsibility of the Chief Constable, now appointed Billeting Master, as well as the camp on the Lower Cricket Ground, and later at the Agricultural Ground (now Showfields) and Culverden Castle, and the temporary VAD hospitals now being created, mostly in private houses. The first casualties were conveyed by car from Tonbridge station.

The Council received directions and requests directly from the military as well as from Whitehall; in addition to the camp on the Common, North Farm was made available for a rifle range, while produce from the Council's farms was donated to the Fleet. Trenches on the Common and in Calverley Park were used for bayonet, and other, training. With the aid of public subscriptions the Council set up a soldiers' laundry, also in Rock Villa Road.

Private charitable efforts overlapped with the official response, and were often under official patronage. Besides the constant appeals for men and accommodation, there were financial appeals for the Belgians, for the Red Cross, and for the relief of distress at home; and for clothing, tobacco and razors for the troops in France, and for POWs in Germany; there were appeals for eggs, blankets and newspapers for the wounded, for cricket gear and footballs, for vegetables and fruit (especially rhubarb for the Fleet), for horse chestnuts for munitions, for nutshells and fruit-stones for use in making gas masks, for ambulances for men and horses, and to make sandbags at home[11]. From 1916 waste paper was collected. Reflecting its historic links, the town was said to be third in England in the funds raised for Indian troops fighting in France.

From the start the town recognised the war as an unprecedented national emergency - a *'cataclysm'* (Lady Matthews), *'the greatest struggle of modern times' (Courier)* - and tried to respond to the multiplicity of needs for which

---

[10] *Minutes 9.11.14: the precise number does not seem to have been recorded, but a later letter from the Advertising Association indicates at this stage it was 'up to 8,000' (Courier 12.11.15).*

[11] *Advertiser 28.8.14 et passim: Courier 7.8.14, 2.7.15 et passim: in a later war some of these campaigns might have been intended to boost morale, but not it seems in this one.*

there was no, or inadequate public provision. The early years of the war now appear as a key moment in recognising the social needs, however amplified by war, for which over the next half-century the state assumed responsibility. Meanwhile Tunbridge Wells was conscious of its reputation as a wealthy and charitable town, and shouldered the burden with more or less informal efforts, often inspired and co-ordinated by the Council.

The Liverpool Scottish Band 'in action'.

Tunbridge Wells also remembered its tradition of receiving visitors and welcomed these, especially the Liverpool Scottish with their band; for their part the Lancastrian soldiers were 'very cheerful and friendly with the population' [12], but the National Union of Women Workers organised patrols of the Common 'to prevent soldiers being pestered by bad women'. Those concerned formed themselves into what they called the 'corps of police-women'.

By May 1915 the strain was beginning to tell and the Union asked the Council less euphemistically to provide the patrols 'to prevent the commission of acts of immorality and indecency'. The Council's response is not recorded, but police resources were stretched: following a successful visit by Army recruiters from London they found they needed thirty (male) special constables to fill the gaps. The Council said they were proud of the police's patriotic spirit.

As time went on a more practical response was shown by 'very devoted lady residents', who patrolled the streets at night 'to make friends with the young and excited girls, and protect them as far as possible from the dangers and difficulties that must arise under the existing abnormal conditions…'. A house at 13 Quarry Road had been lent by Alderman Gower as a club for girls 'where their soldier friends will also be welcome'; there were already facilities for tea and coffee, a piano, ping pong and bagatelle, and a writer to the *Courier* appealed for more games and furniture.

Six months of disastrous military news and the arrival of casualties had not affected the public mood. In February 1915 the Lancastrians started to leave, to general regret. Lady Matthews was 'very sorry to lose them… such nice steady fellows… (they) have friends everywhere'. The *Courier* was more heroic: 'the bearing of the men as they left the railway station… showed that they were heartily glad to be away and doing'. And when the Liverpool Scottish marched to Church Parade at Emmanuel: 'It was with a little difficulty that the spectators restrained their natural inclination to cheer the troops as they marched past'[13].

---

[12] Lady Matthews 9.11.14: possibly Tunbridge Wells had not met working class northerners before.
[13] Presumably it was improper to cheer a church parade.

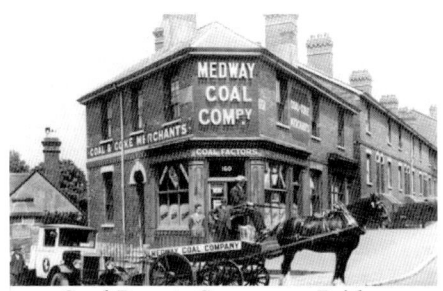
Coal Depot, Grosvenor Bridge

At the Council, peacetime concerns and peacetime divisions were not forgotten, especially the need to minimise the call on the rates for revenue spending, or borrowing for capital. Early on, the Council faced a demand from the local War Emergency Workers Committee[14] to control food prices, provide meals and clothing to needy children, supply milk to nursing mothers, and organise public works at trade union rates. The Council resolved to take no action.

After five months the Council decided it could only afford to light two faces of the new Trinity clock. They debated the cost of providing a separate ward for TB cases at the Sanatorium, as requested by Kent County Council and strongly recommended by the Medical Officer; there was Government help and Alderman H. H. Cronk offered his architectural services free, but the tradesmen's lobby was concerned about the effect on the town's reputation for health and the TB ward was not built. The tradesmen also deplored 'the decline of Tunbridge Wells as a spa', and emphasised the urgency of improving the appearance of the Pantiles.

By 1915 increased prices[15], and the loss of men to the forces, brought discontent in the Council workforce to a head, with more than 100 employees appealing for a wage increase; manual workers had not had an increase for thirteen years. The Council voted a penny in the shilling 'war bonus', up to a maximum of 28 shillings a week. When it was realised that this eliminated the advantage of those required to work on Sundays, there was another protest but the Council kept to its decision. To meet the cost,, the grant to the Band Committee was cut after the band was hired for the summer season, causing protests from the Tradesmen's Association and their allies on the Council.

By spring 1915, the Council also faced complaints from Rusthall[16] about the `evil and annoyance` caused by Sunday trading, specifically the sale of newspapers and ice-cream. Surprisingly the Council was advised it had no powers to act on ice cream (possibly because being sold in the street it was a matter for the magistrates).

The principle of the 1888 Act was that specific powers were conferred on the Council by national legislation, but increasingly these definitions were strained by the demands of the war. When the Government took control of pithead prices for coal, it fell to the Council to negotiate with local coal

---

[14] In effect, a Trades Council.

[15] Lady Matthews claims food price inflation for 1914-15 of more than 50%; the Council admits to 45% for 1914-16 for food and rents (Minutes 2.8.16). 28/- *a week* equates to about half the 2014 minimum *hourly* wage.

[16] Minutes 14.6.15: Rusthall seems to have been a centre of hard-line Nonconformity.

merchants to fix prices to consumers. When the Drill Club became the Volunteer Training Corps under Captain Beeching (of the Bank) the Town Clerk became the President, and the new force was launched by the Mayor at the Town Hall[17].

The Council found it had a role in what later became known as civil defence. Following instructions from Whitehall it tried to organise a guard for its water works at Pembury. The Army declined to release troops for this, and the matter was referred to the Territorial authorities before it was decided there was no need for a guard.

Thus the Council found it had responsibility, direct or indirect, for the security and welfare of the civilian population, home defence, recruitment, civil order, the enforcement of wartime regulations and the management of public appeals. When rationing came in, the Council was responsible for enforcing the Food Control Order.

The possibility of attack from the air was serious, and public concern about Zeppelins amounted almost to fascination. People had to be warned not to stand in the street watching when they passed over: 'at every street corner groups were congregated'. Following air raids on east coast towns in January 1915 the Army ordered 'all lights' to be extinguished between 5pm and 7.30am, and the Town Clerk's office issued the necessary order. Street lights were not to be lit and shops to lower blinds or use coloured paper on their windows. 'Motor vehicles (were) also darkened'. Only 'some' private houses were treated as exempt.

Within half an hour the Army clarified the order to refer only to lights 'showing skywards'. But when this was understood to mean street lighting the Council was obliged to compensate the Gas Company for unlit columns[18]. Thereafter the police and the courts were kept busy with disputes about what was permissible, and about safety in the blackout, with the Tradesmen's Association demanding whitening of kerbs. At first the public was more concerned about the risk of accidents than of bombs. When the Council agreed reluctantly to whitening kerbs in a few places at a cost of £150 the *Courier* celebrated it as relief for 'gropers'.

> 'There is... no fresh reason for expecting an air-raid, and this is one of the safest parts of the country, (but) crowds should disperse and everyone take shelter, while those in houses should go into cellars or lower rooms. Children should remain in school. Unexploded shells or bombs should not be touched. ..Inhabitants should provide themselves with candles'.   Announcement by Mayor Emson 12.3.15

When war broke out the Council was extending and improving street lighting (gas in the main roads, otherwise electrical), and continued to receive petitions from residents who wanted it. By Spring 1915, it was clear this was incompatible with the danger from the air; the Council now received

---

[17] *Courier* 22.1.15; later the Local Defence Volunteers, the Home Guard.
[18] Minutes vol.410 p.256; it's not clear whether the columns belonged to the gas company.

protests about excessive lighting and in May, after a Government order instructed councils to 'take the necessary steps', street lights were extinguished. The Chief Constable protested about this and investigated ways of darkening the town 'on the approach of raiders', as practised in some other towns, on the principle that the military would receive a warning from the coast and alert the civil authorities, who would determine how to respond.

The Council asked the Gas Company to turn off the gas at the gasworks when a warning was received. The Company replied that this would not have the desired effect: gas in the pipes would continue to feed the streetlights for up to an hour, while there was a serious risk of explosion when the supply was turned on again. They suggested the Fire Brigade should turn the lights off individually, and the Council accepted this.

The street lighting was anyway turned off during the summer months, but the Council allowed the Gas Company to provide lighting from a column outside its new showrooms in the High Street. Presumably this was deemed not to 'show skywards'. In October the Council decided not to relight the streets 'for economy'. There seems to have been little empirical information as to what was visible from above.

Following the chaos of May 1915, successive regulations imposed some order in the matter of lighting, but there remained confusion as to what was required for protection, what was imposed for fuel economy, and black-outs from actual cuts. When a young woman died on the operating table during a power cut she was described as a victim of 'Hun brutality'.

In December 1915, the Council tried again ... *'inside lights must be so shaded or reduced, or the windows, skylights and glass doors so screened by shutters or dark blinds or curtains that no more than a dull subdued light is visible from any direction outside.'* Factories were not subject to the order but were expected to extinguish lights on receiving a telephone warning. Motorists were warned by signs at the entrances to the town. It was not until 1917 that county-wide lighting restrictions were introduced.

With the approach of the first anniversary of the war, Tunbridge Wells faced up to the need for more lasting arrangements. The Grove bandstand was inexplicably surrounded with barbed wire, even though according to the Band Committee, the town was 'well filled with visitors'. In April, the traders appealed for 'girls' to deliver parcels in place of the traditional errand boys, and the railway company introduced 'lady' booking clerks (the distinction is interesting); the latter were commended on their efficiency. 'Girls' were also invited to volunteer to work, apparently unpaid, in the new VAD hospitals. In October, shops were required to close at 10pm as an economic measure.

The conflict between peacetime attitudes and wartime needs could be stark. The manager of the Kosmos cinema applied to hold `sacred` Sunday evening concerts and donate the proceeds to charity[19]. Several members of the Council were outraged at this profaning of the Sabbath. This controversy would rage during the whole of 1916 and a detailed report of it can be found in Chapter 9.

The severe temper of the town was also revealed by the uproar caused by one of the three radical and Quaker Misses Candler reporting (correctly) that the troops in France were given a tot of rum before going over the top. (This is also reported in more detail in Chapter 9.)

Resolution

On 15th July 1915, the Government passed the National Registration Act requiring men between 18 and 40 to register, giving details of their employment, from which it could be assessed how many were potentially available for conscription, which at this stage was still voluntary. Men were invited to 'attest' to their willingness to serve through a scheme, set up by Lord Derby. Those attesting, and accepted, would be enrolled in the Reserve and could be called up immediately, but were able to choose their regiment.

While this volunteer response was encouraging, the Government would soon decide that the armed forces required even more and compulsory conscription was introduced in early 1916. The Council set up a committee under the Mayor to implement this and a Local Recruitment Appeal Tribunal was set up to hear appeals against being 'called up'.

In February 1916, War Savings Certificates were launched nationally, priced at 15/6d but redeemable at £1 in 1925, to be managed by local authorities. These were too expensive for most people and were later complemented by savings stamps sold at post offices. National needs increasingly took over from the plethora of local appeals, but still channelled through the Council.

Knowledge of the war in Tunbridge Wells was limited to what was carried by the censored national newspapers, and beyond that to stories told by those arriving in the town injured or on leave, and on personal contacts with London. In Tunbridge Wells, censorship was in the hands of the military.

With one of the Bandsmen a patient in the General Hospital, news spread that only three of those who played in the 1914 Band season had survived. In early 1915 the town awoke to find the buses missing: they had been commandeered in the night to take troops to the coast in case of invasion.

On the night of 13th/14th October 1915, bombs fell in Calverley Grounds, near Grove Hill Road: Lady Matthews says three, others say four. There were no serious injuries but windows were broken as far away as the clothing depot in Crescent Road. In July 1916 the sound of the guns in France was

---

[20] Council Minutes 1916 p.3; `no comic or dramatic films to be shown`.

heard in Tunbridge Wells *'booming all day long, and rattling windows up to 11.00 at night'.* By early 1918 with air-raids in London this noise could also be heard in the town.

Little evidence of dissent appears in the local papers, while Council attitudes often seem naively high-minded. The camp on the Common was apparently unfenced and the British Socialist Party organised an anti-war rally in close proximity to it; the residents were amused by this conjuncture; and no official action was taken. Lady Matthews was shocked to hear of a young man refusing to register saying 'What has my country done for me?'

However there was an increase in juvenile offences no doubt partly due to the absence of police, but attributed by the *Courier* to a lack of parental guidance, and reports of assaults on women and children. When the blackout was imposed, the Post Office announced telegrams would no longer be delivered by post-women after dark. Accidental deaths increased in the town when the blackout started, but subsequently fell back to peacetime levels.

Grosvenor Road with General Hospital (note Urban's sign on left)

Most group dissidence took the form of demonstrations against Germans. The naturalised watch-maker Louis (Ludwig) Reich had his windows broken[20], and more seriously 'about a thousand young men' were reported as being gathered on a Saturday night outside the premises of J. Urban, a hairdresser in Grosvenor Road. They were dispersed by `a small army` of police, and no violence was reported.

The stresses in the town were reflected in different ways. The Council faced protests from their manual workforce, apparently initiated by the gravediggers who claimed their workload had increased. There was discontent in the police who were allowed no leave in the first three months of the war, and were subsequently refused consent to retire when due. Following the penny-in-the shilling bonus award in March 1915, with its effect on overtime, the manual workers persuaded their employer to pay extra for overtime in May 1916, and to increase war bonus from 2/4d to 3/6d a week.

The Union of General Workers protested again about this meagre allowance, and suggested referring the dispute for arbitration to the Board of Trade.

---

[20] It is sad to record as this book goes to press that L. Reich & Co., Jewellers, of Monson Road, will be closing down shortly, after about 125 years in Tunbridge Wells, as a result of the retirement of the owner, the great-grandson of the original Louis (or Ludwig).

The Council refused, saying the workers were entitled to take their labour elsewhere.

One complication arose from the argument that unmarried men did not need the same increase as married ones, and another from the Council's undertaking to make up the pay of men who joined up, at the time when this was voluntary. However, following further unrest the bonus was increased again in 1917, to five shillings a week, with a maximum of 35/- for married and unmarried. Finally, with a threat of a strike, or mass resignation (a strike being arguably illegal), the Council agreed to meet a delegation, and a 'final settlement' was agreed of an increase of 2d an hour on the pre-war rate, not payable to those in the forces.

The dispute might have been embarrassing since in early 1916 the Finance Committee forecast an unforeseen surplus of more than £10,000 for the year, partly through the departure of Council staff. They felt it would look bad to reduce the rate with the war situation, and worse if it was necessary to raise the rate again next year. They proposed investing the surplus in War Bonds which would produce a dividend; the Council agreed. The Tradesmen's Association protested at the failure to 'hand the money back'. The Council's determination to preserve the town's reputation as a resort was shown by maintaining the grant of £500 to the Band Committee for 1916. But when Captain Beeching appealed for financial help for his corps, they found they had no power to assist.

The strength of the Tradesmen's Association was possibly also illustrated by the response of the Council to the District Auditor who questioned the practice of having named local traders as suppliers to the Council, in place of competitive tendering; the Council deferred the matter 'for six months'. However when the traders appealed to the Council to fix dates for Bank Holidays in February 1917, in place of the two postponed by Royal proclamation in 1916, the Council declined: it was for individual traders to reach agreement with their workforce.

Many of the Council's workers joined up early on, a factor no doubt in the industrial unrest. Following the disaster of the Somme, the Government appealed for the release of doctors under 45, and Tunbridge Wells released its Medical Officer, Dr Linton. Its regular operations were also handicapped by the loss of horses. The Council was already facing the extra burden, and cost, of collecting refuse from the military. With the prohibition of bonfires there was more garden and similar waste to be collected from all sources, and the Council appealed for it to be burned.

The principle had been agreed that the Council would be reimbursed for providing services for the military, but there was much room for negotiation, and it is perhaps surprising that relations with the Army seem to have remained cordial. The Council had to improve roads, repair the existing and build new ones, for example on the Agricultural Ground (now Showfields). It had to unblock drains in houses where soldiers were billeted, and turn schools over at short notice for billeting troops overnight, notably during the invasion scare in early 1915.

Weekly Bath Parade

As mentioned already it made towels available for soldiers using the public baths, followed later by costumes, supplied in bulk by Weekes. The hills of Tunbridge Wells were said to be hard on soldiers' feet and Mayor Gower made a room in his house available for chiropody. War damage was also supposed to be compensated by Government, but this caused dispute with the Council when the Government tried to introduce an insurance scheme.

It is noticeable that domestic questions determined by the Council were on what might be called the pre-war basis of welfare, rather than concerns about morale or efficiency; perhaps this reflected the individualist mood of the population, at least until late in the war with increasing hardship for civilians and the acceleration of casualties.

Ely Lane c. 1910

The housing of the working classes remained an issue, but was seen as a problem for after the war. The Mayor's Emergency Committee agreed to give free medical treatment in cases of need, while the Surgical Aid Society provided false teeth. But when the Workers Committee asked the Council to use its powers to feed those school children 'who by reason of want are incapable of benefitting from education', the Council declined. When, at the same time as losing their Medical Officer, the Council was urged by Government to increase maternity and child welfare visits, the worm turned: the problem 'shall have attention after the war'. Following intervention by the Town Clerk, they agreed to extend the service 'where possible with present resources'.

Survival

By mid-1915 there were widespread appeals to introduce compulsory conscription. The numbers coming forward voluntarily were inadequate, and it was felt that the effect was unfair. There were claims in the press of men doing 'women's work', and from 1915 on cases were reviewed by the

Recruitment Tribunal. From late 1916 the *Courier* printed official weekly lists of those required to register who had not done so, ostensibly to help the Recruiting Officer complete his records. Anyone knowing of their whereabouts was invited to report them anonymously. By 1917 the military were patrolling places of amusement rounding up unregistered men.

The Tribunal, with the power to exempt essential workers, comprised the Mayor, the Town Clerk, an alderman and four magistrates. This composition was attacked by the Tradesmen's Association, who wanted one of their members included, and on the Council by Councillor Berwick who thought labour should be represented. The Council also refused a request from the NUWSS for women to be included.

The cases were overwhelmingly appeals for exemption on grounds of economic or domestic hardship, not conscientious objection, and often brought or supported by an employer. Over three years the West Kent Tribunal heard 2500 cases for 'withdrawal of a certificate' (of conscription) issued by the military; 194 cases were appealed, of which only 57 were successful.

George Dutch at the age of 78 in 1972

One unsuccessful appeal was that of George Dutch, a shop assistant and conscientious objector, who at the age of 21 had founded in 1915 the Tunbridge Wells branches of both the No Conscription Fellowship, and with the Candler sisters, the National Council Against Conscription. Although reputed to be a founder and leader of the Tunbridge Wells 'Soviet' in 1917, no evidence has yet been found to support this.'[21].

While the Government resisted compulsory conscription, the Council was operating the Derby scheme[22], and the Town Clerk appealed for volunteers to distribute and collect the registration forms 'from those who are not already engaged in war work', while the police were also going from door to door. When in January 1916 compulsory conscription was finally announced, the Tribunal was already hearing appeals.

There had been a rush of volunteers at the end of the original period for voluntary attesting in December, and Sir John Matthews, as a JP, was kept busy for nine and a half hours at the Recruitment Office processing men in batches of eight.

The supply and distribution of food was handled by the Food Controller enforcing the Food Control Order. By late 1916 the submarine campaign

---

22 Of seven appeals heard on grounds of conscience in 1916, four were upheld; these were all cases of formal religious commitment. Dutch, whose case was a matter of private conviction, was unsuccessful.
23 Matthews 12.12.15; the Derby scheme was actually extended by 3 months (*Courier* 3.3.16)

was having a marked effect on food supplies, with a corresponding effect on civilian life. Tea was pooled; the Government set a maximum price for meat, and recommended a limit for bread consumption. Bakers were limited to producing loaves in two formats, the controlled price was increased, and a letter to the *Courier* complained about the effect on a soldier's family living on the 24/6d a week separation allowance, of which 6/- was due in rent. From July 1917 coal was rationed according to the number of rooms in a house, and from September 1918 wood fuel similarly, while tradesmen were instructed to close early and halve their use of coal.

The Government initially tried to ensure fairness in food by controlling prices. Milk and livestock farmers protested to the Food Controller that they were producing at a loss but received little sympathy and were threatened with DORA. There were appeals for people to eat less wheaten bread, and more oatmeal, barley and, surprisingly, rice. The *Courier* was at a loss to understand why people were not complying; they were 'unpatriotic'. In November maximum prices were set for all cuts of meat, but butchers complained they couldn't get supplies because immature stock had been slaughtered.

The Mayor led a large crowd on the Common in making a 'ration pledge'. In November 1916 the normally phlegmatic Lady Matthews commented 'the only thing that approaches with certainty is famine'. On finding Calverley Road jammed with women queuing at the food shops, and no food being sold, she summoned the Food Controller who sent the women home. A Yorkshire newspaper, possibly teasing, reported that women in Kent were being instructed in making wheatless, sugarless and currantless cake, lentil sausages, and haricot bean pie.

Calverley Road with street market

In 1915 the British had been reassured by reports of food riots in Berlin, and appeals for food for British POWs in Germany. But in 1916, shortages began in Britain. Margarine was commandeered by the British Government and distributed in bulk to local authorities. By the winter of 1917-18 the 'food problem has grown cruelly'; butchers were closed several days a week, and 'mainly empty'; doors were kept locked and 'forlorn groups of women stand waiting and waiting'. 'Butcher's meat' was rationed but not sausages, chicken or rabbit, if available. But in January the *Courier* reported there was 'no meat in the shops'.

The Government introduced successive orders during 1917 in an attempt to regulate food production and distribution, but this did not deal with the problem of malnutrition in poorer areas and among munition workers. By the autumn of 1917 some overall rationing was becoming inevitable. The Workers' Committee demanded it 'for fairness'.

In fact shopkeepers were already required to register with the Council, and householders with retailers; now sugar 'tickets' would be issued to householders for use in the shops[23]. Eventually there would be four tickets, for sugar, meat, bread and margarine, later combined into a ration book, and householders were supposed to shop where they were registered. Other measures restricted milk, potatoes, tea and bakery products. The Council appointed officers to implement the Order and prosecute offences.

Rabbit clubs (breeding rabbits as meat) were started, including one at Hildenborough. When there was briefly a glut of milk in May 1918, 'the women of Kent' formed a cheesemaking army. Also by this time there were almost 1000 allotments, a fivefold increase from before the war.

In February the Government offered loans for communal kitchens to economise in food and fuel, while supplying 'nutritious meals at reasonable prices'. Four were started in Tunbridge Wells by volunteers regulated by the Food Controller, but by July they were in difficulties and the Council had to step in, eventually supporting six[24]. The Mayor, now Gower, said he hoped 'all classes will not mind mixing with the masses in a public restaurant'[25].

In spite of these obligations, for the Council some earlier themes continued. The pressing need now was for money for national purposes; pressure to buy War Bonds, intensified, and the *Courier* (presumably with central prompting) took to publishing a comparative table of the amounts raised by similar towns: Tunbridge Wells was respectable but a long way behind Harrogate, and embarrassed when overtaken in this league by Maidstone. The Tradesmen's Association appealed for funds to pay for a submarine; this was so successful that they eventually bought a destroyer[26]. The Council resolved to apply for a war trophy or trophies 'in due time'.

As early as 1916 the Tradesmen's Association demanded the Council identify a 'home for the band as soon as peace is declared', and discussion continued intermittently about the provision of a winter garden. In early 1917, A. Brackett, the leading Tunbridge Wells estate agent at the time, led a discussion on property values after the war, and the Council was asked to help find employment for disabled servicemen.
In April 1918, the WEA addressed the question of post-war reconstruction in a meeting at the Town Hall. The RSPB was concerned at the loss of

---

[23] *Courier* 24.8.17; the scheme was introduced in October.

[24] They were set up originally by voluntary effort, but regulated by the Food Controller and taken over by the Council when they got into difficulties. By 1918 there were kitchens in North St (St Peter's), Quarry Road, Cambrian Road (High Brooms), Down Lane, Rusthall High Street and Varney Street.

[25] Lady Matthews 10.3.18; the distinction is worthy of W. S. Gilbert.

[26] *Courier* 14.1.18; at the end of the war, sixty of these were moored in the Medway.

woodlands, and the Canadian Forestry Corps undertook replanting. In August 1917, the Council reverted to the issue of housing the working classes, and the following July a housing conference called for 'radical measures' to deal with the housing shortage[27]. The Council discussed the form and location of a War Memorial, and agreed to site it at the Town Hall[28].

In Spring 1918 the clergy appealed once more for the abandonment of Sunday entertainment 'considering the serious and critical times in which we are now living' [29]. In August, with the failure of the German offensive, in spite of a last-minute invasion scare, there seems to have been a sense of an ending, and the *Courier* printed a letter from Sir Arthur Conan Doyle about how to deal with a German surrender. In June 1918 a letter from Amelia Scott and others proposed the creation of a Council of Social Service *'to promote the idea of co-operation... in view of the unknown conditions that will ensue upon the conclusion of peace'*. Meanwhile the Council resolved to provide a site for 'gardens and buildings (for) musical and other performances'.

In November 1918 the 'Spanish' 'flu epidemic was recognised by the closure of places of entertainment. Mayor Gower was disabled by it, but actual deaths in Tunbridge Wells were few compared with the losses during the war. While still active, the Mayor announced peace from the Town Hall at mid-day on 11th November to a town which was weary and relieved, rather than triumphant. The bells pealed for the Armistice, and according to Lady Matthews, Tunbridge Wells *'burst mysteriously into bunting. Flags and banners were showing everywhere... Everyone greeted everyone else with smiles and sometimes tears'*.

News of the death in action of Lt. Richard Prankerd, aged 27, of St James Road, the last man from Tunbridge Wells to be killed in the Great War, was received after the Armistice. Through the grim winter of 1918-19 Tunbridge Wells continued to face social disruption, food and fuel crisis, news of foreign upheavals, and the return of those maimed by the war, as well as bereavement. Just as at the outbreak, there was an immediate down-turn in trade, and the Council turned its attention to the possibility of disorder from the dispersal of large numbers of troops, and the return of Tunbridge Wells' own.

---

[27] *Courier* 12.7.18; the conference heard that the rent on an `urban cottage` had more than doubled since 1914.
[28] *Courier* 9.11.17; the Town Hall was not then on the corner of Upper Mt Pleasant., but in Calverley Road.
[29] Apparently evidence of divine disapproval.

CHAPTER 5
THE ARMY IN TUNBRIDGE WELLS
by Stephen Bates,
with Pat Wilson, Mike Fradd and Edward Gilbert

It is almost impossible now to get back into the mindset and lives of the people of Tunbridge Wells – or indeed anywhere else – in 1914. Despite a peace demonstration on the Common in the early days of the war, very few people seem to have questioned why the country was going to war – even though quite a few queried whether they personally were needed to fight. Otherwise, why would shopkeepers advertise in the *Courier* in 1914 that they had not lost staff to the war so it was service as usual; and why the anguished periodic remarks in the paper about the town not doing its bit in recruitment?

Part of the answer to the first question was that people across Britain had grown used in the previous decade to seeing Germany as a likely enemy in any war. They had been fed a diet of literary scares about a possible invasion, of which Erskine Childers' *The Riddle of the Sands* of 1903 is the best-known and most enduring example and William Le Queux's *The Invasion of 1910* – published in 1906 and serialised in the *Daily Mail,* with the author making sure his narrative highlighted towns where the paper's circulation was flagging – as leading examples.

If war was unexpected in August 1914, the enemy was not. Germany was seen as an aggressive threat, almost for the first time in history and had supplanted France as the traditional enemy, especially since the Entente Cordiale of 1904 had bound the British and the French together against the threat on France's eastern borders. This was despite the fact that in places, such as Tunbridge Wells, there was a long-settled, well-integrated, law-abiding and English-speaking German population. The waiters who served them their teas in the hotels and cafes were German, so were barbers and shop owners such as Mr Reich who had lived in Britain since the age of six in 1878. Reich had stones through his windows once war broke out and faced discrimination even from the congregation at his Catholic Church. Doubtless Appenrodt's Continental sausages, advertised before the War, were soon withdrawn from sale at London & Raiswell's grocery stores on Mount Pleasant and Grove Hill Road.

At the start of the war, Britain had a relatively small professional army of about 180,000. Of its ten divisions, of about 18,000 men each, six infantry and one cavalry division (of approximately 125,000 men) were based in Britain and available to fight; the rest being needed around the world to guard the Empire. So it could put about 125,000 regulars into the field immediately in Europe, which was a very small number compared with Germany and France's huge conscript armies of 1.8 million Germans and 1.6 million Frenchmen who were immediately mobilised in 1914. Until mid-way through the First World War, British forces were made up of volunteers. The British army – which was about the same size as Serbia's – had not fought in western Europe since the battle of Waterloo 99 years earlier; and the wars it had engaged in since, had been mainly relatively short-lived, distant and colonial campaigns. Even the wars conducted on the European mainland by other countries, such as the Franco-Prussian conflict of 1870, had been brief affairs, over in a few weeks. So the idea that what would become eventually the First World War, would be *"over by Christmas"* and hence not too serious or bloody, was widely-held – and although political and military leaders such as Prime Minister Asquith and Lord Kitchener did not believe that, many of those who flocked to the Colours did.

The British public had been shocked by the poor physical calibre of army recruits during the Boer War (1899-1902). Many of those who had come forward were under-fed, under-sized and unfit. So in 1908, reforms were introduced to re-organise the Regular Army and to create a voluntary Army Reserve which was meant for defence, not offence, since Britain was an island.

This Reserve was designed to replace the existing part-time, voluntary and somewhat uncoordinated and haphazard system of essentially local militia, which had existed since the 18th century. However, the change-over from 'militia' to Territorial Army was neither instant nor smooth, and there is evidence that the previous system continued well into the War.

In 1914, the Army Reserve was made up of 145,350 part-timers, who were paid three shillings and sixpence (17½p.) a week and required to keep up to scratch, by attending 12 training days a year.

There was also the Special Reserve of a further 64,000 men who had signed up for six months in barracks, and then were on call for the next seven years, with the requirement of attending a month's training each year: they too were paid. All these Reserves included men who were either Territorials (i.e infantry), or Yeomanry (i.e cavalry, comprising men who owned horses, or were able to ride).

In total, there were about 215,000 of these 'part-time' soldiers. They attended annual training camps and also one or two evening training sessions a week, while living at home and continuing with their civilian occupations. They would be the first to try and find a solution.

Legally, membership of this new 1908 Territorial Army had no legal obligation beyond opposing any invader of Britain, but in fact in the euphoria of the situation, they would be swept up into fighting in Europe.

In early August 1914, the Territorials of the 3rd battalion of the Royal West Kents had been in training at Shorncliffe near Ramsgate; and the 500 cyclists of the 5th battalion of the Regiment had been pedalling around Broadstairs. How rigorous such camps usually were, is hard to tell: for many they must have been the nearest they got to a holiday with their mates, usually under canvas in high summer: *"to this day,"* wrote one veteran from a northern regiment, *"the smell of crushed grass, which is always to be found inside marquees, reminds me of the rough and ready meals on the bare trestle tables, slightly flavoured with smoke from the cookhouse fires...It was natural that groups of school friends should be drawn together."*

Schools, such as Skinners' too, had their cadet forces, in training to provide the junior officers who would lead their men over the top – and suffer disproportionate casualties accordingly. Indeed, at the start of the war, only boys from schools such as Skinners' and Tonbridge public school were considered for officer training, though the rules were loosened later to allow in grammar school boys and even those who had started in the ranks, to win commissions. The Skinners' School War Memorial, designed by C. H. Strange, would have 81 names on it when it was unveiled in 1920.

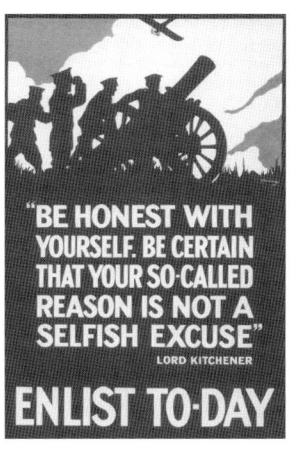

The professional troops of what the Kaiser called *"the Contemptible Little Army"* were the first to be transported across to Belgium after war was declared and the West Kents in particular were one of the first units into action on the first day's fighting, 23rd August 1914, as they guarded the Mons-Conde canal which loops round to the north of the south Belgian town. The regiment's Regular first battalion had been stationed in Dublin that summer and sailed for the Continent on board the SS Gloucestershire on 13th August. Within ten days, they were under fire and would soon be joining the British retreat, back the way they had just marched, along the long, straight, tree-lined avenues of northern France.

Back home, what made men volunteer that summer? Some joined the queues at army recruitment centres, to be welcomed in Tunbridge Wells by Sergeant Instructor Callaghan and Quartermaster Sergeant Hickmott, who signed up 80 men in the first week of the war. Others stepped forward at open air meetings such as that held at Five Ways on the second weekend in September when a Mr Ard sang a solo rendition of Soldiers of the King – "*a good many young fellows handed in their names,*" the *Courier* reported. Clearly moral pressure was exerted: perhaps some had listened to the Rev. C.H. Bellamy preaching a sermon at Holy Trinity on the value of sacrifice. There were other intangibles, such as serving with your friends, not being left behind, or failing to share in the great adventure.

Alan Thomas, a former public schoolboy who served with the 6th Battalion of the West Kents, wrote later: "*I suspect what really moved me to volunteer was less a feeling of patriotism than a desire to stand right with my fellows. To have been a conscientious objector...even if I had wanted to be one, would have been unthinkable.*" But patriotism and a sense of duty also played a considerable part, as letters home by volunteers across the country throughout the whole war attest.

There were other advantages as well: a sense of adventure and a break from the drudgery of normal working life – and the pay was reasonable too. A man earning perhaps ten shillings a week in a labouring or lowly clerical job received a shilling a day: seven shillings a week, from the army, a ration allowance of 14s 7d a week and 3s 6d uniform allowance. If your company patriotically continued to pay half wages, as many did, that meant you were three times better off.

Some employers positively pressurised their men to join up: a landowner named Slater in West Kent drove his footman, cowman and 43 year-old butler into Maidstone to enlist and probably consoled himself that he was personally fulfilling a national service by doing without their services. Tunbridge Wells did not have a single industry as some of the great northern cities did, so it did not recruit pals battalions, made up of groups of friends all joining up together, but there is no question that the Borough Council and other local authorities expected men to do their bit.

Landowners and local aristocrats still employed large numbers of people, both in their houses and on their estates, deference still ruled, and they could demand that their men join up, just as their own sons were doing: thus Sir David Salomons' announcement that he would equip at his own expense 100 volunteers from Southborough and Tunbridge Wells to follow his son, also called David but known as Reggie, into the military.

An emotional 1915 recruitment poster

Recruitment meetings were shovelling men into the forces all over the country. Lord Kitchener's appeal for a hundred thousand men by the end of the year was met well before the end of November – by then a million had joined up - but the enlistment far exceeded the capacity of the military to cope.

The existing barracks all over the country were full within a fortnight and there was a major logistical exercise to house, clothe and feed the volunteers – hence the *Courier's* obsession with where the troops who were being sent to the town as a holding and training centre on the way to the Continent were being accommodated and how they were being fed. In the early days in some units the troops had to find and pay for their own food, which may account for the *Courier's* satisfaction at the end of October 1914 that the presence of the Territorials billeted in the town "*should at least be a help to tradesmen.*"

The town's position made it a suitable concentration point for troops for training purposes and for gathering before they left for the Channel ports and the Western Front. The Tunbridge Wells architect, C. H. Strange, who later wrote a short history of the town, recalled: *"It was made the headquarters of one of the new armies; soldiers were collected here from all parts of England to be drafted across to France. The impression of a military centre was increased by the proximity of a large camp on Ashdown Forest, the men coming into town for evening recreation; by a camp of Canadian foresters who cut down thousands of fir trees to the south of the town for pit-props and sleepers and by the aerodrome at Penshurst."* That was not the only local airfield. There was also one at Liptrap's Farm at the north end of Sandhurst Road, which had been set up before the war and had been a stopping-off point for flying competitions such as the Daily Mail-sponsored round Britain race of 1910. Aerodromes in those days were of course no more than mown fields.

DURING THE WAR

Messrs. JENKINSON & SON
NAVAL & MILITARY TAILORS,
MOUNT PLEASANT,

Have been favoured with the patronage of Officers serving in the following:—

The Royal Navy.
" " Naval Division.
" " Marine Artillery.
" " Marine Light Infantry.
21st Lancers.
Royal Horse Artillery.
" Field Artillery.
" Garrison Artillery.
" Engineers.
" Engineer Services.
The Royal Scots.
" Royal West Surrey Regt.
" East Kent Regt.
" Royal Lancaster Regt.
" Northumberland Fusiliers.
" Royal Fusiliers.
" King's Liverpool Regt.
" King's Liverpool (Scottish).
" King's Liverpool (Irish).
" Norfolk Regt.
" Devonshire Regt.
" Lincolnshire Regt.
" Suffolk Regt.
" Somerset Light Infantry.
" West Yorkshire Regt.
" Leicestershire Regt.
" Yorkshire Regt.
" Lancashire Fusiliers.
" Cheshire Regt.
" Royal Welsh Fusiliers.
" South Wales Borderers.
" King's Own Scottish Borderers.
" Gloucestershire Regt.
" Worcestershire Regt.
" East Lancashire Regt.
" East Surrey Reg.
" Duke of Cornwall's Light Infantry.
" West Riding Regt.
" Border Regt.
" Royal Sussex Regt.
" 5th Royal Sussex (Cinque Ports) Regt.
" Hampshire Regt.
" South Staffordshire Regt.
" Dorsetshire Regt.
" South Lancashire Regt.
" Welsh Regt.
" Black Watch (Royal Highlanders).
" Oxford and Buckinghamshire Light Infantry.
" Essex Regt.
" Nottinghamshire and Derbyshire Regt.
" Loyal North Lancashire Regt.

The Northamptonshire Regt.
" Royal Berkshire Regt.
" Royal West Kent Regt.
" Yorkshire Light Infantry.
" Shropshire Light Infantry.
" Middlesex Regt.
" King's Royal Rifle Corps.
" Manchester Regt.
" York and Lancaster Regt
" Durham Light Infantry
" Highland Light Infantry.
" Seaforth Highlanders.
" Gordon Highlanders.
" Cameron Highlanders.
" Royal Irish Rifles.
" Royal Irish Fusiliers.
" Argyll and Sutherland Highlanders
" Royal Munster Fusiliers
" Royal Dublin Fusiliers.
" Rifle Brigade.
" Royal Army Medical Corps.
" Army Service Corps.
" Royal Flying Corps
" Army Veterinary Corps.
" Army Cyclists Corps.
" 1st Kent Regt. (Cyclists).
" Army Ordnance Departm't.
" Intelligence Department.
" Remount Service.
" Army Motor Res. (R.A.C.)
" Chaplains to the Forces.
" 5th City of London Regt.
" 6th City of London Regt.
" 7th City of London Regt.
" 8th City of London Regt.
" 9th County of London Regt
" 10th County of London Regt
" 11th County of London Rgt
" 12th County of London Regt
" London Scottish.
The Dorset Yeomanry.
" Leicestershire Yeomanry.
" Surrey Yeomanry.
" South Nottinghamshire Hussars.

INDIAN ARMY.
The 2nd Lancers.
" 12th Cavalry Regt.
" 18th Lancers.
" 129th Baluchistan Regt.
Officers of the Belgian Army.
The British Red Cross Society;
also Authorised Agents for the Kent V.A.D. (T.) Tunbridge Wells and District.

JENKINSON & SON,
NAVAL & MILITARY TAILORS
& COMPLETE SERVICE OUTFITTERS
MOUNT PLEASANT
TUNBRIDGE WELLS
And at Crowboro' Cross.   'Phone 535

Tailor's advertisement in the *Courier*, listing the military units served, either in transit, training or convalescence.

Tunbridge Wells was far from being a military town, unlike Maidstone, but what it did have were hotels and boarding houses for the tourist trade and large holiday villas and houses which could accommodate the officers. It also had training facilities of a sort: there was the Common and High Rocks and a firing range, numerous woods and plantations for military exercises around the southern fringes of the town and Ashdown Forest was only a route march away. And its strategic position was good, with two railway lines. It was inland but still close to the embarkation ports at Dover, Folkestone and Portsmouth (and not too far from London for the officers). This made it an ideal centre.

Most of the visiting regiments only stayed in the town briefly as they waited their next orders: first came the Royal Engineers in September 1914, then the Liverpool Scottish Regiment, the King's Liverpool Regiment and the South Lancashire Regiment arrived in November 1914, followed by the West Lancashires in the Spring of 1915, the South Lancashires again in May and July, followed by the Home Counties Division and so on. The Welsh Regiment was in town from November 1914 to February 1915 when they were moved to Scotland. Some of these men would not see their distant homes again: the Liverpool Scottish troops who so impressed the locals with their kilts and their drill in the first weeks of the war would end up

Liverpool Scottish relaxing

sacrificed at the battles of Neuve Chapelle and Loos in 1915.

The arrival of several thousand troops in the town was not regarded by all with unmitigated pleasure. A letter in the *Courier* of 5th November 1915 from a Mr F. A. Spencer of Woodbury Park Road strikes a familiar-sounding note: "*We are not discussing the treatment of the 'Tommies'…in our midst but how many troops the town can reasonably be expected to accommodate. It seems that a high official of the Advertising Association after consulting with sundry other high officials in the town met a high official at the War Office and arranged that Tunbridge Wells should take 8,000 troops. My contention is that 8,000 is too many…living as I do in an 'atmosphere' of billets I have no hesitation in saying that many of the billets were overcrowded and 'unwholesome.' …As each billet must accumulate garbage in a day about equal to what the ordinary or garden householder gathers in the course of a week it follows that each additional billet adds considerably to the difficulties of a collecting department already overtaxed…I know of many who view with dismay the possibility of a visit from the billeting officer. I know of two families who have given up their homes and left the town in consequence of the billeting in their neighbourhood…*" Perhaps Mr Spencer was fortunate if all he had to cope with during the war were the local billeting arrangements and rubbish collection.

The experience of a Tunbridge Wells man enlisting in the West Kents' reserve battalion, stationed at Crowborough in April 1915 would probably have imitated that of the Kitchener army recruits across the country: endless drill, physical exercises, daily kit cleaning, equipment inspections and route marches to toughen them – and their feet - up. Many recruits gained weight and height in their first months of training, because of better food and healthier exercise: it was estimated that on average working class recruits gained six inches in height during the course of their first six months.

They needed to: the average recruit weighed 132 lbs and would be expected routinely to carry about 60 pounds of equipment and accoutrements: 77 pounds in winter: two blankets, two pairs of boots, three pairs of socks, a greatcoat, a shovel or wire-cutters, mess tin, gas mask, rifle and bayonet, entrenching tool, 150 rounds of ammunition and field dressings, as well as uniform and personal toiletries such as comb and wash bag. This was less weight than French soldiers (85 lbs) or Germans (up to 100lbs), but was still very hefty, especially if regular route-marches of 15-20 miles were required. Officers were also allowed 45 lbs of personal luggage, but this would often be carried on the battalion transport.

Recruits would be kept busy all day, from reveille at six a.m, until lights out at ten p.m. Not only square-bashing and route marches - there would be bayonet drill too, the charging of dangling sacks of sand to instil martial spirit by spearing the dummy enemy, just as their great-grandfathers had done in the Napoleonic wars a century earlier. Lines bearing the imitation enemy to be bayoneted were strung up on the Common and in Calverley Park. Such drills encouraged aggression, but often came at the expense of more useful skills such as map reading or trench warfare techniques. The amount of close bayonet fighting in the First World War – which was a war of high explosives, long-range shelling, machine guns and gas attacks – was minute: fewer than 0.03 per cent of casualties (3 in 10,000) in the war were caused by bayonets, although their dramatic use understandably captured the popular imagination as an expression of War.

The emphasis was on encouraging discipline, esprit de corps and obedience. Private initiative had no place: hence the shouting and bawling out by the sergeants and NCOs, the constant repetition and the rigorous regime of punishments for the slightest offence: unshined boots, three days confined to barracks. There was worse for more serious infringements, field punishments and pay stoppages, up to the ultimate: execution at dawn for desertion and other crimes in the face of the enemy. During the war: 304,262 men were court-martialled (nearly six per cent of all those who joined up) with an 86 per cent conviction rate and 3,080 were sentenced to death, though that punishment was only carried out on 346 men, about 10 per cent.

No Tunbridge Wells man was shot at dawn – but 19 year-old Private Thomas Highgate of the West Kents, who came from Shoreham near Sevenoaks, was the first soldier to be executed, on 8th September 1914. Highgate had joined up as a regular the previous year but deserted during the retreat from Mons within a fortnight of the start of the war. *"I want to get out of it and this is how I am doing it,"* he told the gamekeeper who discovered him hiding in civilian clothing.

The Tunbridge Wells War Memorial outside the Civic Centre bears the names of 801 men who died during the First World War and Edward Gilbert has traced brief biographies of most of them. Their names and something of their careers endure because they paid the ultimate sacrifice, but it is worth remembering that, horrendous as the casualty figures were, the death toll in the British army during the entire war amounted to about 12 per cent of those serving: one in eight, approximately 700,000 out of 5.7million men who served in uniform and two per cent of the entire 45 million national population (in addition, 2.2 million were wounded). So, extrapolating, it is likely that at least 6,000 men from the Tunbridge Wells area served in the course of the war.

It is the dead we know most about, though many local people must have their own recollections of relatives who served in the war, then came home and either told their stories to their families, or remained silent about their experiences for the rest of their lives. Not all the names on the memorial's bronze plaques are accurate and not all the men listed there had close connections with the town – some were inscribed because they had relatives locally who wished their names to be remembered in 1923 when the original memorial was dedicated.

K.L.Hutchings

One of the most surprising omissions is that of possibly the most famous young sportsman the town has ever produced: the Kent and England batsman: Kenneth Lotherington – KL -Hutchings, born in Southborough, educated at Tonbridge, one of the finest amateur batsmen of the Edwardian era and scorer of a match-winning century in a Test Match at Melbourne, who was obliterated by a shell on the Western Front in 1916. *"Of all the cricketers who have fallen in the war, he may fairly be described as the most famous...one of the most remarkable batsmen seen in this generation,"* Wisden eulogised in its 1917 obituary. His name is on the Southborough war memorial, but not that of Tunbridge Wells.

Most of those whose names are listed had lived, or been educated in the town: some were living elsewhere (Hutchings for instance was serving with the King's (Liverpool) Regiment because he had been working in the city when the war broke out), or had emigrated and returned, fighting for what were then colonial regiments. Many others were men who had indeed enlisted as a result of recruitment drives locally. There are public school men and Oxbridge students, gardeners and milk-carriers, printers and chemists, farm labourers and greengrocers, butchers and painters, bricklayers and accountancy clerks, errand boys and plumbers' mates: all listed on the plaques without distinction.

Some died after they had returned to Tunbridge Wells or been invalided out of the service because of their injuries but most lie in graves scattered right across the world: in India, Egypt, the Balkans, Iraq – then known as

Mesopotamia – Palestine, Tanzania, Greece, Bulgaria, Turkey, Germany and what is now Pakistan. And, of course, they lie in their hundreds in the military cemeteries in Belgium and Northern France or, if their bodies were never found, have their names inscribed on the great war memorials to the unrecovered dead, at the Menin Gate at Ypres – now known by its Flemish name Ieper – Tyne Cot on the hill at nearby Passchendaele and at Thiepval further south on the Somme. Others were lost at sea while serving in the Royal Navy, the Marines or the Merchant Marine. And a few died as members of the Royal Flying Corps.

What is striking is in how many different regiments and units the men of Tunbridge Wells fought. There are at least 77 different regiments and corps listed on the Tunbridge Wells War Memorial, showing vividly the range of military experiences that the fighters of one town had. While many necessarily joined local regiments: primarily the West Kents, the Royal Sussex Regiment, the Buffs of East Kent and the Royal Engineers; other men served with units from right across the world: the Auckland Regiment, the South African Infantry, Lord Strathcona's Horse from Canada, even the Australian Imperial Camel Corps.

One man, George Hood, whose father lived in Grosvenor Park, distinguished himself by enlisting with the Canadian army then, after being invalided out, subsequently joining the New Zealand expeditionary force and being killed, at the age of 28 in the battle of Messines Ridge near Ypres in July 1917.

Another casualty was Charles Akehurst who had been a young butcher in Rusthall – educated at St James's School and Speldhurst, living with his grandparents in Lower Green Road - before emigrating to Australia in 1913. A year on he enlisted with the Australian army at Adelaide on 16th September 1914 and died eleven months later, aged 20, as a result of wounds he received at Lone Pine, one of the bloodiest and most frantic engagements of the Gallipoli campaign – forever remembered bitterly by Australians – on 22nd August 1915.

Such young men had emigrated in search of a better life and returned to fight on behalf of what many of the colonial troops still regarded as the mother country.

Local men who had stayed at home found themselves in a variety of units. It is possible to work out that those who served with London regiments – the Royal Fusiliers, the Middlesex Regiment, or the City of London Yeomanry – had probably travelled up to town to enlist and that others were working, or had moved, away from their home town, such as those who joined the West Surreys. But what took Tunbridge Wells men into the Gordon Highlanders, the Cameronians, the Border Regiment and the Northumberland Fusiliers? One answer would probably have been family connections. Maybe that was why Ian Mackenzie, whose parents lived in Court Road, Tunbridge Wells, was serving as a second lieutenant with the Highland Light Infantry – poor lad, he died, aged 20, of pneumonia on 12th November 1918, the day after the armistice.

A more common reason was probably that men were transferred to reinforce other units which were short of manpower, or perhaps they volunteered for service elsewhere. The poet Siegfried Sassoon, from Mayfield, who we last saw playing cricket in Tunbridge Wells on the day war was declared, initially joined the Sussex Yeomanry but served subsequently, earning his fame and infame when he came out publicly against the war after he had become a decorated war hero, with the Welch Regiment. It was probably easier to move if you were an officer and were needed to replenish units whose command structures had been destroyed.

The bare biographical details only partially conceal what must have been heart-rending stories. There are the three Goldsmith brothers, all orphaned at an early age and brought up by foster parents in Southborough, who all died, serving with different regiments on the Western Front: Arthur, a lance-sergeant with the Duke of Cambridge's Own, Middlesex Regiment, killed on the first day of the Battle of the Somme, 1st July 1916; George killed eleven weeks later during the last days of the same battle while serving with the Royal Sussex Regiment; and Fred, a lance-corporal with the Machine Gun Corps killed six weeks before the end of the war, on 1st October 1918.

Then there was Dyson Graber, whose family lived in Beulah Road, who signed up at the age of 18 in October 1916, joined the Royal West Surrey Regiment and was sent to the Western Front before the end of the year. He was taken ill for a period early in the New Year and when he recovered returned to the Front where he was immediately killed in March 1917, The Advertiser, recording his death, said: "he was in about his first engagement when he was killed." Graber's commanding officer wrote to his parents: *"He was a good soldier and I only wish he might have been spared as he was one of my most promising men."* Graber's older brother Ellis also served and survived the war, but was invalided out after losing his leg. Some others did not even get to the Front: Reginald Bourner, a second lieutenant with the RFC, a Skinners' School old boy whose parents lived in Calverley Road, crashed his plane in training in June 1918 – a sadly common occurrence – and died from his injuries.

By contrast, Lieutenant William Charles Brown, whose parents lived in Erskine Park Road, was a reservist, called up at the start of the war, who served with the Royal Garrison Artillery. After serving right through the war, he caught dysentery in the trenches in the autumn of 1918 and was sent home where he died from pneumonia. Brown is buried in the graveyard of St. Paul's Church in Rusthall.

Another local man, who died on the terrible first day of the Battle of the Somme, was Edgar Gilbert, who was 28 and whose parents had lived at Little Mount Sion Road. He enlisted on 7th September 1914 in Croydon and so served with the West Surrey Regiment. As he went over the top near Mametz Wood that bright morning after the whistle blew, did he see the men of the next unit from the East Surreys kicking a football towards the German trenches, so confident were they of a walkover? Perhaps not. Edgar, whose great-nephew Edward Gilbert researched many of these biographies, was killed as the Germans emerged from their well-protected dugouts and raked the advancing troops with machine-gun fire.

How fearsome life on the Western Front could be is well caught in a letter to the *Tunbridge Wells Courier* in June 1915, written by Hutchings, the Test cricketer: "*I have been near death two or three times already but it is very hard to realise how near one has been to it when you look round and see your surroundings. In the first place we discovered an enemy patrol the other evening right up in our barbed wire, cutting them, so we got our machine gun ready and about 20 men on the parapets. We then sent up a flare and spied them about 100 yards away and let them have it. I was on the parapet directing the fire of my small squad of men and keeping my head only just above the top, just enough to be able to see in front. All of a sudden I felt a loud crack (a bullet near you makes a crack like the snapping of a branch) just by my right ear. I thought it must have been pretty close and then discovered that the bullet had actually hit and ripped away the top of the sandbag on which I was resting my head.*

"*The other shaves were even closer and I and three officers with me cannot make out why we were not hit – it is simply miraculous. We were talking about being wounded when all of a sudden I thought I heard a shell coming. I shouted 'Look out!' Before we had time to throw ourselves on the ground the shell burst clean over our very heads; in fact when we found we were not hit we looked up and there was the smoke of the burst shell not twenty feet above our heads. We had not got twenty yards before I heard the bang of another gun. We listened for a second, heard the thing coming along and threw ourselves into a ditch which, luckily, was pretty deep, but had a lot of water in it. This time the shell burst ten yards to our left, but we than had managed to get practically under cover and once again we got off.*"

"Our trenches and dugouts are wonderful, with flowers, roses, pansies, ferns etc which we have grown all along our lines...."

Hutchings' luck ran out at Ginchy Wood fifteen months later in September 1916 during the battle of the Somme. A fellow officer wrote: *"Out here you get to know a man very intimately and everyone thought what a fine fellow he was."*

The heartache and grief parents suffered, usually stoically, is well caught in the notes of the Rev. William Parsons, the vicar of St. John's Church and his wife Evelyn, whose son Victor, a lance-corporal in the Royal Engineers, died at the age of 19. Parsons wrote: *"God gave me five lovely children, all strong and perfect in limb; one he took away and I believe Victor is in His loving care."* Victor was killed in an accident at Dover. He had evidently been a reluctant soldier, having had a false start as a subaltern in the Royal Irish Regiment.

His mother left a memoir of him for the family: *"Victor left school and went to Sandhurst. Only a short period was allowed then, I don't think he really liked it, and I am sure he never wanted to fight. He lost his nerve and came out of it and for a time rested on account of ill health. Then he found a nice job in a private school. Here he was greatly loved. I wish he had stayed, but he thought he ought to be in the army, so joined motor cyclists in Dover. How my heart ached. I went and spent a few days in Dover to see him and when I left him it was more sad than ever in my life. I never saw him again. Is there not some instinct in a mother that foretells sorrow? In May 1916 an air raid was over Dover and, returning after to the Castle, my dear Victor came in contact with a motor lorry and he was thrown. His friends took him to hospital, unconscious and bleeding from ears and nose. Shall I ever forget? Poor Dad! The shock was awful to him. He had to go at once to Dover, having received a telegram in early morning of May 21st. I was in bed with an illness. Poor Dad, he arrived only to hear that Victor was dead. He had to identify him at the hospital mortuary. He came home after making arrangements, and he came at once to me in bed. Oh what a meeting! We could not speak..."* Victor is buried in Tunbridge Wells cemetery.

Many families of course did not have the opportunity to see their dead sons or husbands: all they would know of their fate would be the dreaded visit from a telegram boy and later – perhaps – a brief letter of sympathy and regret from their commanding officer. Many of the names on the war memorial have no known grave and some could not: men such as naval lieutenant Robert Faulkner, whose parents lived in Earls Road and who died aged 28 while serving on HMS Black Prince at the battle of Jutland: the one great engagement between the Royal Navy and the German High

Seas fleet during the whole war. The Black Prince, a cruiser, was sunk by German fire late on the evening of 31st May 1916, with the loss of its entire crew of 857 men.

Scanning the brief details of the obituaries, it is possible to trace the whole course of the war and its major battles, through the corpses of the dead Tunbridge Wells men. This started with the army's retreat from Mons and fight back at the River Marne, which stopped the German advance on Paris and led to the defensive stasis of trench warfare as both sides dug in along a line which stretched 450 miles from the Belgian coast, across the western corner of Flanders around Ypres through northern France, across the Somme valley, past the French fortresses at Verdun and down to the Swiss border.

The British army held a segment of about 80 miles from Ypres to the Somme. The imperative was to repulse the Germans and liberate occupied northern France and Belgium, but this was not easy at a time when defensive warfare prevailed and both sides were dug in, shielded by heavy artillery, poison gas and machine guns. Thus the Battle of Loos in September 1915, a drive to push the Germans back that faltered with ammunition shortages, then the Somme in the summer of 1916, which was the British attempt to relieve the pressure on the French beleaguered and under siege by the Germans at Verdun, and Passchendaele in the autumn of 1917, conceived as an offensive to break through the German lines outside Ypres and regain control of the Belgian coast, an attempt which foundered, bogged down in mud following one of the wettest summers on record.

It was only the following year after the Germans' final great spring offensive had petered out in exhaustion outside Amiens that the allies, boosted by the arrival of American troops, were able to roll back the German line and send it into retreat until Berlin sued for peace in November 1918.

The battle honours of the West Kents show the regiment's involvement in all these conflicts on the Western Front and more besides: the second battalion was sent to reinforce the ill-fated Gallipoli campaign in the late summer of 1915 and was also involved in the disastrous attempt to relieve the British and Indian garrison besieged in the town of Kut Al Amara from the Turks in Mesopotamia (modern Iraq) in 1916; one of the most abject and terrible defeats of the war. The British commander surrendered the garrison and retired to gracious prisoner status at an agreeable villa overlooking the sea, while nearly three-quarters of the 13,000 troops he abandoned were subsequently murdered by the Turks or starved to death in the desert.

The regimental history speaks of the men of the West Kents' *"exhausted, emaciated appearance, their soiled kit, shirts 'white with the salt of perspiration, spine-pads and sun-guards half devoured by locusts', of the 'pestilential heat', of the air moist with the exudation of the drying swamp"* – and of the lack of fresh water for them to drink as the level of the River Euphrates fell in the summer heat. But the West Kents also took part in the victorious Palestine campaign, helping to seize Jerusalem and Jericho in 1917.

It was at Gallipoli in October 1915 that Tunbridge Wells suffered the greatest military loss of the entire war: the Hythe disaster. The tragedy was exacerbated because it had nothing to do with enemy action. On the 28th of that month, six months into the campaign to seize the Dardanelles, block the Bosphorus and knock Turkey out of the war, HMS Hythe was in a collision with another troopship, the Sarnia, and 129 men from Southborough, Tunbridge Wells and Speldhurst were drowned. (See the previous Chapter 4 for a more detailed description of the disaster).

Several brothers from Tunbridge Wells were lost in the choppy seas, as were a father and son. The disaster was all the worse because the men were Territorials and had wives and families at home, many of them in Silverdale Road. It was said that the postman delivering the news of the men's deaths along the road became so overcome that he abandoned his round and returned to the depot. The loss of the men was even worse because they were shoring up a faltering operation: within a couple of months the British and ANZAC troops would be evacuated from Gallipoli altogether following the utter failure of the offensive.

The Hythe disaster remains in the folk-memory of Tunbridge Wells: a close off London Road, Southborough is named after the ship and there are two houses in Gordon Road, built in the 1930s for a survivor, named Hythe and Sarnia. A marble monument in St. Matthew's Church, High Brooms, which was originally in the Southborough Company HQ in Speldhurst Road, and which was put up there and paid for by Sir David Salomons, Bt., bears the names of the 129 dead. For many years there was an annual Commemoration Service, but that has now been reduced to decennial anniversaries, and quarter-, half- and full-centenaries.

During the war, some 60,000 men served with the Royal West Kent Regiment, two-thirds of them seeing service overseas, of which approximately 12 per cent were killed or died, 22 per cent were wounded, 2.5 per cent were made prisoners of war and 2 per cent were recorded simply as missing. The regiment gained 70 battle honours and five of its members won Victoria Crosses.

What was life like in the trenches for the men of Kent and elsewhere? Contrary to common perception, there was not constant fighting all along the British sector of the Western Front. Offensives to try and break the German line were relatively few and infrequent and some areas remained quiet for many weeks at a time: troops could go months without seeing an enemy soldier.

The width of the No Man's Land between the trenches varied from a few yards around Ypres – at Zonnebeke in 1915 it got down to seven yards apart – to 500 yards around Cambrai. In these quiet times, days would be spent on sentry duty, kit inspection and trying to keep dugouts and the trenches tidy. Regiments were not endlessly at the front, except in times of crisis or emergency: a unit might spend a week in the front line, followed by a week in the reserve lines further back and then several days at rest behind the lines: perhaps during normal circumstances about two-thirds of the time in the trenches, not necessarily at the front and one third out of them in safety, at rest, recuperation and in training.

In times of battle this would change, but even so they would not be continuously on guard, though the medically-recommended time of no more than 48 hours under attack was often ignored. The rest periods did not mean leave to go home: an ordinary soldier in the ranks might get home about once a year, for about ten days at a time, including travel – the men of Tunbridge Wells, living nearer the coast, would clearly have had slightly more time at home than those who had to journey to the north of England or Scotland.

Once back at home in the town they would have found life proceeding much as normal before the war. They could have gone to the Opera House or one of the local cinemas such as the Kosmos in Calverley Road to watch Charlie Chaplin or Mary Pickford, or selected a book – then as now with troops thrillers were particularly prized - by authors including Charles Garvice and Florence Warden who wrote titles such as The Temptress, Red Rube's Revenge or The Lost Diamonds.

They might even have attended a sing-song organised by the Council at the grand pavilion in St. John's recreation ground – though holding them on Sundays provoked a furious reaction. As architect and Borough Councillor Henry Elwig wrote to the Courier in December 1914: "while whole heartedly commending activities to promote hospitality and pleasure, I regard the concerts as superfluous and unnecessary (and) when of a comic character on the Sunday evening as decidedly objectionable."

Officers generally were allowed two or even three leaves back in England each year, so fared somewhat better than those in the other ranks. Transport links were efficient: it was said a man might be in the trenches in the morning and watching a show in the West End the same evening. The postal service was efficient too: thanks to the education acts, most troops now were literate and able to write home and receive letters back within a week. Letters from the front would be censored by the men's officers: "what a lesson it is to read the thoughts of men, often as refined and sensitive as we have been made by the advantages of birth and education, yet living under conditions much harder and more disgusting than my own," wrote a public school and Oxford-educated second lieutenant in a Midlands regiment.

There must have been many sad partings on the platform at Tunbridge Wells station at the end of leave. One that was perhaps jollier than most was recorded by 17 year-old Private Frank Dunk of the 7th Battalion of the Royal West Kents: *"We were all given ten days' leave before going over to France on 25th July. I remember it was a Sunday evening that I had to return to camp. I had to catch the 6pm train from Tunbridge Wells. My father and both my sisters came to see me off and when the train came in from Hastings it stopped right by where we were standing with a compartment full up with girls going back to Abbey Wood where they worked on munitions. They said: 'Come in soldier, in with us.' I said, 'Not likely,' and got into an empty carriage next door. The train went off but it stopped at the next station and all ten of the girls got out and came in with me, so I had to keep my hand on my kit, the other on my halfpenny. Being only seventeen, I thought I might lose both! But they all made a fuss of me, gave me fags to smoke and told me lots of jokes, some of them pretty near the bone. However, I arrived in London in one piece, still a 'cock virgin'."*

A different world, indeed.

CANADIAN FORESTRY CORPS (CFC) IN THE TUNBRIDGE WELLS AREA

by Edward Gilbert

The presence of a large number of Canadian lumberjacks, operating under military discipline, in the Tunbridge Wells area from 1917-1918 is now a largely forgotten piece of our local history.

In February 1916, the British Government asked the Canadian Government for a Forestry Battalion to be raised in Canada for overseas service. Its purpose was to provide timber for the War effort in the form of planks, duckboards, trench props, logs and telephone/telegraph posts.

224th Cap badge

Within six weeks of the request, some 1,600 men had been recruited and $250,000 spent on logging and milling equipment. The 224th Canadian Forestry Battalion was sent over in several drafts and the first sawn lumber was produced in England on May 13, 1916. Ultimately the CFC would be divided into 101 Companies, with each company having 100-200 men, making the total number of Canadian forestry men in the war about 20,000. They brought with them all of the tools and equipment they needed, including portable sawmills. It is estimated that between 1916-18, Canadian foresters produced 17 million tons of timber from 450,000 acres of woodland, which was half of Britain's productive forest; and this was 70% of all the timber used by the Western allies.

One of these Companies was Company 18, which originated in January 1917, but was renumbered Company 116 in August 1917. It was assigned to District 53 in the south of England, in which Groombridge and Tunbridge Wells were located.

The following extracts from the 'War Diary' of this Company reveal much about their operation:

- **January 16, 1917** the Company arrived in Groombridge and Croseley Villa became their temporary headquarters. A dry canteen was installed for the men.
- On January 17, six heavy horses arrived from Woolwich and suitable accommodation was made for them on farms around Groombridge. Other horses arrived afterwards.
- On January 22 the balance of the Company arrived in Groombridge. Total strength of the company on Jan. 22, 1917 was 5 officers and 126 O.R's.
- From Jan 22 to February 5, there were daily route marches and drills. --
- On Feb 5th a shipment of axes and saws arrived and work on clearing the site began.

Broadwater Forest c.1910
Photo by
Francis Gilbert,1881-1975

- Their first area of operation was a large tract of timber, chiefly Scotch Fir, belonging to the Marquess of Abergavenny *(known to CFC as the Warren Forest, but now as Broadwater Forest/Warren)* situated on the south side of the road from Groombridge to Tunbridge Wells, about a mile from Groombridge. The camp site was on the north side of this road about ¼ mile from the western edge of the timber tract. Clearing and roadway construction commenced Feb 6, 1917.
- the first consignment of huts arrived Feb 16th. Men's dining rooms, cookhouses, tables, and a blacksmith's and a garage were erected. Most of the men however slept in tents erected in the woods. A field adjoining the east side of the camp was given over to growing vegetables and 2,700 lbs of potatoes were planted.
- Pending the arrival of the sawmill, trees were felled and a large quantity of telephone and telegraph poles shipped to France, pit props were prepared and logs skidded. Recreation for the men was provided in a large hut which was in charge of the YMCA.
- On April 10, 1917 The Mill started production. The first day's cut was 4,773 FBM.[1]
- Wash houses and latrines were completed on May 16, 1917, prior to which the Company paraded once a week to the Public Baths in Tunbridge Wells.
- A light railway was built to haul the logs, the cars being hauled by Donkey Engine.

- Pigs were also purchased for raising and subsequent sale, the proceeds going to the Men's Messing Fund.
- All shipments of lumber were by way of a siding on the LB & SC Railway's yard at Groombridge Station.
- Lumber was hauled from the Mill by teams of lorries, a tractor and trailers.

---

[1] The board-foot (abbreviated to FBM [foot, board measure]) is a specialized unit of measurement in the United States and Canada for the volume of lumber. It is the volume of a one-foot length of a board, one foot wide and one inch thick.

•**At Oct 31, 1917**, the Company consisted of 6 officers; 182 other ranks, 52 horses, 12 wagons, 2 water carts, 4 motor lorries, and 1 motor car. By this time, they had produced 45,891 logs cut; 1,726 pickets cut; 19,782 poles cut; 17,308 Ft. Pitwood cut; 480 pointed pickets shipped; 9,638 Ft. Pitwood shipped; 1,593,268 FBM lumber shipped; 2,159,310 FBM lumber cut, and 31,108 logs sawn.

As an aside from the War Diary, the *Courier for 2nd November 1917* recorded that Pte. Charles Homer Heathers, of the Canadian Forestry Corps, but born an American in Nebraska, had died of pneumonia at the age of 35 years, and that the funeral at the Borough (Hawkenbury) Cemetery 'was a most impressive ceremony, the body being carried on a gun carriage drawn by six horses, the coffin being entwined with the American and British flags. Upwards of 200 officers and men from the deceased's Battalion attended, and as the procession passed through the town, Chopin's "Funeral March" was played by the West Kent Regimental Band, who also furnished the firing party ... the Band also played "Abide with Me." A great number of people were present.'

•On December 6, 1917 the first group of Portuguese workers arrived and were quartered in hutments and supplied with a large marquee for their messing. They were found to be very intelligent and hard-working and exceptionally clean in the matter of camp sanitation.

•**Dec 1917**, the Company was given a Christmas Dinner after which songs and entertainment was provided for the men.

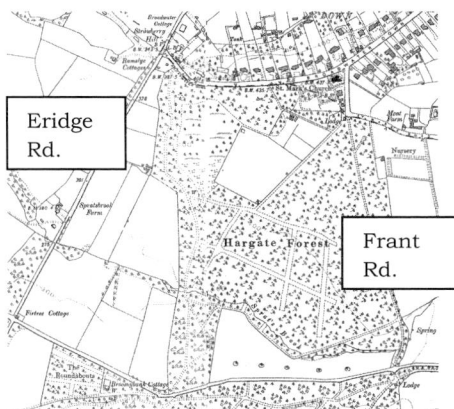

Hargate Forest 1910

•**January 1918**: operations began at the new Hargate Forest camp situated on Eridge Road, the nearest station being Tunbridge Wells S.E.C. Railway which was two miles from the camp. The Hargate Forest was *(then)* some 76 acres and 16,803 trees would be cut down.

•mess rooms, cook houses, stable, garage and latrines were erected and the Armstrong Huts were moved on January 26, 1918 to the new site. A light railway, which is about one mile in length is under construction.

• **February 1918.** The weather was very favourable. Building of the new camp was practically completed this month. The water supply at this camp was a great improvement over the Groombridge camp.

•On Feb 23 1918, another 100 Portuguese labourers arrived and were accommodated at the Groombridge camp, with about half of them

employed at Groombridge camp and the other half in the new camp in Hargate Forest.
- Towards the end of February, a start was made on the plowing of the land at the N.E. end of the camp, mostly clay. Piggeries were erected on the opposite side of the main road to the camp, S.W. of the camp. The new YMCA hut was erected, the one at Groombridge being used to accommodate the Portuguese as sleeping quarters.
- On average one concert a week was given in the YMCA. The general health of the men and horses has been excellent. Total strength of the Company -5 officers, 153 men, 50 horses.
- **March 1918:** Production 261,405 FBM; Shipments 367,053 FBM
- On March 15th the Portuguese threatened a strike, due to the interpreter being taken bodily from the camp. The following day they returned to work.
- Four concerts were held for the men in March. The concert given by the "Kingswood Kippers" on March 14th was very good and much enjoyed by all. The Kingswood Kippers are all Canadian nurses who are doing their bit at the Kingswood VAD hospital in Tunbridge Wells.
- An open air ward was erected by the Company at Kingswood Park VAD Hospital. The building was 96 feet long and 16 feet wide, being equipped with canvas windows which can be opened to the air. It contained 12 beds. Eighty members of this Company had been admitted to the Hospital up to the time of the new ward being opened.
- Lord and Lady Henry Nevill and also Lady Warrington visited the camp. The latter was a very good friend to all members of this Company.
- During the month a recreation room was erected at St Mark's VAD Hospital. The building was urgently needed and so no time was lost in erecting it.

- The log supply for the month of April was very good. The weather was decidedly unfavourable, causing men and horses to work waist deep in mud and water and the transporting of the logs to the Mill became a difficult operation. The steel cable used on our Railway broke and several cars came down the incline and derailed.
- A new area *(for logging)* close to Eridge Castle was measured during the week of April 21.
- **April 1918**: Production 334,456 FBM; Shipments 221,847 FBM.
- **May 1918**: Production 477,079 FBM; Shipments 537,773 FBM.

- May 1918, beautiful weather. May 4th saw the last of the trees in Hargate Forest felled and on the previous day, 30,000 FBM was cut at our Mill in 9 hours.
- May 1918. Visit by two lady inspectors of the RSPCA who congratulated the Company on how well they kept their horses.
- Monday the 10th the first practice on the new ball ground in Tunbridge Wells, which has been donated for our use by the town. It is situated on the Common right in the middle of the town.
- The epidemic of Spanish Influenza which has been prevalent in the town for the past few weeks is affecting the Company.
- **June 1918**: Production 622,357 FBM; Shipments 752,960 FBM.
- **July 1918**: Production 432,056 FBM; Shipments 378,240 FBM
- July 5th first two men admitted to hospital with the 'flu, being the start of a steady admission of Company members to the Kingswood Park VAD.
- On Monday operations at the new camp were commenced, The New Camp is situated on the Marquis of Camden's estate at Bayham Abbey. About 500 logs were cut in the first two days.
- On the 7th in the afternoon we played the American baseball team in Tunbridge Wells, defeating them 7-5. A crowd of about 5,000 were in attendance, the proceeds of the gate going to the Red Cross fund.
- Three members 22 days in hospital. On Wednesday the Canadian Nurses from Kingswood Park Hospital gave a concert in the Pump Room, Tunbridge Wells which was well attended by the Company.
- **August 1918**: Production 387,290 FBM; Shipments 510,627 FBM.
- **September 1918:** Weather unfavourable for work in the bush, rained almost every day.
- The final cut at the mill was made on the 26th September.
- **By Oct 10 1918**, only 42 officers, NCO's and men remained.
- By the end of the month, all machinery as well as stores have been packed and shipped.
- The month of **November 1918** started off quietly on account of the shortage of men.
- The stables are in excellent state and the remaining horses in very good condition. The meals are all that could be required, well cooked, clean and plenty.
- The weather has been good, the rainfall slight with very little cold, every man is anxiously awaiting the time when he shall see his Canadian Home once more!

End of War Diary entries.

It should be recorded that the total production of Company 116 between February 1917- October 1918 was 857,357 cu. ft., or 10,288,044 FBM

○●○●○●○●○

The Canadian Forestry Corps was disbanded in 1920
and reformed in 1940, to be disbanded again in 1945.

Young Men's Christian Association (YMCA)

The YMCA was one of the civilian organisations which provided enormous welfare support to the Armed Forces during the First World War. Both in the UK and abroad, they ran canteens, and provided rest rooms and recreational facilities where troops could gather, away from the discipline of the front line, the regiment or the Army camp.

The YMCA was started in London in 1844 by George Williams as a prayer and bible study group, but quickly began to address other concerns of young men working in the cities, with lectures and education classes, reading rooms and refreshment facilities, to help them adjust to urban life. Its growth was both rapid and international. The first branch in Tunbridge Wells was founded in 1862 with premises in the High Street.

The Pump Room, Tunbridge Wells

In Tunbridge Wells in the First World War, the YMCA took over the Pump Room at the end of the Pantiles, which could hold up to 600 people, as its principal premises; but it also put up a further building in Lime Hill Road, on land owned by Mr. Kutnow, the proprietor of the Kosmos Cinema; and it also ran smaller premises, such as the recreation huts in the Canadian Forestry Corps camps at Broadwater Forest, Hargate Forest and Bayham.

YMCA Hut, Lime Hill Road

The image of the Red Poppy as the Symbol of Remembrance for those lost in the World War, was first devised by an American YMCA worker. Its symbolic relevance was such, that it became the international symbol that it is still today.

JAC

CHAPTER 6
HOW TUNBRIDGE WELLS COPED WITH THE MILITARY-WOUNDED
by John Cunningham and Ed Gilbert

The War soon brought many wounded soldiers back to Britain for longer-term treatment and recuperation and their numbers were such as to create severe problems in providing sufficient beds for them.

The sequence of treatment for an injured soldier was somewhat protracted. He would be treated first at a Regimental Aid Post in the trenches by the Battalion Medical Officer, then at an Advance Dressing Station close to the front line by members of a Field Ambulance, RAMC. If further treatment was needed, he would be moved to a Casualty Clearing Station, generally a tented camp behind the lines and then, if considered necessary, moved to one of the base hospitals. Then the seriously wounded would be taken back to Britain by hospital ship for further treatment. The less seriously-injured would also be taken back to Britain by ferry for further treatment, recuperation and convalescence at one of the thousands of VAD hospitals which would be created in Britain to cope with the situation.

In 1914, there were three military hospitals in Kent - at Woolwich, Chatham and Folkestone. Woolwich had 629 beds and was one of the largest military hospitals in the country.

In 1914-15, the existing hospitals in Tunbridge Wells (see Chapter 1, pages 21 & 22 for their details) did their best to cope with the extra influx. The General Hospital was only able to take about 60 and the other smaller hospitals even fewer, so there could have been a real problem, not just in Tunbridge Wells but throughout Britain.

It had been recognized since the end of the Boer War in 1901 that there was a shortage of qualified nurses in Britain and it was felt that their workload could be lessened if some of the more mundane jobs of nursing such as looking after convalescents could be given to less qualified volunteers, thereby freeing up more time and staff for nursing the patients who needed expert care.

A solution, which would be as yet untried and untested in 1914, was created in August 1909, not for World War I which could not then have been anticipated, but for any major military emergency which might develop. This may be indicative of underlying fears and insecurity at that time, but also possibly of a certain prescience.

This was the **V**AD – the **V**oluntary **A**id **D**etachment – which was a volunteer organisation established by the British Red Cross and the Order of St John (St John's Ambulance) to run *auxiliary* military hospitals in houses, church halls, schools and even tents. However in 1914 while it had been established, it was still a relatively undeveloped and untrained organisation.

The Detachments were originally intended to staff only auxiliary hospitals in the UK and initially they received no payment or salary for these duties. At the beginning, the type of woman recruited would have been in a position to offer her services without pay, since most of the initial VADs, as all personnel were called, were of the middle and upper classes. Subsequently, they would be paid – for the first seven months at the rate of £20 a year, then at £22-10s-0d, with a uniform allowance of £2-10s-0d every six months and quarters, food, washing and travelling provided.

The role of the volunteer was essentially a supportive one. Trained in basic first aid and nursing skills, they assisted qualified nursing staff to keep hospitals and ambulance services operating. Volunteers were required to achieve certificates in First Aid and Home Nursing, issued by one of the various teaching bodies such as the Red Cross and St. John Ambulance Association.[1] They cleaned, cooked and acted as porters as well as undertaking basic nursing and surgical support and care, in order to release the qualified staff for clinical duties. Volunteers additionally spent time with the wounded, and wrote letters for those unable to do so.

The involvement of the VADs in nursing the war-wounded was not without controversy. The nursing profession, who had been campaigning for state registration and professional recognition since the early years of the century, disapproved of the involvement of VADs who they felt, represented an essentially outdated view of nursing as a philanthropic, but not practical approach to the care of the ill and injured. They pointed to the contrast between the three years professional training for a qualified nurse and the much poorer levels of skill of the VADs. Moreover, many qualified nurses feared that the VADs would be competing with them unfairly in the professional employment market following the war.

---

[1] Burr, M., (1915) 'The English Voluntary Aid Detachments' in *The American Journal of Nursing*, 15: 6 pp. 461-467.

While many VADs were expected to be little more than ward maids, many of them eventually became highly skilled military nurses, if only because the sheer volume of patients flooding in, meant they had no alternative but to do more than was originally expected of them.

The patients with whom they dealt, ranged from the bed-ridden to crippled and walking wounded, and some would be terminal cases. One of the worst type of wound was gas gangrene, which could lead to amputation and death, for which the only (then known) treatment was Carrel and Dakin solution, also known as Eusol. Hester Cotton, a VAD at Rust Hall VAD Hospital in Tunbridge Wells records[2] 'I could never get the smell of that stuff out of my nose. I can still smell it even now, a sort of chlorate of lime smell, and the smell of the wounds themselves was terrible. If there was a case of gas gangrene in a ward, you could smell it as you opened the door.'

Most VADs were unaccustomed to both the hardship and discipline of hospital life and when VADs started to be sent abroad, many military authorities would not accept them at the front line and so when they were stationed in France, they were generally placed in hospitals located near the coast.

There were about 50,000 women involved on a fairly light part-time basis in the VAD before the start of the War. It has been estimated that between 70-100,000 served as VADs during the War, most on a full-time basis and some for up to five years.

Detachments were officially numbered by the War Office. Women's detachments were given an even number and the men's detachments an odd number. There would be a total of 32 men's and 95 women's detachments in Kent.

Although the War Office paid a daily allowance for each patient, a large part of the equipment and running costs of the hospitals was met through local fundraising and support.

Kent would have over 127 VAD units during 1914-1918, about a third of them being mixed detachments of men and women. These units provided 4,730 beds, an average of about 40 beds per unit. Each unit had a Commandant who was more often than not a woman, a Medical Officer, a Quartermaster, a Lady Superintendent for the female staff, a Pharmacist and other personnel of all ranks.

---

[2] The Roses of No Man's Land by Lyn Macdonald, Penguin, 1980

Kent would accommodate more wounded soldiers than any other area of the country and by the end of the War, its VAD hospitals had cared for 125,000 patients – about a third more than any other county.

VAD IN TUNBRIDGE WELLS

Tunbridge Wells would eventually have a total of 18 VAD hospitals (not all at the same time), since it was particularly suited to VAD World War I criteria:
- being reasonably close to Folkestone and Dover, both major ferry ports;
- it had a great number of large houses, which could be ideal as auxiliary hospitals and many of which were either unoccupied or occupied on only a seasonal basis;
- its population had a significant surplus of women, who were generally seen as the natural carers of the sick and ill and by inference, the wounded;
- but these carers would be as yet unprepared and untrained for the role which was to be thrust upon them.

It should not be thought that the number of VAD hospitals in Tunbridge Wells was extraordinary – Kent had 127 and Sussex 71; Bromley had over 15; Chislehurst over 10; Brighton 6 [3]; and Eastbourne 9 – so Tunbridge Wells with 18, was not significantly out of the ordinary in this respect.[4]

What is of interest is how many of the large houses which became VAD hospitals, did so as a result of becoming vacant on the death of their elderly occupants. It should also be recognised that other interested parties were competing with VAD hospitals for these large houses - the Army needed billets for the many soldiers in training or transit in the area; and the civil authorities were seeking accommodation for Belgian and other refugees.

The existing four hospitals in Tunbridge Wells at the beginning of the War all took on extra VAD staff during the War to cope with the wounded (the Fever Hospital as an Isolation Hospital could only take 'fever' cases) and they converted buildings to provide extra wards, but this was not enough.

---

[3] Interestingly, all these were only for officers – one wonders why?

[4] It should be said that none of them were specifically for officers.

The General Hospital allocated 60 of its existing 70 beds to the military and converted other parts of the building into further wards to cope with demand, but there were limits and the prime function of the four hospitals was still to care for the civilian population of the town. The General Hospital was however the only one with an X-ray department, and so they took on the responsibility of providing an X-ray service for all the other hospitals. The military patients also created one further but fairly major change in the daily life of the town.

Ward for wounded soldiers, General Hospital

Convalescing Soldiers outside the General Hospital in Tunbridge Wells

St. Augustine's Catholic Church was directly opposite the General Hospital in Grosvenor Road[5] and had had a 68-foot-high Campanile since 1888, containing a clock on two faces, and five bells weighing a ton, which could be rung i.e. swung, or chimed i.e. hit with a hammer. They were rung once an hour and chimed four times an hour, ringing what was known as Westminster chimes, and they could be heard for hundreds of yards. The clock had been designated an official timekeeper under the Factories Act and many people set their clocks by it. The clock would survive 81 years until 1969, but the Westminster chimes lasted only 27 years, since they were silenced in 1915, when the staff of the General Hospital complained that they were disturbing the sleep of wounded soldiers. They never rang again, except once, on 11th November 1918, when Alfred Hubble, one of the Parish's bellringers, rang them at 11 am to mark the end of 'the War to end all Wars'.

---

[5] Both have now vanished, the General Hospital in the 1930s to be replaced by the Post Office and shops (still extant), and St. Augustine's in 1969 by Tesco's Supermarket, when the Church moved to a larger site in Crescent Road, where it still is.

The Tunbridge Wells Eye & Ear Hospital in Mount Sion was by the nature of its work essentially an Outpatient hospital, but it did have some 20 beds and during World War I, it allocated 16 of them to military patients.

The Homeopathic Hospital in Church Road also allocated a number of its beds to the military, but no record has been found of the exact number.

Pembury Hospital (the Sandhill Infirmary) was the infirmary of the Pembury Workhouse which was outside the boundary of the Borough of *Royal* Tunbridge Wells, had over 100 beds before the War, and became a major VAD hospital in Tunbridge Wells, extending its capacity by converting its Outpatients' Department to a ward of 32 beds.

During the war many servicemen were sent there for treatment and recovery. Although the medical care they received was of a high standard, they were perhaps not as fortunate, in terms of lavish surroundings, as other of their comrades who were lucky enough to move into a grand mansion.

But the number of wounded far exceeded existing capacity and consequently there was a great need for temporary and *purely military* hospitals, which would be run entirely by a VAD. Not all of the 18 VAD hospitals set up in Tunbridge Wells existed for all of the four-five years. There were also a great number of VAD hospitals set up within a small radius of Tunbridge Wells. There were 5 VAD hospitals, which were within what are now be the boundaries of the *current* Borough of Tunbridge Wells, as well as another 14 which, while not within either the then or current Borough boundaries, could be considered to be within its 'catchment area'. All these VAD hospitals are listed in the Table at the end of this Chapter. They would all be closed at the latest by August 1919 and their buildings were returned to their owners.

The Kent Nursing Institute (KNI) occupied Holly Lodge at 11, Crescent Road. It had been started in 1875 as a private nursing service and its main work was visiting patients in their homes. After 1903 the Institute also operated under the name of the Tunbridge Wells District Nursing Association (Queen Victoria Memorial Home). Some 14,279 home visits were made in 1913, mainly to the poorer classes, by the Superintendent and her three nurses (an average of 39 calls a day), but they also had beds at Crescent Road. During the War, the hospital had 33 beds for soldiers, in addition to its beds for civilians.

The VAD hospitals in Tunbridge Wells developed in response to demand – although understandably, the response would inevitably be somewhat slower than demand. The first VAD hospitals interestingly were all in the north of the present town and were particularly in Southborough: Bidborough Court, Park House, and the Royal Victoria Hall.

Bidborough Court (originally known as Elm Court) is a Grade II-listed Victorian country house in Bidborough and dates from about 1860. It was lent by its owner and served as one of the original VAD hospitals in Tunbridge Wells, from October 1914 to August 1915. With the VAD number of Kent 74, it transferred to 8 Nevill Park in 1916.[6]

Park House was a large Victorian mansion of 20 rooms at 24 Park Road in Southborough. It had a large 3-storey central building with two 2-storey wings and was constructed of brick and stone, with a slate-tiled

---

[6] It became a boarding school but most recently has been converted into flats.

pitched roof, and had landscaped grounds. In the 1911 Census, Park House was a boys' school run by Percival Humphry and his wife, Jessie, one assistant school master, one matron, and three domestic servants, who looked after the thirteen boys between the ages of 8 and 12 who were boarders. It opened as a VAD hospital in October 1914 and closed in January 1919.

The Royal Victoria Hall in Southborough had opened 15 years earlier in 1900 and was the first municipal theatre to be built in England under the provisions of the Local Government Act of 1894. It was built to commemorate the Diamond Jubilee of Queen Victoria in 1897 and Sir David Salomons, who was the Mayor of Tunbridge Wells from 1894-1895, donated £3,000 of its £5,000 cost. It was recruited as a VAD hospital very early on, in October 1914, since it was a large hall which was not fully occupied with performances, but it ceased to be a VAD hospital in 1915, probably when the supply of other buildings, which were more suitable as hospitals, increased.

St Mark's Military Hospital was the only VAD hospital in Tunbridge Wells to call itself Military and was set up in October 1914 in St Mark's School which was then at 73 Frant Road, which is now the site of the Pantiles Baptist Church (and where some of the original classrooms are now used for Sunday School). It had 66 beds. In March 1916, it took advertising space in the Courier to give a financial report on St. Mark's Military Hospital from 13 October 1914 to 31 December 1915, no doubt with a view to generating donations. Its Income had been £1,343-19s-1d of which the War Office provided 83%; Expenditure £1,033, of which only £47-4s-8d were salaries and wages; and the Balance-in-hand was £310-19s-1d. A total of 513 patients had been treated at an average weekly cost of 17s-9d per head. An Operating Theatre had been completed at a cost of £233. The report was signed: Edith Melba Stunt, Commandant.

The earliest VAD hospitals would not in the end prove to be the biggest, which were:

Rachel Ard

Rust Hall which was offered by Mr. & Mrs. Simon Leeder for five years at a rent which could be afforded. It still exists as a ten bedroom mansion on Langton Road. Rusthall, would prove to be the largest VAD hospital in Tunbridge Wells with a total of 334 beds. The hospital's VAD number was "Kent 154" and under this number, were Rust Hall itself and also its Annex, which operated from April 1915 until the end of August 1919; the Mission Hall, Rusthall which operated in 1916; the Rusthall Beacon Staff Hostel which operated from 1917 until 1919; the Rusthall Girls School in the High Street which operated from 1917 until May 1919 and The Elms Staff Hostel which operated only in 1919.

The house had 12 acres of grounds, which could accommodate tents should the need arise. The hospital was opened in 1915 and following extensions, would eventually have a capacity of 130 beds in the main building and 204 in the annexes.

Rachel Ard, a clergyman's daughter born in Armagh, Northern Ireland, was appointed Commandant. She was awarded an MBE in 1917 for her services to the war effort, and would in due course become one of the first female Justices of the Peace.

There were many in the area who gave freely of their time, money and possessions to assist in the formation and upkeep of this hospital. One of these was Rachel Beer, who was the aunt of Siegfried Sassoon and was known as "The first Lady of Fleet Street", since she had been the Editor of both *'The Sunday Times'* and *'The Observer'*, both titles being then owned by her husband. When her husband died, she moved to Tunbridge Wells in 1903, and lived initially at the Earl's Court Hotel on Mount Ephraim, but then moved in 1904 to Chancellor House, a large and historic house, reputedly the home of Judge Jeffries of Monmouth Rebellion infamy, which was further down Mount Ephraim, and where she remained until she died in 1927[7].

Rachel Beer

Rachel Beer was a major benefactor of the Rusthall VAD hospital and when it became too small to accommodate the huge number of wounded, she paid for the rent of additional grounds, as well as for two hostels for the nurses.

At St Paul's Parish Church, Rusthall, is a cemetery which contains the graves of several men who died at the Rusthall VAD. Private William Martin, as an example, had served for seven months and had been wounded no less than fourteen times, including having his leg blown off above the knee. He had been in hospital for sixteen months before he was transferred to the Rust Hall VAD where he died in October 1918, leaving a wife and three children.

Many letters sent from Rust Hall VAD by servicemen to loved ones can be found in the archives and online, all of which comment on how grand a place it was in which they were staying, and lavished great praise and thanks to those who looked after them. One such letter dated 3 May 1917 was a sad one written by Sgt. James R. Forrest who had been wounded when a shell exploded in his trench. He had the sad task of explaining that his friend, Gunner Harold Moore, who had been reported missing, was actually with him in the trench when the shell landed; and that was the last seen of him. Many letters also talk about the friendships that had been created at the Rust Hall VAD between the soldiers and with the volunteers, whose assistance and care they greatly appreciated.

Lady Matthews' reference to Rusthall as *'our hospital'* was echoed by the *Courier* reporter who wrote the retrospective to mark the hospital's closure. *'It has been'*, he said, *'Rusthall's hospital, upheld - very largely upheld – by Rusthall people of all classes, and in it has centred a big part of the care and interest of the village'*.[8]

---

[7] This Chancellor House was subsequently demolished in the 1930's to be replaced by a block of flats which was given the name Chancellor House and exists to this day.
[8] *The Courier*, 5 September 1919, p. 3.

Nevill Park – No.8, Nevill Park - was a mansion of fifteen rooms in a development of the 1850-1860s by the Abergavenny family following the Park concept created in Calverley Park by Decimus Burton. In 1914, it was occupied by James Harris Sanders and the circumstances in which he 'gave' the house as a VAD hospital are not clear. Certainly the VAD hospital set up in Bidborough Court in October 1914, had been transferred to Nevill Park by October 1915.

This house was listed as one of 12 VAD hospitals in Tunbridge Wells which were in operation in the autumn of 1917. Nevill Park seems to have expanded to a capacity of about 300 beds, since 300 patients were invited to a Christmas entertainment at the nearby Spa Hotel in 1917, and about the same time, there were prizes for the best-decorated-for-Christmas Ward *or Tent,* and in 1917 it was won by Tent No.2. Nevill Park was closely associated with 'The Hollands'. It ceased to be a hospital on 28 February 1919 and was returned to its owner. It still exists today, but it has been divided into flats.

Although most men recovered from their injuries, others did not and some of those who died, did not die from war wounds. One of these fatal casualties was Lt. William Charles Brown of 4 Erskine Park Road, who died at the Nevill Park VAD on 7 November 1915, aged 29. He was the eldest son of Mr and Mrs Brown of Park Road and was a Rusthall School boy, who had joined the Volunteers on leaving school, and later joined the Royal West Kent Regiment. He had arrived home on leave on Tuesday 29 October and on the following Friday was taken, suffering from influenza to the Nevill Park Hospital, where he died from double pneumonia. His parents had three other sons and two sons-in-law in the army, as well as a daughter in the WAACS in France.

The Glengow Archive has online a large number of letters from Sidney Brooks (1871-1957), a Canadian soldier from Alberta, to his wife, with whom he had seven children. He had been injured in France and was sent to the Nevill Park VAD to recover. He wrote every day to his wife in Canada and they give an insight into life at Nevill Park. On 27 June, 1917, shortly after his arrival at the hospital, *"I have enjoyed very much my walk through the principal parts of Tunbridge Wells, including Toad Rock and around the hospital, which is a very fine residence with walks and drives and stables and grounds and, oh yes, a small greenhouse full of tomatoes"*. He goes on in other letters to remark on how well he was being treated; the good food being served, and how *"fine"* all the nurses were. He had nothing but praise for the hospital and the care he was being given.

Crothers was a two storey vine-covered mansion at 74 Pennington Road, Southborough, which was owned by Miss Robertina Crowther and was initially used by Belgian refugees, but became a VAD hospital in 1915 and remained one until January 1919. The building was situated in large landscaped grounds and there was an area where the soldiers could play croquet and other lawn sports.

West Hall was a three-storey Victorian mansion of 19 rooms at 7 Chilston Road in Tunbridge Wells, on the south-west corner of Chilston Road and Queens Road. In the 1911 census, the house was occupied by Martha Harriss-Gustrell, the 73-year-old widow of a British diplomat, James Plaister Harriss-Gustrell, with a staff of five servants. She died at West Hall in November 1912 and so the house was empty and so the house was put up for auction at the Swan Hotel on Friday 17 July 1914, just over two weeks before the start of the

War. Presumably it did not sell and her son offered the building to the Red Cross who occupied it with VAD 94 which had been set up in 1913. West Hall would have a capacity of 50 beds and the first to arrive on 14 October were wounded Belgian soldiers. It remained a VAD hospital until early 1917 when the building was sold to The Skinners' School and patients were first transferred to Crothers and then to Bredbury.

Bredbury, 77 Mount Ephraim, was a 3-storey 21-room Victorian mansion with a 4 storey tower, overlooking Tunbridge Wells Common, which still exists. The last occupant of the mansion before it became a VAD hospital was Francis Gray Smart (1844-1913), a retired physician who was one of the founders of the Homeopathic Hospital in Church Road, and who lived there with his wife and eight servants. His wife died in 1913 and he died eight days later. Upon their deaths, the mansion became vacant and was therefore available for use as a VAD hospital, which it was from 1915 to January 1919. It expanded over time and would eventually have 112 beds.[9]

Broomlands in Broom Lane, Langton Green was a seven bedroom mansion built probably in the 1840s and it had parkland of 21 acres. The last occupant before the war was Col. R.C. Style who was at what was then called "The Broomlands" in 1913. It had a particularly close association the Tunbridge Wells general Hospital. The building has remained in residential use ever since it ceased to be a VAD hospital.

The Hollands, Langton Green is a Regency house designed by Decimus Burton in some 52 acres of grounds, which include a lake and woodland and paddock.

---

[9] It would subsequently be used as the Regional Civil Defence HQ during the Second World War, but is now divided into 12 flats.

Kingswood Park was not in Kingswood Road, as might be expected, but in Pembury Road, just south of Chilston House and Dunorlan. It opened in 1915 and was quickly enlarged. At the end of March 1916, the Courier reported that Kingswood Park Hospital was extending from 50 to 82 beds – the extra 32 being an 'open-air' ward – and by the end of May, the Marchioness Camden had opened the new 'open-air' ward, which was reported to have cost £700. The hospital would be extended further and by the end of the War, had 220 beds.

Shown above are two of a series of 41 photographs taken at Kingswood by John Santo McBride, a soldier from Calgary, Alberta, Canada, who had been sent to Kingswood for treatment. His photographs were put in an album and inscribed "To Nurse Turner with the season's best wishes, and in grateful remembrance from Pte. J.S. McBride, 24th Canadians". Sadly, John McBride only lived another six months after making this presentation, since he was killed in action on 3rd June, 1916, aged 24.

Lilian Teasdale

Also shown here are two examples of entries made by Cpl. H. Earp of the Prince Consort's Brigade and Sapper George Webb, in the autograph book of VAD nurse Lilian Teasdale (1877-1969), who worked at Kingswood, the Kent Nursing Institute (the KNI referred to), and the Eye and Ear Hospital.

Blackhurst, a mansion designed by Decimus Burton and built in 1838, is just off the Pembury Road by Halls Hole Road. Its owner, Frederick Frank, fortuitously died in 1915 and left the estate to his sons. Blackhurst was however not used as a VAD facility until April 1918 and then only until 1919, when it returned to residential use.[10]

Macquarie a large house on the eastern side of Pembury Road, next door to Kingswood Park and just north of Kingswood Road. It was a VAD hospital from 1918 until March 1919. It had been occupied by Edward Ross Fairfax b. 1842 in Sydney, NSW, Australia and brother of Sir James Fairfax, the senior proprietor of the *Sydney Morning Herald*. He died in July 1915, leaving £20,122, and his wife, Kate (Catherine Agnes) died a year later in October 1916. This left the house empty and an obvious candidate since it was next door to Kingswood to be a VAD hospital, which it became early in 1918. After being 'demobbed' as a VAD hospital, it changed it name to Hurstmead.[11]

Calverley Lodge was a large mansion, built in the 1830s on the N.E. corner of the junction of Prospect Road/Pembury Road and Calverley Road /Bayhall Road. It was taken over for use as a VAD Hospital in April 1915 and remained so until 1919.[12]

---

[10] During World War II, the premises were leased to the Ardath Tobacco Co Ltd. who used the building as their office from 1939 to 1944, after moving from London to Tunbridge Wells, due to the bombing of London. The owner of the estate in 1944 was Alfred Cathorne who sold it to the Kent Council, who transferred it to the Ministry of Health, who ran it as a preliminary nurses' training school from 1949 to 1979 and then subsequently as NHS Area offices. In 1994, the building was refurbished and in 1998 it was sold to a development company which turned the buildings into a gated flat residence, which is called Blackhurst Park.

[11] It is now the Salvation Army Sunset Lodge

[12] After the war, Calverley Lodge was acquired by Dr. Percy Charles Law who converted the mansion into a medical centre which continued until 1950. From 1951 to 1969 the building was used as the Calverley Lodge Nursing Home. In 1970 the Salvation Army acquired the

Shernfold Park in Frant, which is outside the boundary of the current Borough, but has always looked to Tunbridge Wells as its centre of gravity, was built in 1855 on the site of an earlier building, to the design of the architect, Lewis Vulliamy. It was a 3-storey mansion of 20 rooms with a central entrance flanked by two wings, constructed of stone with a slate roof. It had a circular carriage drive, rose and flower gardens, parterre, summerhouses, an orchard, fishponds, a lake with boathouses, a centrally-heated winter garden and a park of about 50 acres. The 1911 census shows that it was occupied by Benjamin Mewgass, aged 72, born in 1839 in Derin, Germany, who was a merchant banker. Living with him was his 48-year-old wife, Maria, their two children and five servants. It is not known how it became a VAD hospital or whether the nationality of its occupier had anything to do with it.

War Hospital Supply Depots

All the VAD hospitals needed a supply infrastructure for clothing, bandages, food and other hospital supplies and what is astonishing is that this service was also run and funded by volunteers, largely a mix of married and maiden ladies. There were 2,787 supply depots in Britain and overseas for VAD hospitals, of which seven were in the area of Tunbridge Wells and these are on record as:

Depot No.	Location	Organiser	Organiser's Address
1006	Tunbridge Wells	Miss Lushington	Templehurst, Southborough
4045	Paddock Wood	Mrs.F.M.Sealey	Aycliffe, Paddock Wood
4100	Cranbrook	Miss A.G.Hardy	The Old Studio, Cranbrook
4525	Tonbridge	Miss E.P.Pechey	Homeleigh, Tonbridge
5292	Goudhurst	Mrs. Raikes	The Vicarage, Goudhurst
5360	Lamberhurst	Miss K.Gurr	Hillside, Lamberhurst
5587	Goudhurst	Mrs.E. Wickham	The Firs, Goudhurst

This task must have been a major challenge for women who before the War would have had relatively little organisational or management experience on such a large scale. It is clear that they rose to the challenge

---

property, demolished Calverley Lodge and built their new Citadel on the site (which remains to this day), replacing their former Citadel in Varney Street (which would subsequently vanish under the development of Royal Victoria Place).

magnificently. What is also of note is that most of the supplies were collected, assembled, manufactured or purchased locally by the Depot staff, the cost being met by donations from the staff themselves, or the general public. The Supply Depot in Tunbridge Wells was at 50, The Pantiles and in its first year it had 300 volunteers who supplied 53,370 'Hospital Necessities' including 19,000 bandages, 16,818 surgical swabs, 6,729 Many Tail bandages, 1,262 Moss dressings, 1,375 mittens and 1,030 mufflers. A report in the *Courier* in September 1916 records that Sphagnum moss which was thought to be very therapeutic in dressing wounds was collected at Eridge.

Christmas at the VAD Hospitals of Tunbridge Wells

Every year great efforts were made to make Christmas special for the wounded troops. Wards were decorated with holly, ivy, garlands, streamers and Chinese lanterns. There were concerts, carol services, and other entertainment, including musical chairs and 'other old-fashioned games'. Local groups, such as the King Charles's Girls' Club, toured the hospitals, giving performances of their 'Italian Dance and Minuet' and 'Mrs. Jarley's Waxworks'. On Christmas Day, the Mayor and Mayoress and the Deputy Mayor visited every hospital. The Mayor and Mayoress gave every soldier a diary and the Deputy Mayor gave each a packet of cigarettes. It was reported in the *Courier* that that the 'geniality' of the Mayor and the 'infinite charm' of the Mayoress had made a great impression, while the Deputy Mayor, (who was) Colonel Sydney Sladen, was 'completely at ease with his comrades, as he called them'.

Strafe the Tailor—A Bad Fit of the "Blues."

The Blue Hospital Uniform.

All wounded soldiers had to wear a special uniform when outdoors. It was a blue single-breasted jacket with a white lining, worn open at the neck, with blue trousers, a white shirt and a red tie, to which was added the soldier's own khaki service cap with its regimental badge. This uniform inexplicably had no pockets, and when washed had shrinkage problems – the outer layer which was flannelette, shrank at a different rate from its lining, which produced an unsightly and badly-fitting garment, and led to satirical postcards such as the one illustrated here. There were a number of explanations as to why the uniform was blue, the most cynical of which was that it immediately identified them if they went into a pub.

The presence of these wounded men in their blue uniforms, walking around the town and particularly the three Commons of Tunbridge Wells, Rusthall and Southborough, must have had a significant impact on the town.

Patients at Tunbridge Wells

Available Beds and the Number of Wounded Soldiers Treated.
As far as is known, no estimates exist for the number of military hospital beds in Tunbridge Wells, or the number of military treated in them. But it is worth attempting a figure. Such an exercise introduces variables, which can verge on the imponderable – specifically, the exact number of hospitals within a defined boundary (and how that boundary is defined), the length of time each of them was in operation, and the exponential growth and speed of growth of each hospital over their operational time.

Some partial figures do however exist, which could be extrapolated *with suitable caution* to produce averages which might be applied to the estimated number of beds:
- the General Hospital, which eventually supplied a total of 70 beds for the Military, is on record as treating over 1,700 soldiers during the 4½ year period – an *average* of 24 per bed, which suggests that the *average* length of stay was just over 10 weeks;
- St. Mark's Hospital which had 66 beds, recorded treating 513 soldiers in its first 15 months - an *average* of 8 per bed, which suggests an *average* length of stay of about 13 weeks.
- Rust Hall VAD Hospital, which *eventually* had 334 beds and was almost certainly the largest in Tunbridge Wells, is recorded as treating just under 4,000 soldiers during its four and a half years of existence – an average of about 12 a bed or just under 890 a year, which could support a broad estimate of an average length of about 12 weeks.
- Nevill Park VAD Hospital started with 50 beds in 1915 but seems to have grown to 300 beds by Christmas 1917.
- Kingswood Park VAD Hospital which was operational from 1916 to March 1919, would eventually have a capacity of 220 beds, and while no estimates seem to exist for the numbers it treated, it is likely that they would have been proportionately similar.

If one takes from the above figures an overall average of about 11-12 weeks' length of stay per bed, and applies it to the best estimates of the number of hospitals and beds available, then one could make a very broad estimate of the number of soldiers treated within the defined boundaries of what was then Royal Tunbridge Wells.

The total number of 'military' beds in Tunbridge Wells over the 4½ year period would seem to be of the order of about 1,300, and if one discounts this figure by a quarter, to allow for the fact that they were not all available for the whole period, then it would seem that a very broad estimate of the average number of 'operational' beds was probably about 1,000. If one then takes an average length of stay of about 12 weeks, the total number of wounded treated in Tunbridge Wells was probably of the order of about 14,000, which would have been an *average* of over 700 in any given week of the 4½ years.

The above figures, derived quite independently, tie in broadly with the published VAD figures for the County of Kent. Tunbridge Wells probably averaged 12-14 VAD hospitals operational at any one time, which is about 10% of the 132 recorded for Kent. The County also recorded treating 125,000 wounded patients and an estimate of 13,500 for Tunbridge Wells alone, is also just over 10% of the County total, so the independently-arrived-at estimate for Tunbridge Wells would seem to fit reasonably.

It should be said, although it is probably self-evident to the reader, that it is not surprising that knowledge in Tunbridge Wells today about the VAD hospitals of Tunbridge Wells then, has largely vanished, essentially because it all happened 100 years ago and is therefore outside living memory.

Perhaps the only remaining relics of VAD hospitals in Tunbridge Wells are the VAD Red Cross flags which flew above Rust Hall and Bidborough Court/Nevill Park and which still hang in St. Paul's Church, Rustall and St. Mary the Virgin, Speldhurst.

But there can be no doubt that in their time, the VAD and the wounded for whom they cared, did have a major impact on the town and this must have influenced future behaviour and attitudes.

VAD flag in St. Paul's Church, Rusthall.

TABLE

Temporary VAD Hospitals in Tunbridge Wells 1914-1919

Name	VAD No.	Location	Maximum Capacity (beds)	Operational Period
Bidborough Court	Kent 74	Bidborough		Oct.1914-Aug.1915
Blackhurst		Halls Hole Rd.		Apr.1918-1919
Bredbury		77, Mt. Ephraim	112	1915-Jan.1919
Broomlands		Langton Green		
Calverley Lodge		Pembury Rd.		Apr.1915-1919
Crothers	Kent 94	74, Pennington Rd, Southboro'		1915-Jan.1919
Kent Nursing Inst.		Holly Lodge, 11,Crescent Rd	32	*1875*-1919
Kingswood Park The Hollands	Kent 172	Pembury Rd. Langton Green	<u>220</u>	Oct 1916-Mar.1919
Macquarie		Pembury Rd.		Mar.1918-1919
Nevill Park	Kent 74	8 Nevill Park	300	Oct.1916-Feb.1919
Park House	Kent 98	24 Park Rd Southborough		Oct.1914-Jan.1919
Royal Victoria Hall	Kent 98	Southborough		Oct 1914-Aug 1915
Rust Hall - Main	Kent 154	Langton Rd, Rusthall	130	Mar.1915-Aug.1919
Rust Hall -Annex			204	
The Mission Hall	Kent 154	Rusthall		1916
Rusthall Beacon (hostel)	Kent 154	Tea Garden Lane		1917-1919
Rusthall Girls' School	Kent 154	High St. Rusthall		1917-May 1919
The Elms (hostel)	Kent 154	Rusthall		-1919
Shernfold Park	Sussex 8	Frant		-Jan. 1919
St.Mark's	Sussex	Broadwater Down	66	Sept 1915-Dec1918
West Hall	Kent 94	7 Chilston Rd	<u>50</u>	Oct 1914-Mar.1917
		Total	**1,114**	

There were a further 18 VAD hospitals on the periphery of Tunbridge Wells (although not necessarily within the boundaries of the current Borough) at:

Other VAD Hospitals within the locality

Name	VAD No. (Kent)	Location	Maximum Capacity (beds)	Operational Period
Vestry Hall		Cranbrook	42	Oct.1914 - ?
Harecombe		Crowborough		
Lidwells		Crowborough	35	May1915-Mar 1919
Brandfolds				
Gore Court	122	Goudhurst		- March 1919
Claytons		Mayfield		
Beechlands		Newick		
Village Hall	18	Paddock Wood		Oct-Dec.1914
Green Hill		Rotherfield		Transferred to Claytons
St. John's Hall	56	Sevenoaks		Oct.1914-Mar1919
Cornwall Hall	56	Sevenoaks		Sept1914-Mar1919
Coombe Bank	76	Sevenoaks	46	Dec.1914 - ?
Quarry Hill House	44	Tonbridge		Oct 1914-Feb1919
The Hamptons		Tonbridge/Hadlow	17	
Lyghe Institute	44	Tonbridge		Jul 1915-Dec1918
Somerhill	44	Tonbridge		
Tonbridge School Sanatorium	44	Tonbridge		
Tappington Grange		Wadhurst		
Hill House		Wadhurst		
Beech Green		Withyham		

Note: There were two classes of VAD Hospital:

Class A had trained nursing personnel and suitable equipment for treatment, and they received 'cot cases' from Military Hospitals in Great Britain and from abroad.

Class B had nursing personnel and provided convalescence, but little treatment. They received convalescent and walking cases only. Most of the Tunbridge Wells VAD hospitals are believed to have been Class B.

This classification dates from September 1915.

CHAPTER 7
TUNBRIDGE WELLS WOMEN IN THE FIRST WORLD WAR
by Anne Logan and Catherine Lee

Introduction

Pre-First World War British politics is often said to have been dominated domestically by three themes: the Home Rule for Ireland crisis, the struggle for 'Votes for Women', and the fight between capital and labour, which was played out in high-profile strike action by transport workers and miners between 1910 and 1914. Of these three political issues, the one with the greatest resonance in Tunbridge Wells was undoubtedly women's suffrage. With a demographic gender imbalance firmly tilted towards a feminine majority – according to the 1911 census there were 6,500 more women than men in the Municipal Borough - the town was perhaps unsurprisingly an epicentre of the early twentieth-century feminist earthquake.

The Edwardian women's suffrage movement was made up of a multitude of organisations, many of which had adherents among the people of Tunbridge Wells. The militant societies – whose members were termed suffragettes – were the Women's Social and Political Union (WSPU) and the Women's Freedom League (WFL), both of which had an intermittent presence in the town during the period 1908-14.

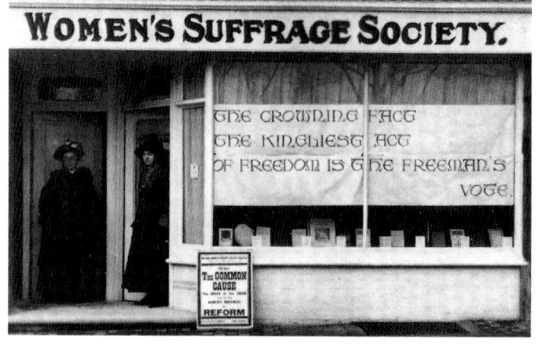

NUWSS premises in Crescent Road c.1910

But numerically the largest pro-suffrage organisation nationally and locally was the National Union of Women's Suffrage Societies (NUWSS), which was an umbrella for the constitutional, non-militant section of the movement, that is, people who went by the title 'suffragist'. Formed nationally in 1897, the NUWSS was so strong in the south-east by 1913 that it formed a Kent Area Federation in that year. Of all the branches in the county, Tunbridge Wells had the second highest membership (165), and significantly also boasted 278 'friends', working- class supporters who could not afford the full subscription but who nevertheless expressed support for the society's aims by signing a pledge.[1]

Not only was the NUWSS the town's largest suffrage organisation, it was also by far and away the most active and significant. Officers included many of Tunbridge Wells' most prominent ladies, including the social reformer, Amelia Scott; a celebrated novelist, Sarah Grand; and Lady Annette Amelia Matthews, a recent arrival in the town as the recently-married second wife of a retired colonial legal officer, Sir John Matthews.[2] The local NUWSS treasurer was Lydia Le Lacheur, the Guernsey-born widow of a former consul-general, who lived at The Wilderness in Pembury Road. Several of Lydia's eight daughters were active suffragettes. As this chapter will show, most of these ladies - and many others - were to play an important part in the war work of Tunbridge Wells' women between 1914 and 1918.

Amelia Scott

While undoubtedly important, suffrage organisations were but a part of a much wider women's movement in pre-war Tunbridge Wells. Early twentieth-century Britain was host to a myriad of women's organisations, set up for many different social groups, classes, causes and special interests. These included ladies' temperance societies, which sought to pressurise the government into stricter controls on the liquor trade; and rescue and preventative societies, whose goal was to help young girls who 'got into trouble' (that is, became pregnant while unmarried). For working class women, there was the Women's Co-operative Guild (WCG), which brought together mainly the wives of skilled manual workers to discuss politics. All these women's organisations – and more - had active local branches in Tunbridge Wells.

As with suffrage, an umbrella organisation which linked many of the groups had emerged: this was the National Union of Women Workers (NUWW), which was established both nationally and locally in 1895. The instigator of the local branch was a Poor Law Guardian, Amelia Scott, who set up the first meeting in the house she shared with her sister,

---

[1] NUWSS Kentish Federation, (1913) First Annual Report, Women's Library, London. Only Ramsgate had more members than Tunbridge Wells (191) but this branch either did not run the 'friends' scheme or else did not specify its number of 'friends'.
[2] Lady Matthews was also the half-sister of Lord Airedale, a Liberal politician and former MP.

Louisa, on 16 May 1895.³ The NUWW, despite its name, was not a body for working-class women, but for ladies involved in philanthropic endeavour.⁴

The Tunbridge Wells branch, which was to last for eighty-nine years, was extraordinarily vibrant for a relatively small town, vying with some of the big-city branches such as Birmingham and Bristol in its level of activity during its heyday. Once again, this was a testament not only to Tunbridge Wells' unusual demography (perhaps a result of the high proportion of unmarried sisters living together, and widows, as well as domestic servants in the population) but also to the high levels of social capital possessed by many of its inhabitants. Like the NUWSS, the NUWW - and its many related organisations - played a vital role in the organisation of women's war work.

The NUWSS 'Pilgrimage' of July 1913

Before 1914 Tunbridge Wells' active women's movement had already scored several remarkable successes. The vote may not yet have been won, but the NUWSS 'Pilgrimage' – a mass demonstration which converged on London in July 1913 from all points of the compass, including West Kent – had demonstrated the determination of suffragists to achieve their goal, notwithstanding the hostility created by the alleged unlawful acts of suffragettes.

Much had also been achieved by Tunbridge Wells' ladies in the field of social work, especially the provision of services for women and children. For example, led by the Scott sisters and a Quaker businesswoman called Sarah Candler, NUWW members had organised a club for young women workers which opened in 1900. Called the 'Leisure Hour Club for Young Women in Business', it aimed to provide safe and appropriate after-work and weekend activities for girls from fifteen years of age who were not

---

³ NCW Tunbridge Wells Branch, *The First Seventy-five years 1895-1970*, Kent History and Library Centre, Maidstone.

⁴ The NUWW was renamed the National Council of Women in 1918.

working in domestic service, but in shops, factories and laundries.[5] The club continued to flourish during the First World War, when it had over fifty members and organised special 'social evenings', to which members could invite 'a soldier friend'.[6]

Before the War, the NUWW branch had also campaigned for safe housing for poor women, opening a lodging house exclusively for women in the premises of a former public house in 1913. This Varney Street hostel was to provide accommodation during the war for the female relatives of soldiers encamped in the town, and in 1917 it became the base for a communal kitchen that fed soup and milk puddings to needy women and children.[7]

This chapter demonstrates that, far from putting aside their political and social campaigns for women once the war broke out, Tunbridge Wells' ladies continued to promote activities which while supporting the war effort – or at least ameliorating its human consequences – also served to advance the same causes that they had worked for pre-war. The suffrage society and the other women's bodies did not disband, but kept a lively presence in the town throughout the war, their members ready to greet and work with any advance in women's rights that wartime conditions could provide, while seeking to defend the members of their own sex whom they regarded as weaker than themselves.

This chapter also looks at changes in the work and role of working-class women, the promotion of both military service and work on the land for women, and some of the more private and domestic aspects of women's lives to be affected by total war.

Women's Voluntary Work in the War

On the outbreak of war in 1914, women's work – nationally and locally - continued along its well-established, philanthropic lines. The suffrage society's offices in Crescent Road were immediately converted into a depot where donated clothing was collected, mended if need be, and distributed to soldiers, hospital patients and refugees via charities such as the Red Cross.[8] By 1917, over 11,000 garments had been handled by the depot.

While suffragists were divided in their opinions about the war, with views ranging from pacifist opposition to the conflict to enthusiastic support for it,[9] they could at least unite around the necessity of a humanitarian

---

[5] http://www.womenshistorykent.org/themes/workingwomen/leisurehourclub.html
[6] *Kent and Sussex Courier*, 2 November 1917, p. 5.
[7] *Kent and Sussex Courier*, 13 July 1917, p. 5.
[8] *Tunbridge Wells Advertiser*, 23 October 1914, p. 8.
[9] See box on 'Women and the Peace Movement'.

response to those injured or exiled by conflict. Thus Tunbridge Wells' leading suffrage women were also prominent in the Mayor's committee formed in October 1914 to help Belgian refugees. This group, which consisted of twenty women and five men, set about the task of finding accommodation for the Belgians, as well as raising money and soliciting donations of furniture and household items.[10]

Lydia Le Lacheur – who was on the committee – immediately assumed responsibility for a group of about thirteen refugees whom she welcomed to the town in early October. Other notable committee members included one of Lydia's daughters, as well as the Scott sisters (who later received the gift of a souvenir album from grateful members of the Belgian community in Tunbridge Wells)[11] and Miss Susan Power, a Poor Law Guardian for Ticehurst. (See Chapter 8 – Belgian Refugees in Tunbridge Wells - for more details.)

In addition to offering hospitality to Belgians, community-minded women threw themselves into organising refreshments and respectable entertainments for the regiments of soldiers who were soon billeted in the town. When the first refreshment tent was erected close to the encampment on the Lower Cricket Ground, it became a great attraction for many of the townspeople. On the first Sunday it was there, members of the public had to be roped off to make room for the soldiers.[12] On 18th September 1914 Lady Matthews recorded in her war diary that she had spent three hours in a 'draughty tent' giving out tea and cakes and washing up for 120 young Territorial Engineers. This recreation tent on the Common was run jointly by the local branches of the National British Women's Temperance Association (NBWTA) and the NUWW.

Lady Matthews did not regard this as pleasant work: on another occasion she mentioned the tent was dirty, greasy and damp. But it was nevertheless a patriotic duty that she must have felt obliged to fulfil. More pleasant perhaps was the 'smoking concert' in the Great Hall that Lady Matthews presided over in November, where men from Lancashire and Wales were entertained with songs and served coffee and buns. On Christmas Day 1914 she toured six different large premises where a total of 2500 soldiers were served a festive dinner of turkey, roast beef and pork, apple sauce, boiled and baked potatoes, Brussels sprouts, cabbage, Christmas pudding and mince pies.[13]

Tunbridge Wells' women were obviously capable of undertaking mass catering operations during the first months of the war. Altogether, the

---

[10] *Tunbridge Wells Advertiser*, 16 October 1914, p. 10.
[11] In the Women's Library.
[12] 'Women and War Work', Amelia Scott Papers, 7/ASC/2/1/4/1, Women's Library.
[13] Lady Matthews' war diary, Imperial War Museum.

NUWW was involved in running eighteen canteens in Tunbridge Wells throughout the war years and these provided an estimated 720,000 meals at an average cost of 4d. a meal.[14] In addition to the facilities provided for the use of encamped and billeted soldiers, others catered for wounded and disabled men and another for the visitors of wounded men at the General Hospital.

These efforts of respectable Tunbridge Wells ladies were not only motivated by hospitality but also by a perceived need to keep the young men busily engaged in safe recreation, away from public houses and - crucially - from any chance of creating mischief through unsupervised contact with the town's young girls. Soon after the outbreak of war 'khaki fever' was identified nationally as an affliction affecting particularly young women and girls, especially those in the thirteen to sixteen age bracket, who, it was feared, would lose all inhibition in the presence of lusty young men in uniform.[15]

Tunbridge Wells saw more than its share of cases of 'khaki fever', a result of the large numbers of soldiers regularly billeted in the area. Their presence was believed to be causing the local girls to lose their heads, and it was said that on the nights when drafts left for the front, the girls were to be found marching in the ranks with their arms round the men.[16] The alarm over khaki fever prompted a number of women's voluntary war work initiatives. It is notable, as historians have pointed out, that the 'social ... and sexual independence' of female teenagers was associated in the public and official mind with prostitution and immorality, and was imagined and described accordingly, as a social problem in need of a remedy.[17]

Women Police Patrols and the Soldiers' Laundry
Tunbridge Wells had long been home to a branch of the Rescue and Preventative Association, which ran a shelter in Upper Grosvenor Road and provided assistance to so-called 'fallen' women. In the year before the outbreak of war, fifty-three girls had passed through the doors of the shelter, and after this its work was felt to be even more necessary owing to the 'great wave of unrest, excitement and emotion' provoked by abnormal wartime conditions.[18]

---

[14] 'Women and War Work', Amelia Scott Papers, 7/ASC/2/1/4/1, Women's Library.
[15] Angela Woollacott (1994) '"Khaki Fever" and its Control: Gender, Class, Age and Sexual Morality on the British Homefront in the First World War, *Journal of Contemporary History* 29, 2.
[16] 'Women and War Work', Amelia Scott Papers, 7/ASC/2/1/4/1, Women's Library.
[17] Woollacott, p. 343.
[18] *Kent and Sussex Courier* 20 March 1914 p. 9.

At the Association's Annual General Meeting in 1916, Sir John Matthews, in attendance in his capacity as a committee member, made a short speech of thanks to the Chairman. His words reflect very enlightened views, possibly influenced by his wife's feminist politics. He said that he deplored the sexual double-standard, but was thankful that this was changing. The term 'fallen women', he believed, should be replaced by 'betrayed woman'.[19]

As the war progressed, the Association extended its work to making home visits to soldiers' wives, which suggests that, with their husbands away at the front, some of these women were also believed to be in danger of falling prey to sexual temptation.[20]

However, not all young women seemed appreciative of the 'help' they were offered. In 1917 the *Courier* carried the story of seventeen-year old Doris Kingswood, who had been found sleeping rough, and subsequently absconded from a 'home' in London, to be discovered soon after in the East End, in the company of a Canadian soldier. Doris was placed in a Tunbridge Wells home, only to be discharged for misconduct, after which she spent a few weeks in the workhouse at Pembury, before once again sleeping rough on the Common. She was sentenced to a month in prison with hard labour, but according to the reporter, *'seemed unconcerned'*.[21]

Another response to khaki fever - in Tunbridge Wells and nationally – was that the NUWW began to lobby forcefully for women to become involved in voluntary patrolling and to be recruited into formal policing as a means of safeguarding girls' and young women's morals. In September 1914, central government authorised the NUWW to organise women patrols which, as *The Times* put it, were designed to keep girls and young women safe from the *'results of the excitement aroused by the war'*.[22] This initiative has been interpreted as well-meaning interference in the lives of others but, as will be seen later in this chapter, with the problem of 'war babies' the focus both of national and local attention, it becomes more understandable.

The local branch of the NUWW, one of only two in Kent at this time and probably one of the most dynamic in the country, responded immediately to its parent organisation's call for volunteer patrollers to deal with the exceptional war-time conditions. Thirty-three local women (13 married, 20 unmarried) enrolled and the first patrollers took to the streets of Tunbridge Wells in October 1914. These included Sarah Candler, one of

---

[19] Ibid., 18 February 1916 p. 7.
[20] Ibid., 16 March 1917 p. 6.
[21] *Kent and Sussex Courier*, 20 April 1917 p. 5.
[22] *The Times*, 31st December 1914, p. 3.

the proprietors of the Woodlands Laundry; Dr Edith Neild, the first female member of the British Homeopathic Society; Ethel Beecroft, daughter of a local JP; and Maggie Fenn, secretary of the Tunbridge Wells branch of the Christian Social Union. Subsequent recruits included Margaret (Daisy) Masterman, sister of the Liberal M.P. Charles Masterman. Patrollers had no powers of arrest and wore no uniform except an NUWW arm band. They carried an authorisation card signed by the Chief Constable and undertook to patrol at least twice a week for two hours at a time, always in twos.

It is clear that the patrols met with the approval of the local elite as can be seen by the letter written to the *Courier* by Margaret Empson, the Mayoress. She explained that the patrollers' aim was to *'make friends with the young and excited girls'*, to persuade them away from the streets at night and so protect them.[23] Violet Harris, the patrol organiser said that she and the other patrollers wanted to dispel the idea that the patrols were spying on the girls.[24] Amelia Scott believed that the patrollers' presence on the streets was 'a protest against rowdyism and a plea for decency'.[25]

At the same time, it was recognised that the most effective way to prevent girls and soldiers from being on the streets together at night was to provide an alternative venue for them to socialise together. Empson said: *'There is no counter-attraction to "Tommy", but there should be a counter-attraction to the streets at night'*. As has been seen, the Leisure Hour Club for Young Women in Business continued to run throughout the years of the war. Additionally, a Comrades Club was set up by the NUWW patrol committee in the early months of the war with the aim of keeping *'boys and girls off the streets'* in supervised safety. Accommodation at 13 Quarry Road was provided and by March 1915 there were forty-three members.

The club provided them with somewhere to invite their soldier friends to enjoy non-alcoholic refreshment and entertainments such as a gramophone and a piano. Soldier guests were forbidden to leave the club and then return later, to prevent them from visiting the public house in the interval. The social evening organised at the club in February 1916 gives us some idea of the entertainments that were on offer to rival the temptations of the pub. They included name-guessing, apple-bobbing and hat-decorating competitions.[26]

---

[23] *Kent and Sussex Courier*, 5th March 1915
[24] *Tunbridge Wells Advertiser*, 19 March 1915, p. 5
[25] 'Women and War Work', Amelia Scott Papers, 7/ASC/2/1/4/1, Women's Library.
[26] *Kent and Sussex Courier*, 11 February 1916, p. 5

In the meantime, the voluntary NUWW patrols continued in Tunbridge Wells until the end of the war and Maggie Fenn and Ethel Beecroft, having each achieved the distinction of patrolling continuously during the whole period, were decorated in recognition of their service. Fenn accompanied Amelia Scott to the garden party for war workers that was given by the King and Queen at Buckingham Palace in 1919, an event that was described by the *Daily Mirror* as *'essentially a woman's day'*.[27]

In addition to their unsettling effect on the younger members of the opposite sex, the resident troops became the focus of another problem during the first months of war. This was the matter of their laundry, since men were reported to be leaving for the front in dirty and worn clothing. Once again, this problem was understood to be linked to women of loose morals since the camps were reported to be over-run with women, some of whom were alleged to be *'undesirable characters'*, offering to do soldiers' washing to earn some money. To make matters worse, dirty clothing was said to be scattered *'up and down the cottages'* in the town and thereby causing a health risk.[28] So in 1915, the NUWW decided to set up a central laundry to provide washing and mending services to the thousands of soldiers camped in the town.

The scheme was given the backing of the Mayor, the military authorities and the Medical Officer of Health. Premises were found and an appeal launched to raise the £120 needed to cover initial expenses. Writing to the press in June 1915 to appeal for funds, Lady Constance Coote, local women of the town *'to do their bit by seeing that soldiers' clothes were properly washed and mended'*. In addition to preventing soldiers suffering from *'unnecessary miseries'*, she explained that the laundry would additionally provide paid employment for a number of women in need of work. This was no doubt welcome news to the poorer *'cottagers'* of the town, who had been earning money from doing the soldiers' laundry and who expressed dismay that they were to be deprived of this source of income.[29]

With forty paid staff and two hundred voluntary helpers at the height of its activities, the laundry washed, mended and sorted as many as 20,000 garments for over 2,000 men every week. Soldiers were initially charged 5d a head for five items: one shirt, one pair of socks, one towel, one pair of pants and three handkerchiefs. Khaki trousers, khaki tunics and cook's suits were charged at 6d each.

---

[27] *Daily Mirror*, 26 July 1919, p. 1
[28] *Kent and Sussex Courier*, 11th June 1915, p. 5.
[29] Ibid., 18 June 1915, p. 5.

National Union of Women Workers.

SOLDIERS' CENTRAL LAUNDRY AND MENDING ROOM

Office: 44, GROSVENOR ROAD, TUNBRIDGE WELLS.

1. Washing done at 7d. a head. (This allows for six articles:—one shirt, one pair socks, one towel, one pair pants, one vest, three handkerchiefs.)
2. Khaki Trousers, 6d. each.
   „   Tunics, 6d.   „
   Cooks' Suits, 6d.
3. The Laundry cannot hold itself responsible for any man's bundle **unless his Name, Regimental No. and Company are clearly written on his list of articles sent,** and no claims for deficits can be considered after two weeks have elapsed.
   [NOTE.—It is urgently advised in addition, that each man's Clothes should be marked with his Regimental No.]
4. Sacks are provided for the Soldiers' bundles, and are the property of the Laundry.
5. Each Battalion's Clothes will be washed and packed in separate Companies.
6. **Terms: Weekly Cash Payment.** Bills will be sent to the Q.M.S. of each Company.
7. Clothes will be mended **FREE** by Voluntary Workers as far as possible. If mending of all clothes must be guaranteed, some charge must be made

(Signed)
AMELIA SCOTT, *Hon. Manageress of Laundry.*
SUSAN POWER, *Hon. Manageress of Mending Room*
J. M. POWER, Esq. *Hon. Treasurer.*

BALDWIN, PRINTER, TUNBRIDGE WELLS.

NUWW Central Laundry workers at 44, Grosvenor Road, Tunbridge Wells

Among the regiments to benefit from the services provided at the laundry were the Royal East Kent, the Lancashire Fusiliers and the Worcestershire Yeomanry. At its premises at 44 Grosvenor Road, *'old-fashioned, skilled, hand-washing'* was carried out by many women who had previously been made redundant by the move to highly-mechanised commercial steam laundering processes.

At the turn of the century, laundry work had employed the largest number of the town's girls and women after domestic service. But washing soldiers' kits was not likely to have been a pleasant occupation. Lady Matthews told of a quartermaster who had to go through soldiers' belongings when they were admitted to the hospital, burning the *'unmendable'* and sending the rest for washing. *'She has to finger the things as little as possible, for some [men] come from the trenches, with clothes quite alive. When her unpleasant work is done, she goes home and bathes in "sheep wash" as she put it. To my mind,* added Lady Matthews, *'vermin must be the most terrible part of war conditions'.*[30]

The laundry was supported with contributions from the public, and a Gift Day in February 1916 attracted donations of money, shirts, socks and

---

[30] Lady Matthews' War Diary, 25 December 1915.

other items. Emmy Brown and Rose Pavey, young girls who started as under-hands, each became heads in the sorting department. Pavey was only 14 years old at the start of the war; she appears to have been keeping up a family tradition as her own mother had contributed to the family income by taking in ironing.[31] Mending was done free of charge and offered the women of the town a way to contribute to the war effort. The mending room eventually became officially recognised as a provider of Voluntary War Work, with eighty of the voluntary helpers proudly wearing Government Volunteer War Workers' badges.

The Mending Room

The women worked for the duration of the war, through difficulties such as the time all the pipes froze one winter, and another when almost all the staff went down with the 'flu. Through the war years the laundry handled 167,863 garments. Among the letters of thanks received from the soldiers was one that said: *'Thank-you for mending my shirt, I now sleep in peace, before I slept in pieces!'*[32] When, at the beginning of 1918, it was proposed to set up a Women Voters' and Citizens' Association in Tunbridge Wells, it is interesting that a room at the laundry was suggested as a possible meeting place.

By January 1918, the NUWW in Tunbridge Wells had earned sufficient funds from the laundry enterprise to create the position of a paid Patrol Leader. Eleanor Plumptree was therefore sent to undergo training at the Bristol Training School for Women Patrols and Women Police. Described in contemporary literature, this specialist three-month course consisted of visits to police courts, report-writing practice, and first-aid and elementary criminal law.[33] Graduates from the training school took up positions either as paid patrollers (generally attached to the Metropolitan Police) or as women police officers on borough or munitions police forces.

---

[31] 1911 Census Returns RG14: 4062, 184.
[32] 'Women and War Work', Amelia Scott Papers, 7/ASC/2/1/4/1, Women's Library.
[33] *The Times*, 24 October 1916, p. 5

Despite the success of the voluntary patrols, the need both for women police officers and for additional officers in Tunbridge Wells generally was repeatedly voiced by the NUWW. As early as October 1914 it was suggested that women constables should be appointed 'during the sojourn of the military' but this did not meet with the approval of the Town Council. Seven months later a representation from the NUWW, consisting of Maud Mackintosh, Amelia Scott and Sarah Candler, attended a meeting of the Tunbridge Wells Watch Committee to urge that rangers or police officers should be placed on the Common after nightfall in order to prevent the commission of *'acts of immorality or indecency'*.

More widely, calls for women to be recruited into regular policing gathered pace during the war years. Police forces became progressively more depleted as men were encouraged to enlist. Following the introduction of conscription in 1916 under the Military Service Act, it was even more difficult to maintain manpower levels. The Mayor of Tunbridge Wells addressed the police force in May 1918 to persuade the younger members that they would be serving the country more effectively by joining the army, and nineteen members volunteered as a result.[34]

When, therefore, the Tunbridge Wells Rescue and Preventative Association once again raised the question of women police with the Watch Committee in March 1918, they met with a positive response. The decision was made to recruit three women police officers from the Women's Police Service in Eccleston Square, London. In May 1918, Norah O'Sullivan, Annabel Dalziel and Mary Cameron were sworn in as members of the first class police reserve of Tunbridge Wells, at a salary of 35 shillings a week plus an additional war bonus, together with an allowance of £9 per year for uniform.[35] Amelia Scott took the opportunity to state, through the columns of the *Courier*, that the NUWW voluntary patrols hoped to work 'in perfect harmony' with the newly-appointed policewomen.[36]

That the new women officers were quick to make their presence felt, is suggested by a letter written to the *Courier* in August. Protesting against the 'high-handed' manner in which they were carrying out their duties, the writer claimed that he and a *'well-known and perfectly respectable young lady resident'*, *with whom he had been sitting one day on the Common, had been instructed by a policewoman 'to sit much further apart, as we could be seen from the road'.*[37]

---

[34] *Kent and Sussex Courier* 10 May 1918, p. 6.
[35] Tunbridge Wells Watch Committee Minutes, 16 May 1918.
[36] *Kent and Sussex Courier* 10 May 1918, p. 5.
[37] Ibid., 23 August 1918, p. 2.

Thus the protection of women's morals and the maintenance of orderly behaviour in public, which had prompted the NUWW's voluntary patrolling initiative, remained at the heart of women's roles in policing throughout the war years.[38]

Women and the Army

The sorts of voluntary work described above, together with opportunities to serve as members of the Voluntary Aid Detachment (VAD) in emergency Red Cross hospitals, provided many middle-class ladies with satisfaction that they were 'doing their bit' in wartime. However, those in the women's movement who were most enthusiastic about Britain's involvement in the war remained disappointed that the authorities apparently put so little faith in the ability of women to step into the shoes of men and play an active and less gender-stereotyped role in warfare.

For example, when a Scottish medical practitioner, Elsie Inglis, offered her services as a doctor to the War Office, she was turned down. Undaunted, and supported by fellow suffragists, she instead organised the Scottish Women's Hospitals for Foreign Service Committee, and travelled to Serbia to practice on the front line there. Inglis' work was enthusiastically supported by NUWSS members all over the country, and in January 1916 a packed meeting in Tunbridge Wells heard all about the Scottish Women's Hospitals. The event's organiser, Lady Matthews commented that *'these suffrage women, Doctors [and] Nurses, have done marvels of work in France [and] undoubtedly have gained the sympathy and admiration of everyone, whether for women's franchise or not'*. [39]

But perhaps Lady Matthews' feminist sympathies caused over-optimism concerning attitudes towards women's active involvement in the war, as

---

[38] The apparent success of the campaign for women police was short-lived. Following a period of post-war retrenchment, Emily Price was sworn in as the first female member of the Tunbridge Wells Borough Police Force in the 1920s, and by the Second World War there were two women officers. Full equality of employment, however, was still another thirty years away.

[39] Lady Matthews' Diary, 31 January 1916.

there is plenty of evidence that controversy about women stepping into men's roles only began to abate in 1917, when the War Office reluctantly launched the Women's Auxiliary Army Corps (WAAC). On another occasion Lady Matthews expressed frustration: *'our best blood is being spilt at the front'*, she wrote in July 1915, *'[but] our women [are] still not admitted into the Nation's Councils, their wisdom lost, [and] their experience unused'*.[40]

Early in the war some former suffragists and suffragettes decided not to wait for official approval and formed the Women's Emergency Corps (WEC), initially as a means to co-ordinate women's voluntary efforts. One aim was to safeguard working women's income since there was a good deal of concern that, in the rush of the middle classes to knit and sew on a voluntary basis, working women's livelihoods could be threatened.

At a meeting in January 1915 chaired by Mrs Robertson of Knight's Place, Pembury, former suffragette Margaret Kineton-Parkes – last seen in Tunbridge Wells as a representative of the WFL-affiliated Tax Resistance League - gave an address on the WEC's work. Some concerns were voiced about the overlapping of local initiatives since, as Lady Matthews and Sarah Grand were quick to point out, women's volunteer efforts in Tunbridge Wells were already being successfully co-ordinated by the Mayor's central organisation.

The ensuing discussion, as reported by the *Courier*, reflects some tension between the visitors and the Tunbridge Wells activists, particularly when Mrs Kineton-Parkes had to confess to not being familiar with the details of local circumstances. However, the discussion resulted in the formation of a local branch.

The WEC soon spawned a paramilitary wing, called the Women's Volunteer Reserve (WVR). The WVR was highly controversial as members were regarded as appropriating masculine symbols of militarism, for example by sporting khaki uniforms, and stipulating that no make-up was to be worn on the face. They were often stereotyped as 'upper-class Amazons'.[41] A battalion of the WVR was also soon established in Tunbridge Wells under the leadership of Mrs Silcock, an Alderman's wife and former Mayoress, and by April 1915 it was said to have 130 recruits organised into two companies, with a fifty-strong auxiliary made up of girls too young to join the main organisation.

---

[40] Lady Matthews' Diary, 22 July 1915.
[41] Janet S. K. Watson, 'Khaki Girls, VADs, and Tommy's Sisters: Gender and Class in First World War Britain', *International History Review* 19, 1, p. 38.

Members trained in some less obviously feminine activities such as signalling, driving, motor mechanics and cycle dispatch riding, as well as in first aid, nursing and cookery. In the event of an emergency, the cyclist section was ready for deployment in calling the Corps together to await orders at the railway station yard, whilst the first-aiders were expected to prove their worth in the event of an air raid. Above all, they took part in regular drill sessions and even went on military-style route marches, such as the one through Tunbridge Wells which was organised by Mrs Silcock and Lady Matthews in June 1915. The occasion was sufficiently remarkable (a *'mild sensation'*, according to the *Courier*) to attract a large

WVR officers on their first Route March, June 1915

crowd of spectators to Vale Road to watch with 'mingled admiration and curiosity'.[42] The route march was led by Captain Florence Manser, the wife of medical practitioner Dr Frederick, while Commandant Mrs Silcock opted to motor to Bishop's Down, where she was saluted by the corps as they marched past.

Such controversy reigned over the WVR's motives that organisers tried to justify these activities in feminine terms: Mrs Silcock claimed that 'Swedish drill' had beneficial effects on the girls' *'carriage'* [43], but such justifications could not obscure the potential such militaristic activity held for challenging traditional gender roles.

---

[42] *Kent and Sussex Courier*, 4 June 1915.
[43] *Tunbridge Wells Advertiser*, 30 April 1915, p. 5.

Tunbridge Wells postal staff Misses Wood, Baker (standing) and Harding, went to France with the Signalling Corps of the Women's Auxilliary Army Corps June 1917

Some historians have claimed that while the WVR was largely middle and upper-class, the subsequently-formed official WAAC was necessarily made up of mainly working-class recruits. The Tunbridge Wells evidence is ambiguous regarding the social status of WVR members. On the one hand, a riding dispatch corps was founded, with three members wealthy enough to provide their own horses. On the other, the local Reserve members decided to make their own uniforms, purchase the khaki fabric in bulk, and help those who could not afford to supply their own uniforms with the cost.[44] Thus there seems to have been some genuine attempt to open the WVR to women of all classes.

When the official WAAC was finally launched in 1917, it was not the *'middle-class Amazons'* who were encouraged to join, but women of more humble backgrounds required to fulfil tasks such as cookery and clerical work. Yet twelve Tunbridge Wells WVR members immediately joined up, while Mrs Silcock, Lady Matthews and Rachel Ard turned to organising WAAC recruitment drives.[45]

Agriculture

In addition to the unprecedented formation of women's military organisations, the First World War is also remembered for the encouragement of women to take up agricultural work, especially through the formation of the Women's Land Army. Yet, like the WAAC and the other uniformed women's services, the Land Army was a development that came very late in the war, prompted not only by labour shortages, but also by an increasingly serious crisis of food supply.

As an agricultural county, Kent was likely to be in the forefront of any innovations in the use of female labour on the land. The employment of women in farm work was by no means unprecedented, although women's labour on the land had declined in the mid-19th century, to such an extent that many contemporaries believed it was a novel idea. Moreover Kent residents were accustomed to the annual migration of women and children from London to take part in the county's hop harvest.

---

[44] *Ibid.* 5 March 1915 p. 5.
[45] *Kent and Sussex Courier*, 26 October 1917, p. 5.

Yet again, the women's movement, in its desire to increase the opportunities for women to earn an independent living and to contribute to the country's wealth in peace and its security in war, was to be found not far behind moves to expand women's role. In 1899, the Women's Agricultural and Horticultural International Union (WAHIU) was formed by the International Council of Women, to which the NUWW was affiliated. The WAHIU's British branch aimed to promote agriculture and horticulture as suitable occupations for educated, middle-class women, perhaps with emigration to the colonies in mind. Around the turn of the century establishments offering courses for women in horticulture began to spring up, most notably the college at Swanley, which admitted female pupils from 1891 onwards.

Interestingly, two of Lydia Le Lacheur's Tunbridge Wells-bred suffragette daughters took up a career in farming before the War, with one running a dairy farm near Reading, and another producing vegetables and cut flowers in Sussex. Yet when war broke out, male farmers were allegedly reluctant to employ women, who they doubted would have the staying power to do rough and dirty work.[46]

This obstacle did not face Ada Wansbon, of Mark Cross, as she worked on her parents' farm. With five sons enlisted, three of whom had previously been employed about the farm, Wansbon's parents were unable to find male workers to take their place. Ada, described by the *Courier* as a *'patriotic Mark Cross Girl'* and dressed in her brother's working clothes, laboured from 8am until 5 pm cutting swedes, caring for 30 bullocks and dressing hops.[47]

Meanwhile, undaunted by most farmers' reluctance to employ women, the WAHIU began to train women for labour on the land. Again, a voluntary body was stepping in where the State was reluctant to tread. As the

---

[46] The Times History of the War, part 221, Vol 17, 12 November 1918, p. 447.
[47] Kent and Sussex Courier, 14 April 1916

conscription of men into the army began in 1916 and the food crisis worsened, the Government set up the National Land Service Corps as part of the Board of Agriculture, to improve labour supply in harvest periods. Meanwhile, Women's War Agricultural Committees were established county by county, under the auspices of the Board of Trade. It was not until the end of 1916 that these two organisations were brought together and a Women's Branch of the Board of Agriculture was set up in January 1917. The Women's Land Army was launched just two months later.[48]

Under the new arrangements, women over eighteen years of age would receive a month's training; a clothing kit of two overalls, one pair of breeches, one pair of boots, leggings, clogs and one hat; and a guaranteed minimum wage of eighteen shillings a week (a lower rate than the pay in the WAAC). Moreover, they were promised the prospect of extra training and promotion to *'skilled milkers, thatchers, tractor drivers, Group Leaders, Instructresses etc.'* and even the possibility of assistance with settlement on the land at home or in one of the Dominions after the war.[49]

In May 1917 Mrs Silcock chaired a public meeting in Tunbridge Wells aimed at urging women to come forward for service in the Women's Land Army. One of the guest speakers was Miss Courtauld, a member of the renowned textile manufacturing family, who was a leading light in the WAHIU and herself a *'lady farmer'* in Essex. The other speaker, Miss Bagnall, the travelling inspector for the Board of Agriculture in the South East, said that only *'very strong, fit and intelligent women'* would be accepted.[50]

A further local recruitment drive took place in March 1918, when there was a procession through the town accompanied by a military band.[51] Nevertheless, there were still difficulties in persuading farmers to accept their labour. In a letter to the *Courier* in April 1917, Lord Wolseley argued that if women left other occupations to join the Land Army, then they should be found jobs as soon as their training was finished. Farmers needed to notify their County Committee of vacancies immediately. *'Some seventeen years' experience of women gardeners has taught me that women, when well-trained, can help very materially in gardens and on farms'*, he wrote.[52]

---

[48] *The Times History of the War,* part 221, Vol 17, 12 November 1918.
[49] *The Times History of the War, part 221, Vol 17, 12 November 1918* pp. 448-9.
[50] *Kent and Sussex Courier,* 18 May 1917, p. 6.
[51] Ibid., 1 March 1918, p. 7.
[52] Ibid., 20 April 1917, p. 5.

Women ploughing using traditional methods

By November 1917, the *Courier* could report that there were nine thousand women registered as land workers in Kent, and two to three hundred enrolled in the Land Army. The newspaper reported on a demonstration of women's agricultural work that had taken place at Allington, near Maidstone, which showed that women could do all kinds of agricultural work, including ploughing, fruit planting, grading and packing.[53] Kent certainly must have played an important part in the training of women for agricultural work: many of the prize winners at the Allington event were students at Swanley, or at Wye College, where Land Army members were trained to be land bailiffs, and even the Land Army's tractor training school was only just over the Surrey border in Oxted.

We do not know how many Tunbridge Wells women answered the call to join the Land Army, but the mobilisation of temporary harvest-time labour was every bit as vital in maximising food production. In 1918 a thousand women were organised in the county to thresh the *'good corn harvest'* of that year, and in October the work of the West Kent Women's War Agricultural Committee (WAG) in co-ordinating village communities' food production and conservation efforts, was celebrated in an exhibition of produce in Maidstone.[54] Moreover, the Board of Agriculture encouraged the growth of the Women's Institute (WI) movement in villages across the country in order to promote women's skills of food production and preservation.

Women ploughing using modern means

In December 1917 the West Kent WAG hosted a meeting at which Lady Denman spoke on the subject of village institutes in Canada, which was from where the idea for Women's Institutes (WI) had come. It was announced that such an organisation had been recently

---
[53] Ibid., 30 November 1917, p. 3.
[54] *Kent and Sussex Courier*, 11 October 1918, p. 7.

formed in the village of Kemsing,[55] which may have been the first branch of what soon became the West Kent Federation of the WI. Still in existence today, WIs have become a lasting legacy not only of the early twentieth century women's movement, but also of the food production crisis and the pressing need to involve village women in agriculture during the First World War.

Women and Paid Work

So far, this chapter has concentrated mainly on the activities of the army of middle-class female volunteers who were capable of performing vital tasks in Tunbridge Wells and on the quasi-military organisations that sprang up during the war. But what of the working-class women, many of them very young, and most of whom worked as domestic servants? The First World War had a transformative effect on their lives by giving them new work opportunities, even if many of these proved to be short-lived, for the duration of the war only.

Much was made by middle-class employers of the growing servant shortage during the war. As young men were at first encouraged to enlist in the army – and were later conscripted – so young women were to be found taking their place. Yet the initial impact of the war was to throw women out of work, especially those who worked in shops, dress-making and similar trades, who were laid off when the wealthy suddenly cut back on perceived luxuries in the name of patriotism. This process may well have affected Tunbridge Wells' normally busy retail sector, as Lady Matthews noted the 'slack' trade in local shops by the end of August 1914.[56]

Suffragists were aware of the problem: one aim of the WEC in the early months of the war was to avoid doing on a voluntary basis the kind of work – like some types of sewing – which would otherwise earn poorer women a wage. Within a couple of weeks of being set up, the local branch was inundated with as many as twenty requests a week for paid employment from dressmakers and shop assistants, all of whom had been laid off by their employers. The WEC tried to assist by finding them knitting or sewing to do and by selling their work through local shops.[57] Lady Matthews herself drafted a letter, signed by the Mayor of Tunbridge Wells, appealing to residents to buy from local retailers when purchasing

---

[55] Ibid., 14 December 1917, p. 3. A former suffragist, Lady Denman became the first president of the National Federation of Women's Institutes and in the Second World War she took charge of the revived Women's Land Army.
[56] Lady Matthews' war diary, 22 August 1914.
[57] *Kent and Sussex Courier*, 5 February 1915, p. 4

materials to make goods for the Red Cross. She also criticised some of the 'amateur sewing' that was wasting materials and time.[58]

However, as more men left for the armed forces, increasing numbers of women began to be employed in their place, as both substitution and so-called 'dilution' of labour took place. As already mentioned in the case of farming, women could take over the jobs of male relatives as they left for military service. In May 1915, Lady Matthews recorded in her diary that the milk delivery boy had enlisted and been replaced by a girl. But not all substitution went smoothly. Less than two years later the *Courier* carried the tragic news of the fate of one Rhoda Harland, a twenty-year old woman who had left domestic service also to deliver milk, in order *to ' do something for her country'*. After only two weeks in the job lifting large milk cans, she had collapsed and died, while crossing the Common with two soldiers and a girlfriend.[59]

Women railway workers at Tunbridge Wells.
Note the four men – 3 of them officers

Another opportunity that opened to women substituting for men, was transport work. The South Eastern and Chatham Railway took women on as booking clerks from 1915 and trained the daughters of railway employees in the 'duties of punching tickets' to replace ticket collectors who had joined up.[60] Later in the war, Lady Matthews reported seeing girls replacing men on the trams in St Leonards-on-Sea - *'a bonny red-haired girl [who]…was dealing most ably with a car, greatly over-crowded'* – as well as waitresses in place of waiters in a Bexhill hotel.

The feminist in Lady Matthews even applauded women bus conductresses in London who were striking for equal pay, but the employer in her fretted about the servant shortage, allegedly caused by the lure of other forms of female employment in wartime.[61] Nevertheless the patriot in Lady Matthews, who understood that the conflict, however unpleasant, had to

---

[58] Lady Matthews' war diary, 15 August, 4 October 1914.
[59] *Kent and Sussex Courier,* 23 February 1917, p. 5.
[60] Ibid., 23 April 1915, p. 5, 15 July 1915, p. 5.
[61] Lady Matthews' war diary, 31 January 1916; 14 May 1916; 1 September 1918.

be won whatever the cost, would have acknowledged that working-class women's labour was needed for the war effort, not only in the newly-created women's services and in the Land Army, but also in munitions.

By far the largest provider of employment for women in the First World War was munitions work. It is estimated that the munitions industry (defined to include tank and aircraft production, as well as chemical explosives and shell manufacture) may have employed around 750,000 women nationally. As Woollacott observes, manufacturing the weapons of warfare, effectively the '*first stage in the production line of death*', was the single activity that brought '*Tommy's sister*' the closest experience the war could offer her to that of the soldier.[62]

It was dangerous work: many women munitions workers died or were injured in the war, not only from factory explosions but also from TNT poisoning. Yet the work was attractive to many women despite the inherent risks and long shifts, and not just because of the relatively high pay. Becoming a *'munitionette'* was seen as directly supporting *'Tommy'* in the war effort, by literally providing him with the ammunition he needed.

WOMEN MUNITION WORKERS IN TUNBRIDGE WELLS.

There were no munitions factories in Tunbridge Wells, but in 1917 a scheme for training women as munitions workers started in the town. Run by Dr Lister, the principal of the town's Technical Institute, the scheme gave women two weeks' training after which they would be transferred to work in a munitions factory elsewhere. There is no indication where they may have gone: there were gun manufacturers in Erith, Crayford and Dartford, and an explosives factory in Faversham as well as the vast ordnance works at Woolwich Arsenal, but recruitment was national and women were expected to live in hostels, so Kent and Sussex women could have been sent almost anywhere.

---

[62] Angela Wollacott, (1994) *On Her Their Lives Depend: Munition Workers in the Great War,* University of California Press, pp. 1-2.

In September an exhibition of, and about the trainees' work was shown in the High Street, accompanied by a recruitment meeting supported by the mayor and the county education committee. The *Courier* reported that a visitor to the exhibition would be struck by *'the comparative ease and simplicity with which complicated machinery can be worked by women and the splendid results obtainable'*, a tribute perhaps to the principle of *'dilution'*, in which complicated engineering processes were simplified for hastily-trained women operatives.

A speaker at the recruitment meeting assured anxious mothers that their daughters would be carefully looked after if they signed on for munitions work, and that the reported *'early difficulties'* with the hostels were being overcome. Perhaps hinting that the VAD hospitals were overstaffed, the speaker alleged that some women in the hospitals would actually be more suitable for munitions work, and she hoped they would be *'graded out'*.

There is definitely a suggestion too that women from Tunbridge Wells were not especially keen to take up work in munitions factories, as the speaker claimed that conscription would be needed if not enough volunteers came forward. Interestingly, none of the women in the accompanying photograph were from the town itself: they were captioned as residents of Brighton, Eastbourne, Bexhill, Groombridge and Farleigh.[63]

However, by the autumn of 1917 young women had quite a range of remunerative war work open to them,

---

[63] Kent and Sussex Courier, 14 September 1917, pp. 3 and 7.

and local girls may have been more attracted to the WAAF or to nursing than to dangerous and unpleasant factory labour, however patriotic it was. Doubts also lingered about the nature of the hostel accommodation provided, and the NUWSS began to raise money for better huts and recreational schemes. As late as February 1918 the Technical Institute was still advertising its training scheme, promising free training, a maintenance allowance for trainees and 'good prospects' *for those who completed the course.*[64]

Domestic and private life

1915 recruitment poster

This chapter has so far considered the war's impact on the public dimensions of women's lives. For many women of all classes, however, this impact was felt in other ways, at the level of family and domestic life and of personal relationships. With husbands, sons and lovers enlisted or conscripted, for many women war meant isolation, living on army separation allowances, of running a home and feeding a family on reduced income and securing food supplies during a time of severe shortages.

In the early years of the war, women had been used as a tool in the campaign for recruitment into the armed services. A government recruitment campaign poster carried the slogan: *'To the Women of Britain: Some of your men folk are holding back on your account. Won't you prove your love for your Country by persuading them to go?'*[65] In some places in Kent, incidents of women presenting white feathers to men not wearing uniform were reported.[66] In Deal, the Town Crier made a public call *for 'Ladies [...] to present to the young men of Deal and Walmer, who have no-one dependent on them, the Order of the White Feather for shirking their duty...'*[67] Women in Tunbridge Wells were persuaded of their responsibility to free their husbands and sons to do their duty in more subtle terms. At the regular recruitment meeting in December 1914 Mrs. Spender-Clay, wife of the local Member of Parliament, told the women in the audience that it *'did not become them to ask their men to stay at home'.*[68]

---

[64] Ibid., 22 February 1918, p. 1.
[65] Parliamentary Recruiting Committee poster, 1915, Imperial War Museum Collection (Art.IWM PST 4884).
[66] *Whitstable Times and Herne Bay Herald* 5 September 1914 p. 6.
[67] *Birmingham Daily Mail* 2 September 1914, p. 3.
[68] *Kent and Sussex Courier* 18 December 1914 p. 11.

Once their menfolk had enlisted, or later on had been conscripted, women could find their home lives profoundly altered. A Home Club was set up in Tunbridge Wells where soldiers' and sailors' wives could seek companionship, obtain refreshment and recreation, receive up to date war news and write letters. Crucially, the club also provided a nursery room to look after their children while they were doing so.[69] By November 1915 there were over 400 members.[70] In addition to the physical absence of their husbands, working-class service wives were also faced with the prospect of living on the army separation allowance in place of the income of a male bread-winner. The rates of this allowance were increased in early 1915 to between 12s 6d and 31s 6d a week according to the rank of the woman's husband and the number of children she had.[71] A soldier's wife who corresponded with the *Courier* in January 1918 received 24s 6d a week, of which 6s went on rent. She considered herself *'thankful to get enough to last, without any extras'*.[72]

To address such difficulties, as has been seen, the Salvation Army Varney Street Citadel was transformed into a communal kitchen to provide meals to the needy during the food shortages. Other sites soon followed. By February 1918 the fourth such kitchen was opened, at which time 3,500 meals were being served weekly at all four facilities.[73] The kitchens practised economies of food and fuel and were taken over in November 1918 by the Tunbridge Wells Corporation as National Restaurants run according to Ministry of Food policies.[74] In opening one restaurant, the Mayor thanked Amelia Scott and the other *'patriotic ladies'* whose efforts had made the scheme possible.

Shortages in food supplies and the need to queue for what was available was a problem faced by housewives at all income levels. Shoppers reported not being able to find tea, and having to queue for items such as meat and margarine.[75] Lady Matthews wrote frequently in her diary of the difficulty in obtaining supplies of sugar, butter and tea, and of having to have a meat-free diet some days. *'Always first of all The Food Question draws my pen',* she wrote. On a visit to London in 1915 she was horrified by the waste and self-indulgence she saw there, asking in her diary: *'How can we expect economy from the less wealthy, when rich people are so utterly heartless in their extravagance?'* That Christmas she did her bit by serving only turkey and plum pudding, but no almonds or raisins.

---

[69] Ibid., 4 February 1916, p. 2.
[70] Ibid., 12 November 1915, p. 5
[71] Parliamentary Recruiting Committee poster, 1915, Imperial War Museum Collection (Art.IWM PST 5160).
[72] *Kent and Sussex Courier* 11 January 1918, p. 3.
[73] Ibid., 8 February 1918, p. 4.
[74] *Kent and Sussex Courier*, 8 November 1918, p. 6.
[75] Ibid., 11 January 1918, p. 3; 25 January p. 5

When, towards the end of the war, rationing was introduced, Lady Matthews as employer and housekeeper, found the bureaucratic administration hard to grapple with. When one of her maids fell ill, she complained that she had to not only give her *'four different tickets'* – a National Insurance card, and meat, margarine and sugar Rationing Cards – but also arrange with the temporary replacement maid about her cards. *'It is all extremely harassing'*, complained Lady Matthews. [76]

By 1917 the authorities were also trying to offer advice to hard-pressed, working-class housewives on how to avoid food waste and make the best use of scarce resources. In June a food economy exhibition was opened at High Brooms parish hall by Lady Rhondda, wife of the Minister of Food. Lectures were given to town-dwelling women on bottling fruit and jam-making. Each evening local schoolgirls gave cookery demonstrations. In addition, mothercraft lessons were given in the afternoons where nurses demonstrated how to dress a baby and furnish a nursery with minimal expenditure. [77]

Women's personal lives and relationships were also affected by the social and geographical dislocation created by war-time conditions. At the November 1918 Kent Assizes, half of the cases tried were for bigamy. [78] Much more common, no doubt, was the experience of Lady Matthews' cook, who married suddenly and had only a twenty-four hour honeymoon, because her fiancé wanted to be able to leave his name and pension to her. [79]

It was seen earlier in the chapter that anxiety about the moral welfare of young girls and women was caused by outbreaks of 'khaki fever', an anxiety that becomes somewhat more understandable in the context of the problems resulting from liaisons between local women and soldiers living away from home. A conference was convened in April 1915 in London by the Women's Imperial Health Association, in which many philanthropic organisations including the NUWW and the Mothers' Union participated, to discuss the problem of 'war babies'. [80] This term appears to have been applied variously, by some (see Lady Matthews' comment, below) to any baby born during the war years, by others to the babies of absent fathers serving in the forces, but by most to the babies born as a result of liaisons between soldiers and unmarried mothers, such as the Brenchley baby at the centre of a bastardy hearing in January 1917,

---

[76] Lady Matthews' war diary 11 October 1915; 25 December 1915; 18 March 1918.
[77] *Kent and Sussex Courier*, 15 June 1917 p. 4.
[78] Ibid., 29 November 1918 p. 3.
[79] Lady Matthews' war diary, 11 February 1917.
[80] *Daily Express*, 22 April 1915, p. 1

whose mother claimed it was the child of a sapper in the Royal Engineers.[81]

Locally, Tunbridge Wells Salvation Army workers attested to having worked with a number of women who had become pregnant in this way, and their testimony is supported by statistics showing that the number of illegitimate births rose in Tunbridge Wells during the war years.[82] One case involved a man who had 'represented himself' as a single man but who was, in fact, married. In this case the woman was able to give birth at the Salvation Army's maternity home.[83] Others were less fortunate.

In August 1915 Dorothy Hazeldene, who had formerly lived at Bedford House, Mount Sion, was found drowned in the River Medway. In her pocket there was a letter from a soldier who had recently departed for France, saying that he regretting not having let her know of his impending departure. His last message to her was: 'I have only one wish, and that is that you will meet with someone that will love you with a true love, and make you happy all your life." [84] The post-mortem results revealed that Dorothy was pregnant.

There was an equally tragic outcome to the liaison between domestic servant Margaret Heath and the young man to whom she had hoped to be married. Margaret gave birth to a child that was found dead, upon which the young man enlisted and Margaret was charged with murder.[85] In other cases soldiers, both single and married, were made subject to affiliation orders by magistrates. Whilst, of course, these are extreme examples, they illustrate the difficulties faced by unsupported mothers at this time. In other cases soldiers, both single and married, were made subject to affiliation orders by magistrates.

The conditions of wartime were therefore experienced by women at a number of different levels. Whilst social change and the cause of sexual equality were both gathering pace, in part thanks to women's war-time efforts in the public arena, for those women whose lives were constrained by poverty and reproduction, little appeared to have altered. These women were, however, the focus of plans for post-war reconstruction work, as the final part of this chapter will show.

---

[81] *Kent and Sussex Courier,* 5 January 1917 p. 3.
[82] Medical Officer of Health Annual Reports, 1914-1919.
[83] *Kent and Sussex Courier*, 3 September 1915 p. 6
[84] Ibid., 6 August 1915.
[85] *Tunbridge Wells Advertiser* 27 November p. 7

The End of the War and Female Enfranchisement

In February 1918 the Representation of the People Act became law, which enfranchised all the men who had fought for their country and most women over the age of thirty. This was not the vote on equal terms with men, but it was nevertheless a victory for suffragists. Lady Matthews recorded in her diary that the Cause had triumphed, with the suffrage measure passing the House of Commons on the very day that her third child (*'my small war baby son'*) was born, 19th June 1917. *'The relief to us all is enormous'*, she wrote. *'Now we can devote ourselves to our homelife because we are a recognized part of the nation even in that quiet sphere'*. The following March she attended the great women's suffrage celebration at the Queen's Hall in London.[86]

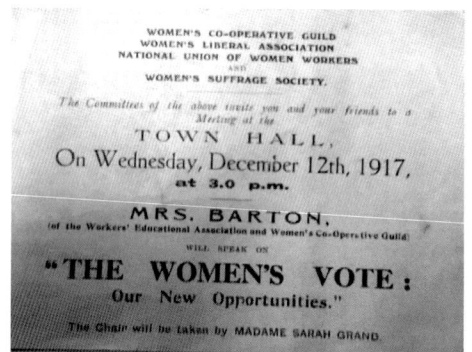

Meanwhile, in Tunbridge Wells the NUWW decided to establish a 'Women Voters and Citizens Association' to *'foster a sense of citizenship in women and to encourage the study of political, social, civic and economic questions'*.[87] Once again, Amelia Scott was one of the new society's officers, this time serving as treasurer. An early meeting included discussion of the Defence of the Realm Act Regulation 40D, which feminists strongly opposed, as it was seen as affecting the civil liberties of women merely in order to protect men from venereal disease.[88]

By the late autumn of 1918, when the first General Election for eight years was called for 14th December, the Suffrage Society was ready to put questions to candidates on a variety of political issues, including not only feminist demands such as the admission of women to the legal profession but also general political questions, for example the establishment of a League of Nations. Moreover they tried to ensure that all eligible women were on the voters' register through the offices of a *'non-party bureau'*.[89] On 20th December the *Courier* reported that women had exercised their *'new privilege'* in large numbers. The newspaper's description of the way in which Tunbridge Wells' suffragists chose to mark this momentous occasion is worth quoting at length:

---

[86] Lady Matthews' war diary, 26 August 1917 and 17th March 1918.
[87] *Kent and Sussex Courier*, 25 January 1918 and 3 May 1918, p. 5.
[88] Ibid., 14 June 1918, p. 5.
[89] Ibid., 22 November 1918; 6 December 1918 p.1 and p. 6. For further details on campaigning for peace, see the box on 'Women and the Peace Movement'.

' *During polling day at Tunbridge Wells a picturesque incident took place during the afternoon, when a procession of women electors, with artistic banners, marched from Calverley Park gates through Monson Road and by the Five Ways to the Town Hall. In spite of the miserable weather a number of people, including the Mayoress (Mrs Vaughan Gower) and the deputy Mayoress (Mrs Silcock) had gathered together to see the ladies start. The Constitutional Women's Suffrage Society, which did so much to promote the enfranchisement of women, was represented by Madam Sarah Grand, who carried a bouquet of red, white and green, the women's suffrage colours. She marched in the centre of the procession supported by Miss Amelia Scott, PLG, and Lady Matthews. At the Town Hall Madam Sarah Grand entered to record her vote, and on returning was received with cheers by the ladies, whose faces showed how profound was the satisfaction felt by them that the long struggle for political freedom was over, and that women had at last entered into full citizenship.*' [90]

The ladies of the NUWSS, with their colours of red, green and white, which had been so visible five and a half years earlier as the suffrage Pilgrims marched from Tunbridge Wells to Tonbridge, surely deserved their day of celebration.

It was often said at the time that women had won the vote, not on account of their vigorous pre-war campaigns, but as a result of their war work. Yet many of the women who actually conducted the trams, joined the WAAC, filled the shells, dug the land and built the aircraft were still too young to vote in 1918. It was also claimed that campaigners put aside their drive for citizenship when war broke out to concentrate on patriotic work. The story of women in Tunbridge Wells illustrates that this assumption is also incorrect.

Ladies threw themselves into the voluntary work associated with the war, but this was very much in tune with their previous philanthropy, with much of their activity strongly focused on the perceived needs of women and girls. Meanwhile, the suffrage and other women's groups in the town remained strong and vibrant throughout the war, with regular meetings as well as practical work. The feminist theme continued in the post-war period, when Amelia Scott and Susan Power were both elected to the Tunbridge Wells council on a women citizens' manifesto. They launched a campaign for a maternity home and for a hostel and day nursery for the children of widows, of deserted wives and of unmarried mothers as a 'thank offering' for victory in the war.[91]

---

[90] *Kent and Sussex Courier*, 20 December 1918, p. 6.
[91] For further details on their post-war activity, see http://www.womenshistorykent.org/themes/post-war/index.html

Closing her wartime diary, which she had kept for her children to read when they were older, Lady Matthews hoped that some good had come of the war. *'It has taught Rich and Poor to know and respect each other'*, she claimed, perhaps optimistically, and had *'nearly brought woman to her right place in the state'*.[92] Only time would tell whether these were to be temporary changes, or whether there would be a real alteration in the direction of post-war society.

1918 Women's recruitment poster

Women's Land Army recruitment poster

---

[92] Lady Matthews' war diary, 11 November 1918.

WOMEN AND THE PEACE MOVEMENT

In 1915 nine women resigned from the NUWSS National Executive Committee due to their unease with the organisation's whole-hearted support of Britain's war effort. These women believed that there should be a higher priority given to the quest for a peace settlement, and wished to travel to The Hague to take part in a women's peace conference made up of representatives from the women's movements in all belligerent – and some neutral - countries. In the event, the government refused to let them leave England and only two of the resigning suffragists (who were already in the Netherlands) were able to attend.

In Tunbridge Wells most active NUWSS members seem to have supported the war, but many nevertheless were desirous that once the war ended, there should be a just peace settlement. In July 1915 the Council for the Study of International Relations, which supported the creation of an international peace-keeping organisation, held two meetings in Tunbridge Wells, one at the home of the NUWSS treasurer, Lydia Le Lacheur. The speaker, Sir Percy Alden (1865-1944) was a progressive Liberal MP and opponent of conscription, who acted as British government commissioner for Belgian refugees in the Netherlands.[1] Alden visited Tunbridge Wells again in September, this time at the invitation of the town's Women's Liberal Association, which was led by the Quaker businesswoman, Sarah Candler. The Association then established two study groups on international relations, with Candler herself leading the one based in High Brooms.[2]

Candler's commitment to peace went even further in 1916 when she became president of the 'Tunbridge Wells and District Council Against Conscription'. Affiliated to the national organisation, the No Conscription Fellowship (NCO), this group vowed to oppose the Military Service Act, watch the work of the tribunals that were set up to deal with men's appeals against conscription, and assist anyone who wished to object on grounds of conscience to the call-up.[3] Among those personally assisted by Sarah Candler and her sisters was the first secretary of the local Council Against Conscription, George Dutch. Following the arrest and imprisonment of Dutch and other local male conscientious objectors, the Candler sisters kept the organisation in existence, although there is little

---

[1] *Tunbridge Wells Advertiser*, 30th July 1915. For Alden, see *Dictionary of National Biography* (online edition).
[2] *Tunbridge Wells Advertiser*, 24th September 1915; 28 April 1916.
[3] *Tunbridge Wells Advertiser*, 25th February 1916.

evidence of it in the local press, presumably because of the unpopularity of the pacifist cause.[4] Women NCF supporters were primed and ready to take over as soon as the men were arrested. This was true of the national NCF too, where Violet Tillard, a former suffragette from a Tunbridge Wells family took over as General Secretary in early 1918. Violet was sent to prison later that year when she refused to disclose information to the police regarding the printer of the NCF newsletter, *NCF News*.[5]

The controversial nature of Sarah Candler's views can be gauged from an incident in 1916 when she was practically forced to apologise for allegedly claiming in a speech at a meeting of the BWTA that soldiers were given rum before they charged in order to 'arouse their animal passions'. The Mayor of Tunbridge Wells took offence, and although Miss Candler claimed that she had been misquoted, she apologised for the 'anxiety and trouble which my words have caused.' Nevertheless, she continued to support the causes of peace and freedom, and in November 1918 was reported as taking the chair for the local branch of the Council for Civil Liberties.[6]

Sadly, Sarah Candler died the following year and so did not live to see the establishment of the League of Nations, a development she would have thoroughly welcomed. However many of her former colleagues in Tunbridge Wells' women's organisations also enthusiastically supported the League. In 1918 the NUWW was renamed the National Council of Women (NCW) and embarked upon a lengthy campaign for 'a League of Nations for the prevention of war and the settlement of international disputes' and for the guaranteed involvement of women in any such organisation. Already in 1918 the local NCW was quizzing General Election candidates on their attitudes towards the proposed League.[7]

During the First World War and after, many feminists believed that women had a special interest in the creation and maintenance of peace. Activist women also wanted to play their part in ensuring that the conflict really was 'the war to end all wars'. Yet Sarah Candler's story suggests that even passionately-held, religiously motivated pacifist views were barely tolerated by the fervently patriotic British public during the Great War.
AL

---

[4] Oral evidence of George Dutch, Imperial War Museum.
[5] *The Tribunal*, 25th July 1918.
[6] *Kent and Sussex Courier*, 6th October 1916; 15th November 1918.
[7] *Kent and Sussex Courier*, 6th December 1918.

CHAPTER 8
BELGIAN REFUGEES IN TUNBRIDGE WELLS
by Alison Sandford MacKenzie

Introduction

On 4th August 1914 the German Army crossed into Belgium, and by 15th October, Zeebrugge and Ostend on the Belgian coast were under German occupation.[1] During those two and a half months, town and cities were besieged and captured - Liege, Brussels, Namur, Louvain[2], Malines, Termonde, Antwerp, Ghent, Bruges, and town and villages in between, were overrun and in many cases all but destroyed. The British newspapers were full of the brutality of the invading army - innocent civilians killed and tortured, their homes ransacked and razed to the ground, women and children used as human shields - and of the bravery of "gallant little Belgium" in holding up the Uhlans, thereby buying time for Britain and France.

On 17th August, the Belgian Government left Brussels to set up first in Antwerp, then Ostend, and finally on 13th October in the French port of Le Havre. And 1½ million Belgians - almost a quarter of the population - also fled their country to escape the terror - to Holland, to France, and about 225,000 of them to Britain.

There were many tales of brutality by the invading forces and while some of the worst of these were subsequently discredited, they were a useful propaganda tool at the time. The personal stories of those refugees who arrived in Tunbridge Wells bear witness to what happened. Some 300 Belgians spent time in Tunbridge Wells between 1914 and 1919 [3]. Though relatively small in number, this self-styled "Belgian Colony" made a huge impact on the life of the town at the time, but has been largely forgotten since.

---

[1] Note re place-names: where there is no Anglicised version of a Belgian place-name, the version most commonly used by the Tunbridge Wells refugees themselves at the time has been opted for, almost invariably the French rather than Flemish version.

[2] The congregation of St Augustine's Church in Tunbridge Wells had a particular interest in the sacking of the University city of Louvain (Leuven) on 26th August 1914: the church's assistant priest, Fr Calnan, had gone to the University there in October 1913.

[3] In total 78 men, 144 women, 35 boys, and 40 girls were looked after by the Tunbridge Wells Belgian Refugees Committee *[Archives de la Guerre. Comité officiel belge pour l'Angleterre (réfugiés belges en Angleterre). Archives Générales du Royaume, Bruxelles]*. The maximum at any one time was 96 adults and 35 children *[1919 Report of Belgian Refugees Committee, Borough of Royal Tunbridge Wells]* This number was augmented by those who were able to support themselves, or who were given hospitality privately.

The 'peaceful invasion' of 1914

On 3rd August 1914 *The Times* reported that the Flushing steamer "had been very late reaching Folkestone" and had landed a large number of Dutch and German women and children who had been sent to England for safety. By mid-October, refugees fleeing the fighting in Belgium were arriving at a rate of 11,000 a day - some well-off and able to pay their own way, many more quite destitute.

Soyez le BIENVENU en l'ANGLETERRE.

Vous irez à LONDRES

Tout sera arrangé pour vous.

VIVE LA BELGIQUE.

Gij Zijt wel gekomen in Engeland.

Gij gaat naar LONDEN
ALLES zal gereed zijn voor u.
Welcoming leaflet given to Belgian refugees

Folkestone bore the brunt to start with, and the pastor at the French Protestant Church, Adolphe Peterson[4], set up a Committee to coordinate efforts. Meanwhile in London the decision was taken to offer hospitality to refugees, and a delegate was sent to Ostend to organise the evacuation of several hundred people. On 22nd August, Lady Flora Lugard, a well-connected writer and journalist, was offered the use of a vessel by the Board of Trade. Adapting the contingency network that had been put in place to welcome possible refugees from Ireland earlier in the year[5], she called on the help of personal friends and a War Refugees Committee (WRC) was set up. Its first public appeal on 24th August met with a "magnificent and instantaneous" response and within 14 days the WRC had at its disposal hospitality for 100,000 refugees.

On 9th September 1914, Herbert Samuel, President of the Local Government Board (LGB), announced in Parliament that the British Government had offered the "hospitality of the British nation" to Belgium's war victims, and that the WRC had consented to cooperate with his department in the reception and distribution of the refugees - it had become clear that the work was too much for a private organisation to undertake.

Appeals for offers of hospitality around the country were published in the press, and the mayors of large boroughs and the chairmen of County Councils and large Urban District Councils, were asked by the LGB to

---

[4] Pastor Peterson was from Belgium and had been in Folkestone since 1901. He was appointed a Belgian Vice-Consul in September 1914 in recognition of his work.

[5] Preparations for possible civil war in Ulster in 1913 foresaw the removal to safety of thousands of women and children: registration, transport and safe homes were organised. The Ulster Committee placed at the disposal of the WRC all its preparations, down to the very same registration forms. [*Report by W.E. Dowding on work of War Refugees Committee, Women at Work Collection IWM, BEL 14/4*]

form Local sub-Committees for the purpose of establishing whether people in their district would be willing to offer hospitality to Belgian refugees[6]. Those committees would become the recognised authorities for the reception and allocation of all refugees within their area, and they were asked to communicate directly with the WRC who would be responsible for the distribution of refugees from London to various local centres.

Advice was issued to Local Committees on how to care for the refugees allocated to them, and also to the refugees themselves on how to behave. All homes offered were to be inspected beforehand, to ensure they were of a "desirable character" and particular care was to be taken in the accommodation of girls and young women; arrangements should be such that the refugees could do their own cooking; visits should be organised from people who could speak French or Flemish; Catholic clergy should be given the opportunity to visit and the refugees assisted to attend the nearest Catholic church. And as for food: "The Belgian customs with regard to meals differ somewhat from English. The Belgians usually have three meals a day only, the diet depending on their position in life"[7] and coffee please, never tea[8]. In return the Belgians were urged to be "good patriots", enlisting in the Belgian Army as soon as possible, and "good citizens", obeying an authority which was to be chosen by and from their number. They were also required to register their names and addresses by means of forms available from the Registrar General at Somerset House

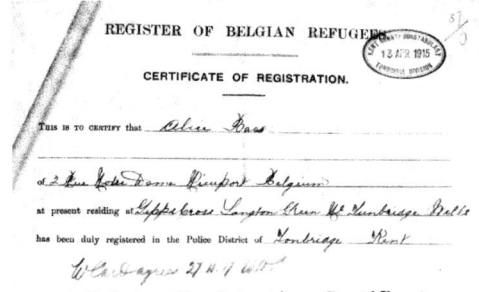

A Belgian Registration Certificate

Britain's great tradition of philanthropy (as well as that of "keeping up with the Joneses") swung into action - everyone wanted a refugee, and offers of help poured into the offices of the Committees in Folkestone and London. London stations were

---

[6] On 25th September, a circular from the LGB announced that 6,000 refugees had so far been provided with accommodation, "fewer than expected" and that offers of hospitality so far exceeded demand. On 12th October, after the fall of Antwerp, a circular went out asking for further offers.
[7] Suggestions to Local Committees regarding the feeding of Belgian Refugees [IWM BEL 2/1/4]
[8] 'The Star 'of 18 February 1915 elaborated on the Belgians' perceived food idiosyncrasies : They "do not like oatmeal which they call 'chicken feed'", they regard tea as 'medicine', and they "scorn marmalade, while retaining high affection for jam of every other kind" [IWM BEL 15/2/31]

reported to be "thronging with well-intentioned men and women all determined to carry off in triumph a refugee", ignoring the instruction to coordinate with the WRC[9]. Tunbridge Wells, though, seems to have obeyed the rules, and also had a very clear idea of the sorts of people it would welcome.

Tunbridge Wells responds

The town already had Belgian connections, and they no doubt provided firsthand accounts of the situation in Belgium. For example, the Countess de Baillet, the elderly widow of a Belgian count[10], had lived for some years at Nevill Court in Nevill Park, and probably the first refugee arrivals in the town were 10 employees from her late husband's estate in Sempst, near Malines. They had fled to Antwerp as soon as hostilities broke out, and then travelled on to England when it was clear Antwerp would fall. The Countess put them up in a house in Rusthall. News would later reach them that the property in Sempst had been completely overrun.

Another connection was that of William Wooding Starmer, the internationally renowned campanologist and composer, organist at St Mark's Church and conductor of the Tunbridge Wells Vocal Association, who was a personal friend of M. Josef Denyn, the bellmaster ("carilloneur") of the Cathedral in Malines. A letter to him from M. Denyn, quoted in *The Courier* of 25th September, vividly described the destruction to the town caused by the Zeppelin raids, and the behaviour of the invading forces, relating how friends of his were taken hostage, made to dig trenches and then marched ahead of the attacking troops as a human screen. *"Happy you,"* wrote his Belgian friend, *"surrounded by your seas and bulwarked by your formidable Navy. Never will you be called upon to experience misery like ours."* Josef Denyn, his wife and six children would eventually flee Belgium and make their way to Tunbridge Wells, first staying with the Starmers at 20 Warwick Park, and then moving to 3 East Cliff Gardens, one of the houses provided by the Mayor's Refugees Committee[11].

Josef Denyn

---

[9] The Times, 5th September 1914
[10] Henriette or Harriet Streatfeild in 1875 had married in second marriage Edmond de Baillet who died in 1913. She was staying with her relative, the Marquess of Abergavenny.
[11] The Denyn family spent most of the war in Tunbridge Wells and played a full part in the life of the town - hardly a concert seems to have taken place in the town during those years,

First to offer hospitality, judging by reports in the *Kent and Sussex Courier* of 4th September 1914, were Mr. and Mrs. Johnstone of Burrswood in Groombridge, who, with the approval of the Belgian Relief Committee in London, offered Clayton's Farmhouse near Ashurst station as a temporary home for 25 refugees, provided the necessary funds could be collected[12]. A small committee[13] was set up to oversee the preparations which included work on the house, and the solicitation of gifts of furniture and other household items, of regular financial support and of food. Mrs. Johnstone in her turn went up to London to discuss arrangements with the Belgian Legation where she learnt firsthand of the "terrible and pitiable" cases of distress among the refugees. It was proposed to appoint a woman "of the better class" from among the refugees to act, in return for a small salary, as interpreter, manager and helper to the community. Gifts of items requested were to be taken to the offices of *The Courier* or directly to Clayton's Farm, and Messrs. Waymark offered to collect and deliver heavy items free of charge.

Clayton's Farm, Ashurst

Donations poured in, a number of local residents undertaking to cover the weekly cost of maintaining individual refugees, and soon the house was ready, the Sanitary Inspector having declared arrangements in the house to be "thoroughly satisfactory". Two refugee Sisters of Mercy from a Convent in Malines, were found to look after the occupants - their duties were to include teaching the children and they were to be assisted by a Catholic Canon from Haywards Heath, himself a refugee from Louvain.

---

but the name Denyn was on the programme in some capacity. Tragically M. Denyn lost two members of his family during those years - his 12 year-old daughter Emma in September 1916, and, almost exactly a year later, in September 1917, his wife Helene. Both were buried in Tunbridge Wells Cemetery. 'Jef Denyn and the remaining members of his family returned to Malines after the war, and in 1922 he founded there what has since 1959 been known as the 'Jef Denyn' Royal Carillon School - the first institution of its kind in the world.

[12] It was estimated that 6/- per head per week would be required - at that rate, £7.10/- would keep 25 people for a week.

[13] Committee members : Hon. Mrs. Field, Ashurst Park; Mrs. Pardington (Glynlee, Tunbridge Wells); Mrs. Iredell, the wife of the Vicar of St Barnabas, Tunbridge Wells; Mrs. Johnstone Honorary Secretary, and Colonel Herbert, of Wyvern, Groombridge, Honorary Treasurer [*Courier*, 11th September 1914]

Meanwhile, the men of the newly-formed Tunbridge Wells branch of the St Vincent de Paul Society, a Catholic charity for the poor, appealed to Catholics in Tunbridge Wells for temporary homes for the refugees, asking for details of the number of rooms available, the class of person desired, whether food or lodging or both would be offered, for how long, and whether payment would be required.[14] It was expected that most of the refugees would be Catholics and that it was therefore only right that they should be helped by their brothers in faith. It is easy to imagine that in such a strongly Protestant town as Tunbridge Wells, there might initially be worries that their religious needs would not be met, if the work of welcoming them was left to non-Catholics.

In mid-September 1914, as requested by the WRC, the Mayor of Tunbridge Wells, Cllr. Charles Whitbourn Emson, held an exploratory meeting with a view to opening a Municipal Fund and forming a Borough Committee to coordinate the reception of Belgian refugees. Two categories of refugees were to be expected: the destitute who were arriving mostly in family groups (which included men), were of the "peasant" classes and probably only spoke Flemish; and "educated persons of good families" who would probably be able to support themselves financially, at least for a while.[15] The Mayor had visited the London Committee earlier in the week, at which time it was stressed to him that any scheme should ensure the housing of whole families together, or at the very least, in the same street. The meeting heard that in addition to the excellent progress being made by Mrs. Johnstone and her Committee at Clayton's Farm, preparations were underway to receive refugees at Grosvenor Lodge (under the direction of Mrs. Le Lacheur *(See also Chapter 7)*; at 32 Upper Grosvenor Road, a house offered by Canon Keatinge of St Augustine's; and at 72 Pennington Road[16] which had been offered by Miss Robertina Crothers. It was decided that as offers of hospitality were actually exceeding demand, no further action would be taken for the time being.

By the end of September 1914, three parties of refugees from Louvain and Malines, had arrived at Clayton's Farm, and a further cottage was being prepared for arrival of two further families. They were all village tradespeople and small farmers, "men of some importance in their small villages", including Frans Grietens, the Mayor of the village of Herent,

---

[14] *The Courier*, 11th September 1914
[15] At that time, the language difference almost invariably signified a class difference: the educated spoke French. People who spoke Flemish at home would speak French in the street. Until 1883 all secondary education was in French, and it was only after the War that it was possible to study in the Flemish language for a University degree.
[16] This house would in 1915 become part of VAD Hospital Kent 94 (an annex to West Hall on Chilston Road, and, when that was sold to Skinners' School in 1917, to Bredbury on Mount Ephraim).

near Louvain, who had left his wife behind in Belgium with their son who was in hospital and too ill to be moved. When the enemy had arrived, M. Grietens had protested at their behaviour[17] and soon heard that he was to be arrested and shot, leaving him no option but to flee.

The arrival of the Belgians in Tunbridge Wells clearly caused great excitement and curiosity amongst the local population as the *Courier* was asked to announce that there were too many visitors at Clayton's Farm and the Sisters were unable to do their work[18]. The Committee was therefore forced to restrict visiting to Tuesdays and Thursdays, and then only on presentation of a card obtainable from its members.

On the 4th October 1914, Lady Matthews mentioned in her diary the presence of Belgian refugees in the town for the first time, and by the end of that week there were 13 refugees at Grosvenor Lodge, and 42 at Clayton's Farm. This was soon to be increased as Mrs. Johnstone was reported to be in Folkestone, assisting in the reception of refugees, and selecting the next party to be brought to Tunbridge Wells.

Belgian refugees arriving

Arrivals
The stream of refugees arriving in England was gradually increasing as the German forces advanced. In October following the siege and fall of Antwerp, the LGB requested further offers of hospitality. A telegram sent to the Mayor of Dover on 14th October 1914 warned of the expected arrival of 5,000 refugees that night; and in one week alone after the fall of Ostend on 15th October, 26,000 desperate refugees would land at Folkestone.

It was time to increase efforts. On 13th October, Mayor Emson had written to the Secretary of the *Belgian Relief War Committee* in Folkestone setting out what Tunbridge Wells was able to offer in the first instance:
I am pleased to inform you that arrangements have been made in this Borough to accommodate 30 Belgian Refugees, not of the peasant type, but of the middle class and tradespeople.

---

[17] On one occasion, for example, a house in which soldiers had received hospitality was the following morning looted and razed to the ground.
[18] The Courier, 2 October 1914

I shall be glad if you can arrange for these refugees to arrive in Tunbridge Wells on Friday afternoon, and if you will kindly let me know prior to their arrival the names, relationships, and any other particulars relating to those sent, and the time of arrival. You will no doubt arrange before they are sent that they are medically examined and have a clean bill of health.

The Tunbridge Wells Belgian Refugees Committee - incorporating that set up by Mrs. Johnstone to care for the residents at Clayton's Farm - was re-formed on 15th October 1914 under the chairmanship of the Mayor, ready to receive the first arrivals, who were to be housed at the house on Upper Grosvenor Road, and in lodging-houses. Mrs. Claude Wilson was put in charge of the Furnishing Committee and an impressive list of furniture and other items required sheds an interesting light on what was considered necessary: "*bed linen, table linen and house linen, fenders, fire-irons, guards and coal scuttles, knives, forks, spoons, salt cellars and cruets, large and small trays, coffee pots, hot water jugs and ordinary jugs; candlesticks, cans, reading lamp, toast rack, toasting fork; large-sized pie-dishes, writing-table for sitting-rooms, small tables for drawing-room, clocks for kitchen, dining-room and drawing room, easy chairs. Extras, not necessities - Piano, games - draughts, backgammon, chess, patience cards, flower vases and pictures for walls*".

This was published in both the *Courier* and the *Tunbridge Wells Advertiser*, as was a letter from the Mayor requesting financial contributions - either lump sums, or weekly subscriptions of 1/- or more - to enable the Committee to make use of the offers of accommodation already received. *"These brave Belgian people have nobly done their share in opposing the German aggression, and let us do our best to show our gratitude,"* he wrote, adding that he was confident that "*an appeal to Tunbridge Wells and neighbourhood for monetary help will not be in vain*".

47 Upper Grosvenor Road today

That same day, a party of 35 visibly anxious and exhausted Belgian refugees of all ages, mostly of the "trading classes" and from Brussels, arrived from Folkestone by train, to be warmly welcomed by the ladies of the Refugees Committee and a large crowd of townspeople. The Autocar Company kindly provided transport for them to their new homes on Upper Grosvenor Road, Dudley Road and in Southborough. This brought to 56 the number of refugees placed in accommodation by the Committee, but many more had arrived separately, and were already being given hospitality by local residents.

As appeals for accommodation, funds and gifts in kind appeared in the local newspapers, donations and subscriptions rolled in. In the first week, £1,703 was raised and in October it took barely a week for 47 Upper Grosvenor Road, the former Blessed Sacrament Convent, soon to be known as "The Belgian Hostel", to be completely furnished and ready to house 26 refugees. In addition to donations to the Fund, and subscriptions (offers to support one refugee for 12 months for example), many imaginative ways were found to raise money - 3 local anglers sold their catch for £7 and donated one third to the Refugee Fund, whist drives were regularly organised, in particular by St Augustine's Church and the Mikado café on Varney Street, and local primary and Sunday schools organised collections. At Christmas, Mr Philip Harrington of Mount Ephraim Stores gave 10% of the sales of Christmas crackers to the Belgian Fund.

BELGIAN FLAG DAY AT TUNBRIDGE WELLS. SOME OF THE LADY COLLECTORS WHOSE EFFORTS REALISED £180.

In total, no less than £6,476 was raised by the people of Tunbridge Wells and district between 1914 and 1918, and this meant that the Committee was able to support the refugees until December 1915 without asking for assistance from the *Central War Refugees Committee*. During the following eighteen months, the Central Committee contributed one half, and from August 1917 the whole cost, of maintenance of the refugees under the care of the Local Committee - a total of £6,564.

[19] Committee members: Mrs CW Emson; Canon J. Keatinge; Mrs Ferguson (Commandant West Hall VAD Hospital); Mrs Iredell; Mrs Le Lacheur; Miss Le Lacheur; Mrs Guthrie; Mrs C Wilson; Miss Crothers; Mrs Pardington; Count Rivarola; Mrs WH Leach; Mr Councillor Kelsey; Miss Moinet; Miss Maud Roberts; Miss Pott; Miss Power; Miss McClean (Rusthall House); Miss A Scott; Miss L Scott; Miss Lushington; Miss Monica Robins; Mrs CW Burton; Mme Le Jeune (Belgian refugee); Mr WC Cripps (Town Clerk)

On average, the Mayor's Committee[19] spent £50 a week over the whole period - all monies that were donated by local people. The Belgians who were provided with accommodation by the Committee also received a weekly allowance of 9/- for adults and 6/- for children. £4 was the maximum amount of cash allowed to any one family each week.[20]

These amounts were decided under guidance from the LGB, based on the "separation allowance" received by the families of serving soldiers, and taking into account a refugee's social class and particular needs[21].

Efforts were also made to help the refugees raise funds for themselves, a notable example being the arranging of a sale of lace in November 1914 at the premises of Messrs. Dust & Co. on The Pantiles on behalf of the House of Vandevelde lace manufactory. This was arranged under the patronage of the Mayoress, Mrs. CW Emson, as well as Lady Henry Nevill and other ladies of the town. The Vandevelde family had succeeded in bringing stock with them when they fled Belgium. Mme Vandevelde - "whose brother fought at Namur"[22] - was present at the sale each day, and all the proceeds - some £260 - went to the family, from which they donated 10% to the local Belgian Relief Fund.

Who were they?

It is perhaps not a surprise to find that the majority of the refugees who came to Tunbridge Wells were - to use the Committee's words - "of the better classes": the advice of the Central Committee to "match the class of refugee to the precise class of person who are asked for by the individual lodging-house keepers" seems to have been strictly adhered to. Most allocated to the town (or "hand-picked" by

---

Belgian Refugees.

Under the Distinguished Patronage of
THE
MAYORESS OF TUNBRIDGE WELLS
(Mrs. C. W. EMSON).
The VISCOUNTESS HARDINGE.
The LADY HENRY NEVILL.
The HON. HELEN BECKETT.
MRS. SPENDER-CLAY.
MRS. PAGET HEDGES.
MRS. FRANCIS BISSHOPP.
MRS. T. C. GUTHRIE.
MRS. A. W. OLIVER.
MRS. CHARLES WATSON.
MRS. CLAUDE WILSON.

All hearts go out in sympathy in the present Crisis to our Belgian Allies, who have been subjected to privations, suffering, and unspeakable horrors, unparalleled in the history of the civilized world, and whose only crime was that they had dared to defend the homes of their own loyal children against the brutal savagery of

The Great (?) German Nation,

who herself was pledged by the solemn responsibility of her own signature to obligations of honour to protect the frontier and to uphold the rights in war of Belgium's neutrality.

This appeal is on behalf of a family of Refugees swept by the ravages of the war away from home and business to take refuge in this country, but who were fortunate enough to save a portion of their stock of choice and valuable Lace which they were able to bring away with them.

The
House of "Vandevelde"

are well known in Brussels, Ostende, and other large cities as Manufacturers and Vendors of the richest and choicest production of

REAL BRUSSELS'—MALINES
Point à l'aiguille and Venetian Lace,
including Tablecloths, Handkerchiefs, Collars, Scarves, Blouses, Children's Dresses, Caps, etc., varying in price from

One to One Hundred Francs each.

We have placed at their disposal the use of part of our Establishment and a window from

Tuesday, Nov. 24th. to Sat. Nov. 28th,

to enable them to convert part of their Stock into Cash.

MADAME WILL BE IN ATTENDANCE
FROM

10 to 6.30 each day, except SATURDAY, when the hours will be 10 to 1 o'clock,

and will be deeply grateful if you will give her the opportunity of offering you some of her choice selection at prices far below their value.

THE WHOLE OF THE PROCEEDS

Without any Deduction whatever

will be handed by us to the family, except that 10 per cent. of their takings will be paid to

The Belgian Relief Fund

DUST & COMPANY,
YE PANTYLES and NEVILL STREET,
TUNBRIDGE WELLS.
Telephone 842.

---

[20] Borough of Royal Tunbridge Wells. Report of the Belgian Refugees Committee, October 1915-March 1916
[21] LGB Circular 8th September 1916
[22] *The Courier*, 20th November 1914

Mrs. Johnstone and others perhaps?) were trades or professional people, small farmers, or landowners whose homes had been destroyed and who had fled with a few necessities. Many others were wealthy individuals and families who were able to support themselves without turning to the Committee for help. They would play a prominent role in caring for and entertaining the whole Belgian community, as well as becoming well-known to, and in, Tunbridge Wells society.

The NUWSS Clothing Depot on Crescent Road, set up initially to help invalid soldiers and cases of extreme distress amongst local women and children, soon extended its help to the refugees. Lady Matthews in her diaries mentions a number of those helped, and her descriptions provide a glimpse into their ordeal as well as the help provided. The following are but two examples *(Lady Matthews' own words are in italics)*:

- A young couple - a car mechanic and his wife - came to the Depot and Lady Matthews commented that their story was quite a common one: they and their two children had fled from their home near Louvain to Antwerp, and then when bombardments started in the area, they had been ordered to move on by the military. They took refuge in Ostend and lived in a bathing-machine for three weeks with one blanket between them. *"The rain came through the roof and they had but bread and water to eat and drink. Then Ostend became a threatened mark and they left again and came over to England where the man says they are 'very happy'. We made him comfortable with overcoat, gloves, a suit, etc, and the wife also."*

- *"A Belgian barrister and his dainty little wife came to tea with us on Sunday. Neither can talk English...They were warned to leave their villa [on the coast] about August 18th in a hurry. They left in their summer clothes, each with a small valise, and went to Ostend. There an English gunboat consented to take them across. The transit took 24 hours owing to difficulties and cautions regarding mines. They made their way from Chatham to London where for three months they managed to live in a boarding house on the few pounds they had in an available bank [account], Their income depends on shares in a factory which is now a heap of ruins... M. and Madame each get 7/- a week from the English government for food. The hostels are full of common people and life is most difficult for differing classes in such close quarters...The Bread of Exile is bitter indeed."*

By early November there were nearly 100 refugees in the town, accommodated in four houses, as well as wealthier Belgians who were able to be self-supporting and had taken private houses in the town. The Meeus family were at 4 Nevill Park (see box); Mr and Mrs. Le Jeune and their family were at Stanton House in Pembury; and world-renowned violinist Eugene Ysaÿe had found temporary refuge in the town, after a terrifying journey from the Belgian coast in a fishing vessel.

The MEEUS-de MEURS family from Wijneghem (now Wijnegem)

Monsieur Hippolyte Meeus, was the popular and long-standing Mayor of the small town of Wijneghem on the outskirts of Antwerp, and owner of the MEEUS gin distillery in the town, as well as being a great benefactor to the town. He and his wife Madame Isabelle Adolphine Marie Ferdinande Josephine Meeus de Meurs, were both in their 60s, lived at 4 Nevill Park and took an active part in ministering to the comforts of the Belgian refugees in Tunbridge Wells. Monsieur Meeus became the Honorary President of the Club Albert when it was set up in December 1914, and he was well-known too at the Tunbridge Wells and Counties Club in London Road.

With them in Tunbridge Wells were their widowered son, Robert, and his four small children; and his mother-in-law, Helene Havenith, and her daughter Suzanne who took care of the Meeus children. It seems likely that the children attended St Augustine's Primary School, as in November 1918, when the Headmaster of the school died in the influenza epidemic, two of the wreaths sent were from 'Charles & Frederic Meeus'.

M. and Mme. Meeus-de Meurs themselves both died in Tunbridge Wells in 1915, only weeks apart - Madame in June, and Monsieur in October. Lavish funerals were held at St Augustine's, organised by Kempster's. Detailed reports of the funerals appeared in The Courier and the occasions must have made quite an impact on the town - the streets were described as lined with onlookers as a stream of carriages made the journey from St Augustine's Church; the Requiem Masses were splendid, the church draped in black and the singing provided by a special choir of priests from Westminster. M. and Mme. Meeus were laid temporarily to rest in the Cemetery Mortuary (at a cost of approximately 2 guineas a week) until such time as they could be repatriated. They were duly laid to rest in the family vault in Wijneghem on 19th August 1919.

Housing the refugees in Tunbridge Wells

The great number of large empty houses in Tunbridge Wells would prove to be a boon and in the first year, they would be quickly snapped up as billets for soldiers, homes for refugees and auxiliary VAD hospitals. Accommodation for the Belgian refugees would be provided in furnished houses, houses furnished by the Committee, apartments and hostels. The Committee later commented that *"with regard to the hostel system of housing, some little difficulty was at first experienced by the Committee in meeting the different views and habits of the Flemings and Walloons but this was soon overcome by allotting hostels to each class. (Report of Borough of Tunbridge Wells Refugees Committee May 1919)*

In total, 38 properties were used by the Mayor's Refugee Committee, with at least another 16 either offered to the Committee or rented privately. Of the houses run by the Committee, three were lent rent free: 32 Upper Grosvenor Road by Canon Keatinge and St Augustine's; Grosvenor Lodge by Charles Tattershall Dodd and family; and 11 Linden Park by builder Louis Beale. The Church Army "Anchor" Home on Upper Grosvenor Road, was rented to the Committee for a nominal rent of £1 a week; another, the Old Convent at 47 Upper Grosvenor Road - "The Belgian Hostel" - had its rent generously paid by two members of the Committee, Miss Power and Miss McClean. Six further houses were rented by the Committee, two furnished and four to be furnished by the Committee, and apartment accommodation was provided at 26 other properties in Tunbridge Wells and Southborough. Properties occupied by Belgians were rate-free, in line with a resolution passed at by the Borough Council Meeting in October 1914.

The Belgian Community in Tunbridge Wells

The Constitutional Club (then at 32 Calverley Road) became the regular meeting place of the town's Belgian community. The concert hall was made available for them and the "*Club Albert*", named after Albert, the much revered King of the Belgians, was set up. In addition to serving as a central meeting point for all the refugees, and arranging social functions and entertainment, it provided a forum through which the needs of the refugees could be brought to the attention of the Refugees Committee, and also as a means by which any matters of importance could be brought to the attention of the refugees. The Mayor of Tunbridge Wells was elected joint Honorary President of the Club, alongside M. Hippolyte Meeus.

Sunday 15th November was the Fête du Roi - "The King's Day" - an important date in the Belgian calendar, and the day was celebrated in style in 1914 by the Belgian Community and their hosts. The Belgian flag was flown over most of the town's public buildings, the Belgians themselves sported ribbons in their national colours of black, gold and red, and a full account of the proceedings was given in the press the following Friday.

The day began with a Mass at St Augustine's Catholic Church at which the large congregation spilled out into Hanover Road. A special choir of Belgian refugees, including the Sisters of Mercy from Malines, was conducted by M. Denyn, and Canon Keatinge preached at length on the debt owed to the Belgian people by English Catholics whose forebears had taken refuge across the Channel during the reign of Elizabeth I. After the service, the Belgians marched from the church to their temporary homes on Upper Grosvenor Road, waving Belgian flags and singing their National Anthem, cheered on by crowds of local people who lined their way.

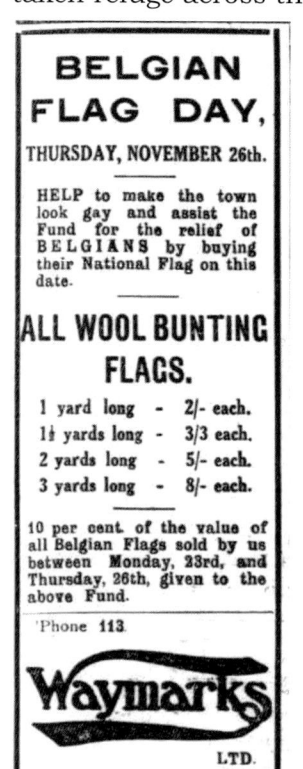

In the afternoon, the Belgians gathered at the *Club Albert*, and the next day a grand concert was held in the Pump Rooms on The Pantiles. Nearly 600 people, mostly Belgians, from all parts of the district, attended, according to the *Courier*, which described it as "a gathering unique in the history of the town". The entire programme was in French with performances by local artistes who kindly gave their services - there was a short play in French, a ballet solo (which was so enjoyed it had to be repeated), recitations, piano solos - and an imitation of farmyard animals by a Miss Parbury. The occasion ended with the Allies' National Anthems and was followed by refreshments: coffee, not tea - of course.

While the *Club Albert* would appear to have been more like a "Gentlemen's Club", albeit one which threw open its doors to all on certain occasions, not far away, on Rock Villa Road, was what could perhaps be described as a "Working Men's Club" - "Le Rendezvous des Réfugiés Belges" - a billiard hall placed at the refugees' disposal by Mr Arthur D Jarvis - a fact he announced in French in the local papers. It is likely that this was the Grosvenor Motor Works' "Chauffeurs' Club" built over the summer of 1914 and which had a full-sized billiard table and a sportsroom.[23]

---

[23] *The Courier*, 24th July 1914

A number of Belgian residents can be found listed in Kelly's and Pelton's Directories from 1915-1919, indicating perhaps that they did not expect to be returning to Belgium in the very near future. A Belgian shop was opened at 79 High Street (formerly Warren's the Tailor's, Bertrand Warren having enlisted[24]). The refugees involved themselves in local activities: for example, at the Tunbridge Wells Charity Carnival in June 1915, Belgian refugee M. Van Haweghem not only entertained with his singing at a concert in the afternoon, but also won the married men's 100yds running race in the Old English Sports event[25].

English lessons were arranged, and the management of the Opera House invited refugees to performances there - one wonders what they made of Hal Bert "the elastic comedian" in 1914. They were granted free admission to afternoon showings at the Electric Cinema on Camden Road. Concerts were organized for and by them - such as a series of concerts funded by a donation from an American friend of Lady Matthews, which took place at the Belgian Hostel in the old Convent building on Upper Grosvenor Road. After one of these concerts in February 1915, Lady Matthews wrote in her diary of meeting a young Belgian couple - a wounded soldier and a Flemish dressmaker - who had been married that very morning, and sat stiffly and no doubt self-consciously, in their new wedding clothes, "the cynosure of all eyes". Research suggests they were 25-year-old Prosper Debergh, a Ministry of Justice clerk from Termonde in Flanders, and 26-year-old Marie Ravijts, residents of two of the houses on Upper Grosvenor Road, who were married at St Augustine's Church on 20th February 1915. It is to be hoped that they returned home safely to Termonde, and enjoyed a long and happy married life together.

Another concert in the Billiard Room of the Constitutional Club must have been particularly entertaining: the programme included the three National Anthems (the Choir of the 5th Welsh singing the French National Anthem, La Marseillaise, in English), piano and violin solos, and a rendering of "Tipperary" by a choir of six Belgians.

The war drags on

As the war went on, life became harder and increasingly costly, and the Belgian refugees were no longer a novelty; living cheek by jowl became a burden for many, and "many a poor Belgian found himself in the position of the much-adored kitten which has grown into an unwanted cat"[26]. In his essay on Belgian refugees in WW1, the Belgian academic Michaël

---

[24] Bertrand Warren reopened his tailoring business following his demobilisation in the Spring of 1919 (see page 262 for advertisement in *The Courier*)
[25] *The Courier*, 11th June 1915
[26] Arthur Marwick : *The Deluge*

Amara identifies a split along class lines in the British population's attitude to their guests: the wealthy took it upon themselves to ease the exile of the middle and aristocratic classes, while the working Briton saw in his Belgian counterpart competition for jobs, rather than an equal needing his help[27]. This caused a reaction in some parts of the country. There were anti-Belgian riots in Fulham in May 1916 for example, but there is no evidence of anti-Belgian feeling in Royal Tunbridge Wells. Perhaps the helpers and those helped, belonged to the first rather than second of M. Amara's suggested categories, and were therefore not seen as a threat to the town's way of life. Indeed the fact that references to them in the local press diminish after 1916 suggests that they were absorbed into local life and no longer an object of curiosity.

Health

All refugees arriving in the country were medically examined, and the possible spread of disease amongst them was often of much concern to local medical committees. In Tunbridge Wells, Drs. Guthrie, Wilson and Campbell Smith gave their services on a voluntary basis and in early 1915 *The Courier* was to report that Dr. Campbell Smith had contracted serious blood-poisoning "in his attendance on Belgian refugees". Happily he would soon recover - unlike others in the refugee community, and the doctors had the unhappy task of certifying the deaths of several Belgian visitors. Perhaps they also assisted at births too, for at least one family, the Van Nulands from Borgenhout near Antwerp, saw their family increase by two during their stay in the town, although they also suffered the grief of bereavement with the death of their two year old son from tubercular meningitis in September 1916.

St. Augustine's Church c. 1960

Religion

St Augustine's Catholic Church was the spiritual home for most of the refugees, and they had the services of two Belgian refugee priests, Abbé Lemmens from Malines and Abbé Josef Peeters from Linth near Antwerp. Homes were found for them - an advertisement in the *Courier* in October 1914 requested a small house of four rooms, 5 not more than £1 a week. minutes from the church, and with a rent of not more than £1 a week.

---

[27] Michaël Amara : *Des Belges à l'épreuve de l'exil. Les réfugiés de la Première Guerre mondiale en France, en Angleterre et aux Pays-Bas* Editions de l'Université de Bruxelles (2008)

In May 1915 the Bishop of Malines, Dr Wachter, representative of Belgium's Cardinal Mercier, visited Tunbridge Wells, an event covered at great length in the local press. In addition to assisting at Masses at St Augustine's, and preaching in English, French and Flemish, the Bishop met his fellow countrymen at St Augustine's School, and was received by the Mayor at a Reception in the Pump Rooms to which all who had contributed to the Mayor's Belgian Relief Fund were invited. In reply to Mayor Emson's introduction, in which he expressed his pride that the generosity of the people of the town had enabled the Committee to provide hospitality for many, Dr Wachter spoke with great emotion of the sufferings of the Belgian people, and expressed his gratitude that although there were only a small number of Catholics in the town, the Belgians had been welcomed, not only as brothers, but as "dearly beloved brethren"; when the Belgians eventually returned home, he was sure that "the names of Tunbridge Wells, its Mayor and Refugees' Committee would be remembered by them, their children and their children's children". The vote of thanks to the Bishop for his visit and kind words, was given by Amelia Scott, on behalf of the ladies of the Committee, for whom, she said, it was a great pleasure "to serve the refugees", and seconded by M. Meeus.

Abbé Lemmens left Tunbridge Wells in August 1915 and expressed his thanks in a letter which was published in *The Courier,* for everything done by the Mayor and his Committee for his compatriots, and in particular for the way in which their religious needs had been respected. Abbé Peeters remained, and was still in the town in the summer of 1916 when Beechwood Sacred Heart Convent records show that he replaced Canon Keatinge as Confessor for the Sisters while the Canon was away on holiday[28]. The Convent and School on Pembury Road had opened in February 1915 with 11 nuns and 9 children - among them Belgian refugees[29] - and in June that year, on the Feast of Corpus Christi, one of the important dates in the calendar of the Catholic Church, Canon Keatinge proposed that the Corpus Christi Procession, which usually took

Beechwood Sacred Heart Convent

[28] Josef Peeters had been appointed Curate in Linth (now Lint) in 1911 and he returned after the war to continue in that post until June 1919.
[29] The first pupils to arrive were Belgian refugees 7-yr old Clementine Willems and her 8½ - yr old sister Christiane, daughters of a Professor from Liege University, Their mother had been educated by Sacred Heart nuns in Belgium and would seem to have been quite involved in the life of the school, both before and after its opening.

place each year at St Augustine's, should take place at the Convent. The congregation of St Augustine's joined the nuns and pupils and other visitors in the grounds, with a guard of honour formed by six soldiers[30].

Not all Belgians in the town were Catholics and only a month after the Bishop's visit, the Reverend Dr Henri Anet, delegate of the Belgian Protestant Churches[31], included Tunbridge Wells on his tour of the UK to raise awareness of the conditions in which the Evangelical churches found themselves. He himself had been arrested on suspicion of being a spy[32]. Dr Anet was not unknown in Protestant Tunbridge Wells having visited some 10 years previously.

Employment
Nationally, this was a tricky subject. It was agreed that the visitors needed to be kept occupied "for their own good", but at the same time they must not take jobs from British people, nor must they undercut wages. That many of the first arrivals found work in the Kent hop-fields[33] did not go down well with English hop-pickers. As early as 14th August, the *Courier* announced that any aliens coming to work in the hop-fields were to be reported. A question in the House of Commons on 15th September 1914 established that hop-field owners were in fact not allowed to employ Belgian refugees, even if English (sic) pickers were not available[34].

In early 1915, a Committee was appointed to make recommendations regarding the employment of Belgian refugees around the country, particularly in industries vital to the war[35]. But the situation in Tunbridge Wells was different from that in other areas: the town was essentially residential and most of the refugees under the care of the Mayor's Refugees Committee were of the middle or upper classes and "not accustomed to work of the nature it was possible to provide".

The ladies of the Refugees Committee set up schemes for keeping the refugees occupied. Mrs. Johnstone and Mayoress Mrs. Emson appealed in the press for funds and materials for the making of items for the Belgian Soldiers Comforts Fund. In December 1914 Mrs. Emson asked for £50 and in May 1915 was able to report that £45.9s.4d had been received

---

[30] Archives of Beechwood Sacred Heart Convent, Tunbridge Wells, held at Barat House, Roehampton University.
[31] Les Eglises Protestantes Evangéliques de Belgique
[32] *Aberdeen Evening Express*, 19th May 1915, and *The Courier*, 18th June 1915 (British Newspaper Archive)
[33] *The Times*, 6th September 1914
[34] IWM BEL 15/3/7
[35] HANSARD House of Commons Debates 16th November 1914 vol 68 cc225-6W

of which £45.4s.5d had been spent. The 11d left would not go far, and she appealed yet again for more, adding that this useful work not only provided comforts for soldiers, but also "comforting employment to many Belgian refugees".

Individual Belgians placed advertisements in the local papers offering their services as French teachers, child-minders, gardeners, chauffeurs, office workers, and even one as a hairdresser. In April 1916 a medically-discharged Belgian soldier was appointed as chauffeur to the Borough Medical Officer of Health Dr Linton, when his chauffeur enlisted. M. Reniers's appointment proved doubly useful when he was called upon to act as interpreter from and into Flemish at the trial of another former Belgian soldier who was charged with being 'drunk & disorderly' in Calverley Road the following month[36].

There is no way of knowing if all these requests for employment were met, but the local Refugees Committee were pleased to report in 1919 that "for some time past every Belgian capable of undertaking work has had employment".

Education
While the adults needed to be kept in employment, the children needed to be educated. In all, 75 Belgian refugee children passed through Tunbridge Wells (though the maximum at any one time was only 35), and arrangements were made with the Borough's schools to give them free education as required. Some children were taught by the Sisters at Clayton's Farm, and most of the younger children attended St Augustine's Catholic Primary School. However, King Charles and Murray House Church of England Schools certainly took in one boy and two girls and the Girls' High School had one pupil who was being supported by the Old Girls of the school. There were boys at Skinners' School and also at Tonbridge School, and from February 1915 a number of Belgian refugee children attended the newly-opened Sacred Heart Convent School at Beechwood on Pembury Road[37].

Assimilation as the war continues
In May 1915 there were around 200 refugees in Tunbridge Wells; by September this number had reduced to 130. The NUWSS Clothing Depot was still being kept busy providing clothing, and the Mayor put out yet

---

[36] The only evidence found of "trouble" in the town caused by a Belgian refugee.
[37] The School Porter's Log Book for the period makes fascinating reading - Belgian family members come and go delivering and collecting children and attending religious services and other events at the school.

another appeal for funds. An impressive £3,400 had been donated over the previous year. Mayor Emson reminded readers of the Prime Minister's offer on behalf of the British nation, of hospitality to any Belgians who sought refuge in the UK, and expressed his satisfaction that Tunbridge Wells had been able to "bear its share of the nation's obligations". He hoped that the town could continue to support the refugees without recourse to funds offered by the London Refugee Committee.

Meanwhile as refugees continued to arrive, others decided to return home to Belgium, or go to France and Holland, no longer able to bear the strains of exile in Britain – the language problem, the high cost of living, the inadequate schooling for the children, and the lack of work for those of the middle and upper classes. On 16th January 1915, an "Absentee Tax" had been imposed by the Germans on Belgians who had left Belgium voluntarily and lived outside the country for longer than two months. This tax was ten times the usual tax due to the Belgian government and despite a call to them by the Belgian and British authorities not to pay the tax and not to return to Belgium, many refugees felt they had no choice but to return. The Mayor of Herent, Frans Grietens, was one of eight refugees from Clayton's Farm who after much soul-searching returned home in March 1915; sadly he died only a year later at the age of 60.

By December 1915, Claytons Farm was closed as all its residents had either returned home, or found employment in other parts of the country. The three Sisters of Mercy had been called back to the Convent in Belgium and with them had gone two elderly women who lived there. All furniture lent for the house had been returned, and any gifts were sold in aid of the Belgian Fund.

In July 1916 the Committee of the *Club Albert* organised a reception at the Town Hall to mark Belgium's Independence Day and in particular to honour the ladies of the Refugees Committee and "all the medical gentlemen of the Borough" who had given their services voluntarily. The President and the Chairman of the *Club Albert* thanked the Mayoress, Mrs. Emson, Mrs. Burton and Mrs. Guthrie, as well as Mrs. Le Lacheur, Mrs. Wilson, Miss MacClean and the Misses Scott. They thanked Drs. Wilson, Campbell Smith and Guthrie for the hours day and night they had spent caring for the sick. *The Courier* reports that a souvenir album was presented to the Mayoress as the representative of the ladies of the Committee.

Although it is not mentioned in the *Courier* report, an album was also presented to the Misses Scott and is held among Amelia Scott's papers at the Women's Library @ LSE.

This was the last great gathering of the Belgians to be covered in the local press and one wonders why. There is no reported celebration of the Fête du Roi in November 1916 or 1917, no New Year celebration in 1917 or 1918, no Independence Day celebration in July 1917 or 1918. However, in November 1916 on the occasion of his re-election as Mayor, Mr Emson mentioned that there were still between 120 and 130 Belgian refugees residing in the town, and of course, that further funds were needed. At the AGM of the NUWSS in December 1916, the Clothing Depot reported that the number of Belgians applying for clothing during the past year had decreased, and that there was more demand by the local population.

But although no big events were reported, small articles in the papers continued to give a glimpse of the Belgians' life in the town. Mme. Le Jeune helped out at St George's Day collections in Pembury, while her husband opened a new drill and rifle range in the village and their son was listed among the prize-winners at Tonbridge School. M. E. Kumps, now at the Front in the Belgian Army, sent greetings to his Brothers of the Druids' "Royal Victoria Lodge". A young Belgian lady asked for the loan of a bicycle during the holidays and others requested a perambulator, a bath-chair, and of course employment. At the Beechwood Convent, an outbreak of whooping-cough in June 1916 meant that the annual Corpus Christi procession was smaller than the previous year, the nuns reporting that the outbreak had "put all the Belgians to flight" [38].

In November 1917 a new Mayor was elected, but Mr. Emson remained as Chairman of the Belgian Refugees Committee, reporting that there were still about 90 refugees in the town and that funds were being provided from London - though he still hoped for help from residents to provide

---

[38] School Journal Tunbridge Wells February 1915-May 1932

extra comforts. In December 1917, the NUWSS Clothing Depot was closed as local refugees were no longer in need of such assistance and it was felt that the people of Tunbridge Wells could no longer be expected to give away clothes "so lavishly" in face of the national demand for economy. One can only sympathise with the local population who were finding life extremely hard themselves, yet still giving generously of their time and money to the many causes asking for help.

Repatriation

Their return home was constantly on the refugees' minds and everything was organised with a view to their eventual return. As early as November 1915, Lalla Vandervelde, the English wife of the leader of the Belgian Socialist Party, had set up the *Belgian Repatriation Fund*. This national fund was to organise help when the time came to re-establish the refugees in their own homes.

The Belgian refugees had to wait nearly three years for the fulfilment of their desires, but by July/August 1918, it became clear that the war was drawing to an end, and their thoughts turned to the 7 million or so who had stayed in Belgium and who were living in desperate conditions. On the 8th November 1918, Cllr. Emson as Chairman of the local Refugees Committee, asked for contributions of blankets and clothing which would be sent to Belgium by the London Committee. 1161 items were received, including 83 pairs of boots, and these were packed up by Amelia Scott and a group of ladies and sent to London. A Belgian Flag Day on 9th November raised £65.

Just two days later the war was over, and members of the Belgian colony of Tunbridge Wells joined the great celebratory parade through the town on 12th November, wearing their Belgian colours of gold, red and black with what the Courier described as "smiling pride", and led by a Skinner's School pupil bearing a banner declaring *"Long live England. We thank you all."*

But though the war was over, it was still to be several months before the Belgians could return home. The return of almost 250,000 people from all over Britain must have been a logistical nightmare. Free passage was offered by the British Government, and between 15th December 1918 and 6th May 1919 when the offer expired, most of the Belgian refugees in the country were repatriated[39].

---

[39] 225, 572 refugees were repatriated and in 1919, 5,608 men and 1,478 women (of whom 111 were nuns) were still in the UK and working – a quarter of the men were metalworkers, and almost half the women were in domestic service (1920 Report of work done for Refugees 1914-1919, National Archives, Kew)

In Tunbridge Wells, repatriation took place under the national scheme. The ladies of the Executive Committee arranged and paid for a farewell reception for the refugees. This was held at Rusthall House, kindly lent by Miss McClean for the occasion. It sounds as though it was a splendid affair; tea was provided and the renowned vocalist, Miss Jean Sterling Mackinlay of London, well-known for her rendition of old songs and ballads, provided the entertainment.

The Tunbridge Wells Belgian Refugees Committee met for the last time on 23rd May 1919 at which time the Chairman, Mr Emson, was able to report that all the town's Belgian refugees had returned home and that he wished it to be publically known that the Report of the Committee's work described not one tenth of the work undertaken by the members of the Committee and their helpers. Not a day had passed when there had not been some question regarding the refugees which needed to be dealt with and he expressed his thanks to all who had subscribed to the Belgian Fund, all those who had lent houses, furniture, and household effects, to the ladies of the Committee, including Belgian refugee Mme. Le Jeune, who were largely responsible for the success of the work.

L'Ordre de la Reine Elizabeth

The Committee's work was also recognised by the King and Queen of the Belgians who presented the Ordre de la Reine Elisabeth[40] to Mrs. Guthrie, Mrs. Claude Wilson, Miss Power, Miss McClean and Mrs. C.W. Burton, and the Palmes d'Or de l'Ordre de la Couronne[41] to Mr. Emson, Amelia Scott and the Town Clerk, WC Cripps.

At the end of the war, there were suggestions from a number of quarters in the town that a carillon of bells would be a fitting 'peace' memorial for Tunbridge Wells, a perpetual reminder of British and Belgian heroism.

Sadly, the suggestion was not taken up, but the town does have another reminder of this period of its history.

This is Paul Van den Kerckhove's stunning life-size bronze bust of Mayor Charles Whitbourn Emson, Mayor of Tunbridge Wells 1913-1917, and Chairman of the Borough Belgian Refugees Committee for the whole period of the war. Paul Van den Kerckhove was a well-known Belgian

---

[40] Order of Queen Elisabeth of the Belgians "The Elisabeth Medal" given for humanitarian work during the war
[41] Golden Palms of the Order of the Crown

artist. A member of the Civic Guard in Brussels, he had fled in September 1914, leaving behind his estranged wife and two young daughters, and had taken refuge in Tunbridge Wells. Local artist, Alexander Kirk, made his well-equipped studio on Cumberland Walk available to the sculptor and while in Tunbridge Wells M. Van den Kerckhove moulded a number of busts of local people.

That of the Mayor was commissioned by the Belgian community in 1915 for presentation to the town as a "personal and permanent and public token of their gratitude" for the welcome given to them in their exile. They paid for it to be cast in London and the finished work was presented at a public gathering in The Great Hall on 22nd September 1915. In his acceptance speech, Mayor Emson, stated that it would be placed in the Town Hall as a *"perpetual memorial of the joint struggle of their nations"* and would *"ever remain as a souvenir of the Belgians' friendship and visit to the town"*.

A further reminder was the Le Jeune Prize for an Historical Essay. Albert Le Jeune, his wife and school-aged children, were from Antwerp and took up residence at Stanton House in Pembury. Mme. Le Jeune joined the Mayor's Refugees Committee, and her husband was one of the Honorary Presidents of the *Club Albert* on Calverley Road.

When they left Tunbridge Wells, M. Le Jeune sent a cheque for £50 to Cllr. Emson, former Mayor and Chairman of the Tunbridge Wells Refugees Committee, as a small token of his gratitude for the kind hospitality extended to his countrymen during the war, asking that it be used for an educational purpose. It was decided to use the money to award two annual prizes of £1 1s (a guinea) each to a pupil of The Skinners' School and of the County School for Girls, for the best essay on an historical subject. In October 1920 M. Le Jeune - who was by then a Member of the Belgian Senate - returned to Tunbridge Wells to present the prize for the first time. He commented in his speech that *"if there was one thing in the Great War which he called a blessing, it was the fact that his boys had been educated in a Skinners' school"* - they had been pupils at Tonbridge School.

The Prize continued to be awarded until the late 1930s.

CHAPTER 9
TUNBRIDGE WELLS IN 1916 – HOPE AND DESPAIR
by John Cunningham

1916 was to prove to be the mid-year of a War which stretched over five years – a War which started out as one which 'would be over by Christmas', but which by 1916 was thought by many could last until at least 1922.

It would be hoped that the stalemate of trench warfare could be overcome with what was called The Big Push in July, but this would turn into the five-month Battle of the Somme with little real outcome except an enormous loss of life on both sides.

Two major factors – the entry of the USA on France's and Britain's side on 6th. April 1917; and the Russian 'October' Revolution of 1917[1] could and would influence the outcome of the War, but neither was on the horizon in 1916.

1916 would be a gloomy year – no victories, many casualties, continuing threats, growing shortages.

Tunbridge Wells in 1916
The year was marked by what might be seen as parochial 'Clochemerle' matters created by the War, compared with what was actually happening in the wider world. The subjects which featured for more than one week (and often for many) in the Courier in 1916 were:
- whether a cinema could hold a musical concert for the troops on a Sunday evening (the Council somewhat reluctantly agreed, but the Bench said 'No');
- what to do with an unexpected surplus of £10,000 of Rate income;
- lists of 'local' casualties every week with photos of most of them, particularly from July onwards.
- a variety of conscription issues - Lord Derby's Scheme for voluntary enlistment; the subsequent compulsory conscription; the weekly meetings of the Recruitment Appeals Tribunal; the weekly publication in the local papers from September of lists of conscription 'dodgers';
- many prosecutions over many weeks for failing to 'black-out' windows adequately, under the Defence of the Realm Act 1914 (commonly known as DORA).
- 'Wartime' restrictions
- the Courier Tobacco Fund for the Troops;
- the activities of the many VAD hospitals (many new since the beginning of the War) with the war-wounded, including the building of new wards;

---
[1] which was actually in November because Russia still used the Julian Calendar.

- reports from June onwards about the proposal to move Charing Cross Station to the South Bank, which caused great uproar and would continue as an issue until 1930, when it finally 'died the death'.
- Outrage at 'the insult' made by Miss Sarah Candler, a Quaker and a proprietress of the Woodlands Laundry, who claimed that soldiers were being given rum to give them 'Dutch courage' before 'going over the top'.
- Saving the Nevill Ground from closure and bankruptcy.

National or World events received little coverage in Tunbridge Wells media. This is probably not surprising since they would have been covered in the National daily media and Tunbridge Wells media was essentially weekly. So much of it would have been anyway old news by the time it was published in Tunbridge Wells. However the *Courier* was connected to the Central News Agency and it did display the Agency's messages at both its Tunbridge Wells and Tonbridge offices. The first mention in print of what we now call the Battle of Jutland which took place on 31st May – 1st June, was on the 9th June when 10 local victims of what was called 'the Great Naval Battle' (note the word Battle, and not Victory) were named. The news about Lord Kitchener's death on 5th June in the sinking of HMS Hampshire was somewhat quicker, since it was also reported on 9th June.

Alderman Elwig

Sunday Concerts for the Troops

The Sunday Concert issue is indicative that the War was not yet changing 'dyed-in- the–wool' attitudes. Early in January 1916, the Town Council received an application from a cinema (unnamed then, but actually the Kosmos in Calverley Road) to hold musical concerts on Sunday evenings from 7-9pm, exclusively for soldiers and their friends. (Cinemas in those days were not licenced for Sunday performances) This aroused great opposition from various elderly Low Church members of the Council, who had all been Mayors in their time :

Alderman Snell

Alderman Elwig: *'It is a dangerous precedent. Tunbridge Wells has a reputation to uphold as a place where Sunday is spent in a quiet way'.*

Alderman Snell did not want 'people to be attending cinema exhibitions at a time when they might otherwise be attending Church'.

Alderman Caley: *'To do evil in order that good might come of it, was a very bad principle.'*

However *Cllr. Col. Hunter.* supported the application. *'The cinema is an innocent amusement which is a counter-attraction to the much greater dangers for a soldier of the public house.'*

But even Alderman R. Vaughan Gower who was much younger, had a Catholic wife and would be the Mayor at the end of the War, said:
'Lack of Sunday observance was becoming a scandal' and he hoped that 'the day was far distant when we would have a "Continental Sunday". It was the thin edge of the wedge.'

The application was however approved 15-7, but was withdrawn a week later, no doubt due to lobbying. The issue did not raise its head again publicly until December, when the Kosmos manager made a further application. The Council then made a counter-proposal that *all cinema proprietors* should be allowed to hold these concerts, (subject to strict conditions: only from 7-9 pm; no film, whether dramatic or musical; strictly music of an *appropriate* nature; and all receipts, less approved expenses, to be given to the Mayor's Charitable Fund).

Alderman Caley

Aldermen Elwig and Caley however continued to oppose this strongly on the grounds that Sunday evenings which should be a time of religious service, were being turned into a time *'of amusement'*. Alderman Silcock said that while he had opposed the application in January, he was now in favour of it, because it *'provided soldiers with something which did not expose them to temptation.'*

Cllr. Edwards said that some safeguards must be laid down about the music to be provided. *'Could not a programme be submitted first, for approval by the Mayor and a Sub-Committee?'*

Cllr. Middleton Chapman approved the application, saying that he did not know *'whether Alderman Caley was afraid that people* (given an alternative) *would leave his or other churches'.* But *'he did not think that it would affect evening services in any way'.*

Alderman Snell said that while he had a great deal of sympathy for soldiers in trying to relieve their *' somewhat monotonous lives'*, it was a matter of principle and he could not approve, since it was 'the thin edge of the wedge.'

Cllr. Colonel Hunter said that one of the Commandments was to keep the Sabbath holy and could anyone contend that *'a Sacred Concert'* violated this? He produced a number of relevant analogies, concluding that opposing the proposal *'would be a most selfish and ungrateful proceeding'.*

The proposal was approved 14-7. However it still had to pass the TW Bench which was dominated by the Aldermen....But then the situation was saved by the Army authorities, who clearly could not understand *or accept* the opposition to it, and who produced a last-minute compromise proposal.

So at a *special* sitting of the Bench on 20th December, the application for a licence was refused by the Bench in favour of a proposal by Capt. Gray, on behalf of General Wilkinson, to hold the concerts at the Opera House instead.

For Mr. Kutnow, the proprietor of the Kosmos, Mr. S.E. Cheale said that the Bench must be aware that there were 3,000 or 4,000 troops in the town. The YMCA had already taken over the Pump Room for the use of soldiers and had also put up a building in Lime Hill Road on land belonging to Mr. Kutnow, with his permission, but these were not sufficient to meet the demand. The Bandmasters of two Regiments were already interested in providing the music for the proposed concerts.

Capt. Gray, on behalf of General Wilkinson, said that the General was very anxious that these Concerts should take place, but felt that they should be held in a larger venue, such as the Opera House. The Management of the Opera House had kindly offered to place the building at their disposal absolutely free of charge.

Rev. James Mountain

The Rev. Dr. Usher and the Rev. Dr. James Mountain of St. John's Free Church both spoke against the application. Both admitted that they had been unable to get professional help in putting forward their case *(presumably no lawyer wanted to be involved with such a 'hot potato')* and they asked for an adjournment, which was refused by the Mayor, who said that there had been enough notice of the meeting and there was no excuse for opposing parties not being properly represented. Dr. Usher imputed that the application was not entirely patriotic or philanthropic, which was denied strongly by the Mayor. Dr. Usher replied: *'If you say that, I bow to your decision, but that is the inference one would have. I don't want to impute motives'* (which was precisely what he did want to do).

The Mayor said that in view of the application which would now be made by the Opera House, the application by the Kosmos would be dismissed, but the Bench fully appreciated the *'excellent intentions'* of Mr. Kutnow and the only reason for dismissing his application was 'that they thought that the Opera House would be a better place in which to hold the concerts.'

The unexpected surplus of £10,000 of income
In January 1916, the Finance Committee reported to the Borough Council that there would be an unexpected £10,000 surplus at the end of next March (1916) - equivalent to a rate of 8d in the £. The Committee did not recommend reducing the Rates because this would be misunderstood outside of Tunbridge Wells. Decreasing one year followed by an inevitable increase the next, would seem poor management at a time of increased 'Imperial' taxation and inflation. This motion was approved 24-1, with abstentions, and the Town Council decided to invest the money in

National War Loans, bringing the Council investment in them since the beginning of the War to £45,000.

It is easy 70 years post-World War II to smile at the paranoia shown in World War I about the potential aerial bombardment of England and the consequent draconian enforcement of lighting regulations. Zeppelin raids on England started in January 1915, and although they caused very little loss of life or even damage to property, their psychological impact was absolutely enormous, particularly since the British had no similar means of retaliation. As far as can be established, there seems to have been only three bombs dropped on Tunbridge Wells, and it is thought they were dropped by accident or jettisoned from a Zeppelin returning to base. They fell in Calverley Park/Grounds, but the fact that there are no accurate records of exactly where they fell, suggests that their impact must have been minimal, although their influence on Tunbridge Wells folklore has been immense.

Every week there were numerous prosecutions brought before the Bench for blackout contraventions. As an example, in the first week of January 1916, there were five prosecutions in Cranbrook for 'unshaded lights', all reported by the diligent PC Hardy; four in Tonbridge; and no less than 15 in Tunbridge Wells. Mrs. Florence Roberts of Hinton Oak, Frant Road, was outraged and demanded to know of the magistrates why she had been prosecuted, when it had been her servant who had left the light on.

Sound of gunfire in France. At the time of the Battle of the Somme which started at the beginning of July, it was widely reported that the sound of the artillery barrage could be heard on the Sussex Downs, a distance of about 200 miles as the crow flies.

Casualty Lists
Page 3 of the *Courier* became over time the page for announcing local casualties, dead, wounded or missing (the latter describing those who could not be traced, but who would generally be found subsequently to be either dead or a prisoner), often with a photo of the individual. In the early days of 1916, there were weekly reports in the *Courier* of 3-6 killed or wounded, but with the beginning of the Battle of the Somme in July 1916, the numbers leapt up. The first casualties - some 20 (7 dead, 13 wounded) - were reported on 14th July under a banner surrounded by Union Jacks:
  'THE BIG PUSH. LOCAL CASUALTIES IN THE GREAT ADVANCE'
(*which advance was actually only between 3-6 miles*). The following week casualties increased to 32 (10 dead, 21 wounded and 1 missing) and 42 on 28th July when the banner was changed to:
  ***PRICE* OF THE BIG PUSH. CASUALTIES IN THE GREAT ADVANCE**,
which is possibly an implicit, rather than explicit, criticism of the event. This banner remained unchanged until 22nd September, when it became the less emotional and more dignified

THE ROLL OF HONOUR

A typical page 3 (32 names) in the *Courier* of 20th September, 1918, (just three weeks before the Armistice)

Casualties remained high, but the weekly numbers started to decline – from 36 on 4th August, to 25 on 25th August, 21 on 29th September, then settled between 20-30 a week until mid-November, falling to 12 at the beginning of December, and dropping to 8 on 22nd and 3 on 29th - a total of 527 in less than six months.

As a sign of the then-prevalent class distinctions, the photos of the Other Ranks (ORs - Privates and NCOs) were grouped together in a block under the banner. From then until November, there were 18-54 names every week in the block, with underneath just their name, rank, regiment and whether they were killed, wounded or missing; while Officers, who actually had a disproportionately high number of casualties, were featured separately and individually with personal and family details.

The proportion of Killed to Wounded and Missing was of the order of 1:3. Later, although OR casualties had barely declined, ORs were given a similar write-up to that which the Officers received.

Page 3 also became the page to feature (generally with photos) an outstanding local family which had three or more members in the Forces. Among the latter with sons in the Forces in 1916 were:

Mr & Mrs. Young, 6, Dorset Road, Tunbridge Wells: five sons and one son-in-law.
Mr. & Mrs. Abraham Adams, Withyham St. John's, Crowborough: five sons and one son-in-law.
Mr. & Mrs. Wall of Ankerwycke, Queen's Road, Crowborough: five sons.
Mr. & Mrs. Edward Loder, Cambourne, Goudhurst: five sons.
Mr. & Mrs. W. Coulstock, Hollands Lodge, Langton Green: five of their six sons.
Mr. & Mrs. W.E.Smith, Medway Villa, 50 Quarry Road, Tunbridge Wells: four sons.
Mr. & Mrs. G. Ayland, Woodlands Cottage, Ticehurst: four sons.

There were also very sad reports. On 18th August, the *Courier* recorded that Mr. & Mrs. Moon of 25, Western Road, Tunbridge Wells had lost all their four sons in the past three months and on 13th October under the somewhat unfortunate headline of *'Rotherfield Family's Bad Luck'* (sic), that Mr. & Mrs. Ralph Minns of Pookham Hill, Rotherfield had had four of their five sons as casualties in the past month.

The *Courier* also reported on 4th August 1916 that Tonbridge School in the past two years:
- had 1,689 former pupils and 12 masters serving in the Armed Forces;
- had suffered 346 casualties (20% of those serving):
    pupils 130 dead, 204 wounded, 9 missing;
    and masters 1 dead and 2 wounded;
- and had received 74 War Honours:
    CB 4, CMG 8, DSO 12, Distinguished Service Cross 2,
    Military Cross 33, promotions in the field 8,
    French & Belgian awards 7;
- and 155 'Mentioned in Dispatches'.

Conscription Issues

Unlike Germany, Austria, Russia and France which had had compulsory conscription since the late 18th and early 19th centuries, Britain did not have such a system until March 1916 and it would take another 6-9 months before a sufficient number of compulsory conscripts had been trained and shipped to the warfront, so they largely missed the Battle of the Somme.

Britain had had voluntary enlistment since the outbreak of the War, and although many men volunteered[2], the numbers were not sufficient to meet the need and so the Military Service Act was passed in March 1916 making conscription compulsory for single men aged 18-41. This was

---

[2] During the whole of the First World War, 2.67 million British men joined as Volunteers and 2.77 million as conscripts.

extended in May 1916 to include married men, and the age limit for both was raised to 51 in 1918.

The voluntary system had problems, largely to do with public understanding and attitudes about the issue. In the jingoistic euphoria which was prevalent in the first 12-18 months, it was not unusual for patriotic, but ignorant and emotional girls to regard any man not in a uniform as a coward. It is sad to record that many of these girls were often associated with the more aggressive arm of the suffragette movement, but in retrospect, their emotional approach is entirely understandable. A.E.W Mason's novel *'The Four Feathers'*, published in 1902, had had as its main setting the unsuccessful campaign to rescue General Gordon in Khartoum in 1885. The book had been a highly popular success and was the prime inspiration for a practice, which was quite widespread in 1914-5, of young, impressionable and immature girls presenting young men not in uniform with a white feather, indicating that they thought they were cowards.

Lord Derby

The Derby Scheme

To counter this and also to generate a stronger sense of commitment to the 'cause', the Earl of Derby as Director-General of Recruiting, in October 1915 introduced the Derby Scheme which was a halfway-house between voluntary enlistment and the compulsory conscription which the Government was reluctant to adopt. Young men would voluntarily register their name, to be called upon for service only when necessary. They therefore 'attested' their willingness to serve their country, and they received a lapel badge and armband to confirm this. Nurse Edith Cavell had been executed in Brussels by the Germans on 12 October 1915 and this caused huge outrage in Britain, and the event was used in all the recruitment rallies. Despite the fact that 215,000 men had actually enlisted in the Forces, and another 2,185,000 attested for later enlistment through the Scheme, it was not thought sufficiently successful for military needs and it was abandoned in December 1915, to be replaced by the Military Service Act which was passed by Parliament in March 1916 and which introduced compulsory conscription.

In Tunbridge Wells, the papers reported every week on the progress of recruitment. The Courier reported on 14th January 1916 that 'nine Derby recruits have opted this week to enlist immediately' and 32 members of C Company of the Fencibles had enlisted and a further 55 attested. The Mayor announced that up to 20th January, 130 had attested. Derby Scheme recruits were being trained at the Ice Rink opposite Skinners' School in London Road. By 4th February, 187 had attested; by 11th February, 236; and by 3rd March, 378, but that Wednesday was the final day that anyone could attest. One of the advantages of attesting was that one could choose one's Arm or Regiment, which would not be possible under the forthcoming Military Service Act. By 24th March, the *Courier* was reporting that there were up to 1,600 men who had attested locally ('local' was not defined), but that only 250 of them were drilling regularly.

Conscription

The introduction of conscription in March 1916 removed the voluntary element from recruitment. Certain categories of worker were exempted from service, but nearly all categories had to provide some recruits, even if their work was considered essential. In hindsight, probably too many farm workers were taken and not all of them would be replaced by women, which would contribute to problems of food supply from the end of 1916. The system of conscription took some time to gear up, but it had at least started, even if it was somewhat delayed by appeals by individuals and employers against it.

Recruitment Appeals Tribunals

On 10th February 1916, there was a Special Meeting of the Tunbridge Wells Town Council to appoint a local Tribunal to deal with appeals under the Military Service Act. Seven members were appointed – the Mayor, W. C. Cripps (the Town Clerk), an Alderman and four magistrates.

The first meeting of the Recruiting Appeals Tribunal on 17th had 9 present, including Col. Sydney Sladen, the Tunbridge Wells Recruiting Officer (and also an Alderman and former Mayor). There were 21 cases – 10 were granted postponement for one month and 8 refused.

The second meeting of the Tribunal was on the 24th had a very pertinent case. The management of a Tunbridge Wells newspaper (not specified, but it could only be the *Courier* or the *Advertiser,* both of which were owned by the same proprietor) asked for exemption for a newspaper reporter called Donati on the grounds that he was the only reporter in Tunbridge Wells. The Mayor: 'Is it not possible to get a woman reporter?' 'No, a woman could not replace him, because you cannot send a woman to Smoking Concerts in Public Houses, or to other meetings which are only attended by men.' His appeal was postponed for one month, but it is surprising that archive searches show no further record of any appeal in the following month (or even later).

The Tribunal continued to meet on a weekly basis and it was reported that it had heard on 23rd March 32 appeals from voluntary-attested men and 15 appeals under the Military Services Act. Thirteen appeals from the voluntary-attested were dismissed and two under the Military Service Act, with a further three being given a Certificate for Non-Combatant Service.

Conscientious Objectors (C.O.s)

While there were a large number of men who did not want to go to war for understandable reasons, there were relatively few who did so on grounds of conscience and they were somewhat unpopular among the British populace. As pacifists they were regarded as unpatriotic and unBritish and they were often given a hard time. It took quite a lot of courage to be a pacifist. 'Conchies' as they were familiarly known, did have the right of appeal against conscription and could apply for a Certificate for Non-Combatant Service which meant that they were forced to contribute to the War effort, even if they did not have to fight as such. The jobs they were given were usually unpleasant and could be dangerous – e.g. as ambulance drivers, hospital orderlies and stretcher bearers on the Western Front.

Tunbridge Wells had its quota of conscientious objectors. Many of them were Quakers who had their Friends' Meeting House in Grosvenor Park where it is to this day. There was also a Tunbridge Wells Council against Conscription. They had their booking of the Town Hall for a meeting in June 1916 cancelled, when the purpose of the meeting was discovered. The meeting was then held at the Friends' Meeting House in Grosvenor Park, but the Press were refused admission.

Not all conscientious objectors were Quakers and probably the most well-known who was not, was George Frederick Dutch, described as a grocer's assistant and 'a Socialist' of 42 Dorset Road, who was Secretary of the No Conscription Fellowship and was later a reputed organiser of a Soldiers' and Workers' Committee in Tunbridge Wells set up on June 24, 1917, which was later called a 'Soviet', after their Russian inspiration. However, despite the fact that Dutch was forcibly conscripted and then court-martialled 'technically' as a 'deserter' and imprisoned, there must be some doubt as to whether he could/would have participated in such a 'Soviet' of *military* personnel.

Notice which appeared every week with a list of 'draft--dodgers'

Government advertising to catch draft-dodgers

It is clear that there were a considerable number of men avoiding conscription and in September the Government took the unprecedented step of advertising in local newspapers the names of the men they wished to 'trace'. It was an early form of 'name and shame' and an implicit invitation to friends and neighbours to 'split' on each other, with the promise that the names of informants would not be disclosed.

The first advertisement appeared in the Kent & Sussex *Courier* on 15th September, occupied two pages of the newspaper and contained about

300 names with their recruitment group/class numbers and last known addresses. The opening paragraphs of the advertisement are reproduced opposite and under the guise of wanting to keep military records straight, asked everybody to provide information. The advertisements were repeated every week and included a 'List of Men *(now)* Satisfactorily Accounted For' which was generally only reproduced for one week. The numbers of names still 'Lost/Wanted' and/or now 'Found' fluctuated each week but by mid-October the 'Wanted' List was down to about 70. The 'Wanted' List continued to be published into the New Year 1917.

Hospital activity
Tunbridge Wells served as a centre for convalescent troops throughout the War. Its four existing hospitals – the General, the Eye & Ear, the Homeopathic and Pembury – took as many military patients as they could, but they still had to service the civilian population. So over time, a total of 17 VAD Hospitals which were entirely for the military were established which probably serviced about 13,000 troops who convalesced in Tunbridge Wells. Readers wanting to know more should go to Chapter 6 where the subject is treated in much more detail.

The *Courier* Tobacco Fund for the Troops
Early on, the *Courier* joined a national subscription fund to provide tobacco to the troops duty-free and it reported each week on who had donated and how much. At the end of January 1916, its Fund stood at £256-15s-9d. By the beginning of October, it had grown to £298-12s-11d which may not seem much today, but it would then have bought over 400,000 'Woodbine' cigarettes (the cheapest brand at that time) or just under 250,000 'Gold Flake', both brands being made by W.H. Wills & Co. (later to be part of Imperial Tobacco)

The poster shown here is by Sir Frank Brangwyn (1856-1956) who was apprenticed to William Morris for four years.

Summer Time (Daylight Saving Time, or DST) is a way of extending the longer evenings in summer by putting the clocks forward one hour, thus allowing the working day to be increased and at the same time, saving energy consumption. It is particularly relevant for outdoor (agricultural) production.

The principle had been discussed in many countries for many years but never implemented until the First World War when its benefits were realised by both sides. Germany and Austria were the first countries to introduce it on 30th April 1916, but Britain followed very soon afterwards on 21st May.

It was a novel concept to which people took time to adjust, and it was discussed frequently in the *Courier*. Lady Matthews expressed support and great interest for it when it was introduced. It was not however popular with the farming community and the *Courier* reported that some members of the Kent NFU were opposed to it. However it seems to have been generally accepted in Britain which has continued the practice ever since, when many other countries abandoned it.

Proposal to move Charing Cross Station to the Surrey side of the Thames in order to provide a site for a National War Memorial.
This proposal started in a very roundabout way. South-Eastern Railways wanted to strengthen Charing Cross railway bridge at an estimated cost of £167,000, in order that it could take more and heavier trains; and to do this they needed permission in the form of an Act of Parliament. It was not proposed to do this until at least 12 months after the War, but as it was thought that as the end of the War might still come quite quickly, it was a sensible piece of forward planning.

The proposed Act provided the opportunity for a number of people to turn it into a much more dramatic issue which would run and run, in one form or another, until the early 1930's.

Hungerford Rail Bridge

Charing Cross railway bridge which had been built as a functional rather than stylish bridge in 1864, had always been regarded by many, and particularly by the leading architects of the day, such as Sir Aston Webb and Sir Reginald Blomfield, as an ugly 'monstrosity', which was unsuitable for its iconic position on the Thames in the heart of London (or should one say, in the heart of the Empire).

Since it was built, the poorer, much more slummy South Bank of the Thames had been considerably improved by the decision of the London County Council to put its headquarters, County Hall, on the South Bank almost opposite the Houses of Parliament (itself a sensible choice, but also an implicit 'political' statement, in view of its 'challenging' position directly opposite the centre of national government).

The building of County Hall was not started until 1912 and because of the War, the south part of its river front would not be completed until 1922 and the north part until 1931-33. However the prospect of a revitalised South Bank was very appealing; and grandiose ideas were put forward about the style and appearance of that part of central London, into which the opportunities provided by the demolition of Charing Cross railway station and the proposed redevelopment of Charing Cross bridge as a new road bridge fitted very well.

In 1916, awareness of the large number of lives lost in the War was increasing dramatically and there was already talk of creating a suitable Memorial for them. This was accentuated in June 1916 with the death of Kitchener, for whom a suitable memorial was demanded. So it is probably not surprising that when the Charing Cross bridge came up for debate in the House of Commons in early July 1916, there were enough protagonists for an alternative view, to turn it into a quite controversial issue.

There was clearly a chasm between those idealistic individuals who were looking for an aesthetic improvement in the appearance of central London and its river and felt that an elegant **road** bridge would be more suitable, and those who lived south of the Thames, and particularly those in Kent, who appreciated being delivered direct to Charing Cross on the north bank of the Thames, and there was almost universal opposition from all the towns in Kent served by Charing Cross Station.

One of the proposals for a Charing Cross road bridge and National War Memorial.

The *Courier* wrote an unprecedented four paragraphs of Editorial about the proposed demolition. 'Any (such) scheme would occupy many years and cost many millions, so that the modest expenditure immediately required by the South Eastern Railway Company for the safety of the public, would not affect any ultimate decision at Westminster.'....'We in Kent are chiefly concerned in the serious inconvenience it would be to travellers to be dumped amid the slums of the Surrey side of the Thames.' ....'a House of Commons Committee (should) not be permitted to so cavalierly ignore the safety and the convenience of the residents of Kent.'

'Wartime' restrictions.
A number of restrictions had to be introduced because of 'wartime' pressures. By 21st century standards, a number of these are laughable but they were very real at the time, since they went against what was then considered to be the 'norm'. Such as:

- The Tunbridge Wells Postmaster announced in March 1916 a reduction in postal deliveries to just two a day and a reduction in Post Office opening hours to 9am to 7pm (from 7am -10pm). This produced the advice by the *Courier* to its readers that 'communications posted *(to us)* on a Thursday, may no longer reach us in time for publication on Friday *(morning)*'.
- In September, the Postmaster announced that telegrams would no longer be delivered by post*women* after dark.
- The Defence of the Realm Act of 1914 had already reduced pub licensing hours to 9.30pm, but in July 1916, these were reduced further to 9pm. This produced the immediate challenge to authority that, since there had been no restriction on playing Billiards in a pub at any time, could Billiards still be played in a pub after 9pm? The short answer was 'No'. The issue also caused the Tunbridge Wells Off-License Holders' Association to hold a meeting at the Clarendon Hotel to discuss and protest about the Restriction Order. Their Resolution was passed and sent to the Prime Minister and the Chairman of the Liquor Board, without any apparent response or effect.
- Tunbridge Wells was very dark without street lighting. In November, the public were beginning to challenge the Town Council: Why was Tunbridge Wells kept in greater darkness than the City of London?
- In November, the Government introduced proposals for the regulation of the food supply, which obviously reflected growing and supply problems, which would get much worse over the next two years.
- In mid-December, the differences between Germany and Britain in agricultural production were highlighted in a speech made by Mr. Albert Bannister to the Tunbridge Wells Farmers' Club. Germany was more self-sufficient. In UK, 60% of farm land is pasture; in Germany 21%. A 100-acre mixed farm in UK and Germany provides food for 45-50 people in the UK; and 70-75 people in Germany. On such a farm, there would be grown:

	In UK	In Germany
Potatoes	11 tons	55 tons
Meat	4 tons	4¼ tons
Corn	15 tons	33 tons
Milk	17½ tons	28 tons
Sugar	Almost none	29 tons

Mr. Bannister called for more land to be made arable in Britain; for better protection of shipping by the Admiralty; for waste to be eliminated; and for the Government to provide more labour and machinery to increase agricultural production.

- A week later, a so-called 'War Conference of Kent Agriculturists' convened by the National Farmers' Union discussed the need for increased production of food. It was not just a question of making more land arable, it was also one of allowing/providing more men (and women!) to work on it – too many had been taken off it for the Armed Forces.
- In December, there was an announcement of curtailment of Rail Services in the New Year. Tunbridge Wells would lose 5 trains a day, down to 12 trains a day to London and 10 trains from London. There would also be a 50% increase in fares, with a concession for season ticket holders within a 40-mile radius of London.

Annual Mayoral Divine Service.
There is a tradition in every Council that each Mayor holds an Annual Divine Service, with the Chaplain of his choice in the Church or Chapel of his choice, and every Alderman or Councillor is 'expected' to attend.

However such were the strong religious feelings of many members of the Tunbridge Wells Council, that many refused to attend the service. In 1916, only 4 Aldermen and 11 Councillors attended out of a total of 32 possible. Two of those unable to attend pleaded 'long-standing engagements', but as the *Courier* pointed out, the date for the Service had been set a full year earlier. For several years, the absence of over half the Council has been a matter of comment. The Mayor had pleaded with Councillors to attend, specifically asking Nonconformist members to give up their prejudices and reservations and attend an Anglican Service for the good of the Town, but they could not agree to do so, which is a very revealing insight into the very strong religious feelings and beliefs still held within the town.

War Savings
War Saving Certificates were on sale at 15/6d each (77½ p.), to be redeemed for £1 after 5 years. The Tunbridge Wells War Savings Association now had 800 members and had accumulated enough to buy 2,500 Certificates. (However, one member had bought 500, another 475, two 200 and two 85, so just 6 members [less than 1%] out of 800 accounted for 62% of the sum raised!)

Miss Candler's 'Insult to the British Army' and Apology
Miss Sarah Candler, one of two sisters who were Quakers and pacifists and who owned the Woodlands Laundry, made a statement when chairing a meeting, held in September in the Town Hall, of the Tunbridge Wells branch of the British Women's Temperance Association which produced a storm of protest. According to the *Tunbridge Wells Advertiser*, she said 'Why were soldiers given rum before a bayonet charge? It was to arouse their animal passions and make them commit acts which they would not otherwise do.' This may have been true, but it was not an acceptable statement to the civilian, Low Church, 'teetotal' and largely female population of Tunbridge Wells.

The Mayor wrote to the Association President, Lady Constance Coote, who dissociated herself from the remark and tried to get Miss Candler to apologise. Miss Candler made a somewhat grudging apology and claimed that she had said 'Was it....?' rather than 'It was ...' but the reporter's shorthand notes confirmed that she had made a statement rather than asked a question. The correspondence, which included letters from serving soldiers, civilians and one who signed himself 'Magna est Veritas', was published in the *Courier* over several weeks. From the latter correspondence, it also emerged that Miss Candler was also the President of the Tunbridge Wells Council against Conscription. The whole issue which lasted about four weeks proved to be a somewhat violent 'storm in a teacup'.

Saving the Nevill Ground.

The Nevill Ground in Cricket Week, 1907

The Nevill Cricket & Athletic Ground in Warwick Park had been opened in 1898 to much acclaim and had brought County cricket back to Tunbridge Wells. Its finances had always been somewhat uncertain, because it did not have enough subscribers and the War certainly did not help.

The Ground was owned and run by the Tunbridge Wells Cricket, Football and Athletic Club Ltd., whose Directors had always been 'the Great and the Good' of the town and they included in 1916 Lord Henry Nevill (the new Marquess's brother) as Chairman, the Marquis Camden, W.C. Cripps (the Town Clerk), Mr. F. Wadham Elers and Mr. Frank W. Stone (both previous Mayors of the town) and Major L. T. Spens.

The Club's financial situation was brought to a crisis level in March 1916 by the death in the previous year of Mr. Harold Beeching, who had underwritten the mortgage of the Ground for £2,000 in February 1899. His Executors now required repayment and this could mean having to sell the Ground.

The Great and the Good rallied round and the 'evil day of reckoning' was postponed, as it would be several more times and in similar fashion over the next 30 years. The Marquess of Abergavenny waived the rent, the Mayor made an appeal for £300 and got £297, a Committee of Management was formed with representatives from the Town Council, the Tradesmen's Association, the Advertising Association and the Chamber of

Commerce (an uncharacteristic and democratic move which shows how desperate the situation must have been) and the Executors were persuaded to withdraw their notice of repayment and accept continued payment of interest. The Army who had commandeered the Pavilion and Stands in 1916, keeping bombs and grenades amongst other things in one of the storerooms, were also persuaded to pay a rent of 15/- (75p.) a week.

Silwood, Court Rd. in the 1890s.
Could it be Mrs. Taylor at the upper window?

Link with 19th century Tunbridge Wells.

In June 1916, the death of Mrs. H. A. Taylor of Silwood, Court Road, was reported in the *Courier* under the headline 'A Heroine of Delhi'. She was the last survivor of the Siege of Delhi in 1857 during what was then called the Indian Mutiny, but is now known, at least in India, as the 1st War of Indian Independence. She is credited with saving nine lives during the Siege, as well as keeping the men's rifles loaded. She was described as 'a woman of much cheerfulness, pleasant and agreeable to all' and had lived in Tunbridge Wells for many years. She is reported to have been a close friend of the Viceroy of India, Lord Lawrence, and his wife and also Field-Marshal Lord Roberts. Her husband was Maj. Gen. H. A. Taylor of the Bengal Staff Corps.

Advertising to the Troops.

In view of the large number of troops in Tunbridge Wells, it is understandable that Jenkinson & Son, the leading military tailor in the town, should advertise regularly to them through the *Courier*, such as this advertisement for the Chemico Body Shield. One does wonder, did the advertising work? And did the Chemico Body Shield live up (if that is the right verb) to its claims?

> **~~15th Great Xmas Show~~**
>
> TELEPHONE 147.
>
> # Thomas Hughes
>
> **4, HIGH STREET, TUN. WELLS,**
>
> Begs to inform his old customers and his many new ones in Tunbridge Wells and the surrounding villages that his
>
> ## FIFTEENTH GREAT
> ## Christmas Show
> OF
>
> **TURKEYS,**
>   **GEESE,**
>   **DUCKS,**
>   **FOWLS,**
>
> From Norfolk and Devonshire and Local Farms,
>
> **PHEASANTS,**
>   **PARTRIDGES,**
>   **HARES,**
>
> From Local Estates,
>
> **WILL COMMENCE ON MONDAY, DECEMBER 18TH.**
>
> **OYSTERS are Cheap**
>
> Try my Special Colchester Natives, in fine condition.
> Per Dozen - 1/-, 1/6 and 2/-
> Per Hundred - 7/-, 9/- and 12/-
>
> I hope to have the support of all my old Patrons again this Christmas.
>
> **ORDERS BY POST OR 'PHONE PROMPTLY ATTENDED TO.**
>
> NOTE NEW ADDRESS—
>
> **THOMAS HUGHES,**
> Fishmonger, Poulterer and Dealer in Game,
>
> **4, High Street, Royal Tunbridge Wells.**

The Year's End

Although there had been clear signs in 1916 of the coming food shortages, this is not apparent in the advertisement which Thomas Hughes (who interestingly was a Fishmonger, Poulterer and Dealer in Game, but not a Butcher) ran in the *Courier* in December 1916 for his customers. What the Hughes advertisement does suggest is that 'luxury' items such as turkey, geese, pheasants and partridges were still readily available, but at a price, while there were clear signs that the staples of everyday living were in increasingly short supply.

Reports on Christmas in Tunbridge Wells.

As in previous and subsequent years, the press reported on the entertainment of troops, both active and convalescent – at the YMCA at the Pump Room; and the Mayoral visits to Kingswood and Nevill Park and other VAD Hospitals – but there do not seem to be any reports of large Christmas Dinners being given to the troops by a doting public, as had been the case in 1914 and 1915. Times and public attitudes would seem to be changing?

The 'War News' column of the *Courier* congratulated the troops somewhat sanctimoniously on 'their exemplary conduct throughout the holiday season. The military police had had practically nothing to do, and no cases of drunkenness had been reported'; and it hoped that the issue of Sunday Concert performances was now definitely settled. On this matter, the Courier rather unctuously said that 'the intervention of the Military Authorities with regard to the Opera House had put it on an entirely different footing.

CHAPTER 10
1917-1918 : The Worsening Situation
by Lionel Anderson

As 1917 dawned against a background of deteriorating military news and continuing food shortages, it might well be thought that the people of Tunbridge Wells were feeling somewhat apprehensive about the future. And yet any review of the local newspapers, particularly the *Kent and Sussex Courier*, gives little indication of such a mood but rather it conveys a spirit of resilience and determination to see things through to the bitter end. However, behind this veneer of bravado on the part of newspapers, there can be no doubting that by the end of 1916 the age of innocence was over for the British people. The remorseless weekly newspaper diet of those killed and injured, the screening in cinemas of the film of the 'Battle of the Somme' which was said to have been seen by 20 million people, and the growing number of families already affected by the loss of loved ones, would have led to a growing concern about the worsening situation.

A world without radio meant that the population was almost entirely dependent on news from the newspapers. Many national newspapers were bound by the restraints of 'D' notices and so were somewhat limited in their freedom but it is generally considered that local newspapers were less subject to scrutiny. For example, letters from the front were often published and, as already mentioned, casualty figures. Jingoistic journalism was a feature of the *Courier's* reporting style when commenting on issues relating to the war, but they were not alone in this, for it was a means by which newspapers could boost morale, and in a sense, 'fight the war'. The importance of this is borne out by the novelist John Buchan, a central figure in British propaganda at this time, who commented: *'the war could not have been fought for one month without the newspapers'.*[1]

As 1917 progressed, food shortages, and the need to queue for food became the norm. Shortages of coal and gas were also being felt and there was a growing risk (small) of being bombed by a Zeppelin. In the view of AJP Taylor, 1917 was to prove the worst year for the civilian population of Britain.[2]

Trying to capture the mood of the civilian population of those times is difficult. An editorial published in *The Times* in December 1916 conveys this:
'In these days it is not easy to obtain a full impression of public opinion but in one direction, the only direction that matters, the people of this country have shown themselves at every possible opportunity consistent and united in that they mean to win the war'.

---

[1] Niall Ferguson: *The Pity of War* p.213
[2] AJP Taylor: *English History 1914-1945* p.88

Lady Matthews's diaries do help throw some light on local conditions and the mood in Tunbridge Wells. Writing in November 1916, she mentions that she is depressed by the news from the front and at the lack of progress of the war – *'all our labours seems to bring peace no nearer'*.

By the latter part of 1916 and the early months of 1917, significant political, military and financial events were combining which would require strong Government policies if Britain was to survive. Arguably, given the seriousness of these problems it can probably be considered the most crucial period of the war years. Therefore, it is helpful to briefly consider these issues before looking at how the people of Tunbridge Wells lived, and met, the challengers of those times.

The Political Crisis
By late 1916 there was a growing realization amongst the populace that Britain's position was very precarious. The public was now fully aware of the likelihood of Germany, having built up its submarine force, imposing a blockade on the high seas and the likely consequences of this policy. At the same time, the problem of financing the war effort was now exercising the minds of senior Government officials since without financial assistance, the war would be lost. Meantime, continuing food shortages were a concern at all levels of society.

The sense of drift and lack of urgency shown by the Government was palpable. Asquith, who had singularly failed to show the leadership necessary in a war situation, was fast becoming a liability and this in turn was leading to a loss of morale. This situation was satirised in song by the music hall comedian George Robey:
> 'Just stem the tide of ignorant conjecture,
> Remain inert and dormant just like me,
> And cultivate spontaneous quiescence,
> In other words: "Wait and See!' [3]

Eventually, a sense of urgency was seen from Asquith who in late 1915 moved to introduce the Military Service Bill. At the same time he bravely (in the opinion of the Times) warned the country of the austerity to come: by this time higher taxation, the banning of non-essential inputs, and abolishing luxuries were now top of the Government's agenda. These measures were, according to *The Times*, *'welcomed with positive enthusiasm by those most affected'* and went on to congratulate the Prime Minister for his courage stating *'that never was any Government so secure of the backing at home in a vigorous conduct of the national struggle'*.

Despite *The Times's* endorsement, it was too little, too late and in December 1916 Lloyd George displaced Asquith. Asquith was by now a broken man, having not only lost the confidence of his colleagues, but had suffered a personal tragedy, losing his eldest son in the Battle of the

---
[3] Stephen Bates:*Asquith* p.124

Somme. One observer wrote at the end of the war 'the effect of this change in direction two years ago may be compared to the substitution of dynamite for a damp squib'.[4]

The Military Crisis

Britain was now engaged not only in a war of attrition on land, which did not seem winnable, but also a war of attrition at sea. To give some idea of the scale of Britain's need to control the seas during the war, British shipping moved over 23 million people, 2.24 million animals and 46.5 million tonnes of military stores during the five years of the War. The key issue though was that despite all efforts to increase home food production, Britain still had to import at least three-fifths of its food requirement and at least one-third of imports to Britain were carried on neutral ships.[5]

British shipping losses had been increasing due to higher U-boat activity but worse was to come, when the German High Command announced that it was going to re-introduce unrestricted U-boat warfare on 1st February. This form of warfare (indiscriminate sinking of all ships without warning) had been previously used by the Germans in 1915, but had been discontinued due to technical problems and the fear of antagonising the USA which had been very disturbed by the death of 128 American citizens in the sinking of the *RMS Lusitania* in 1915.

The decision to re-introduce such a policy reflected Germany's realisation that not only would the USA be entering the War very shortly on the Allied side, but also that Germany could not gain control of the high seas with surface ships. In a memorandum to Hindenburg, the German Naval Commander Holtzendorff predicted that the German U-boat fleet could sink 600,000 tonnes of shipping per month, whilst up to 40% of neutral shipping would refuse to carry goods to Britain. This would lead to food stocks in the UK falling below danger point, strikes and economic chaos.[6]

Admiral Sir David Beattie summed up the position in February 1917:
'France is becoming exhausted. Italy is becoming tired. Neither can keep their factories going owing to shortages of coal, and we cannot keep the supply, because our steamers are all being sunk. Our armies might advance and slay the Hun by thousands, but the real race is whether we shall strangle them with our blockade, before they defeat us by wiping out our Merchant Marine.'[7]

With shipping losses increasing - the Navy was only destroying about one in three of the new U-boats being launched – and the Admiralty continued to vacillate about the most effective way to deal with the threat. Lloyd George, frustrated by the Admiralty's apparent helplessness,

---

[4] AJP Taylor: *Op.Cit.* p.73 (Sir Alexerie Fitzroy, Clerk to the Privy Council)
[5] AJP Taylor: *Op.Cit.* p.84
[6] David Stevenson: *1914-1918. The History of the First World War* p.261
[7] Lawrence James: *Rise and Fall of the British Empire* p.362

effectively took command of the Navy and on the 30th April 1917 ordered the introduction of the convoy system. This was a dramatic and most decisive intervention and it worked. In early 1917, one in four ships was being lost. Following the introduction of the convoy system, there was a significant fall in shipping losses: of 5090 merchant ships conveyed in 1917, only 63 were lost.[8]

The Financial Crisis

This was a crisis that could and should have been dealt with sooner, as it is clear this situation was deteriorating in the early years of the war. On July 8th 1915, *The Times* in a strongly-worded editorial pointed out just how little action had been taken by local authorities to rein back on expenditure and it called on administrators both great and small to grasp the terrible meaning of war. The paper warned of the crunch to come: *'Millions of people in this country still regard the war as an unhappy interlude and seem to think that when it is over they would be able to resume their old placid, probably easy, and perhaps luxurious existence.'* It then calls on people to spend no more money on luxuries, but that they should enforce upon themselves that stern self-discipline which is almost universal in France. It concluded, rather tellingly *'that no revolution in these habits will occur unless the Government takes the lead'.*

The parlous state of the Government's finances becomes evident when considering that between 1914 and the end of the war the National Debt increased from £650m to £7,435 million. Servicing this borrowing meant that half the yield from taxation was taken to do so, compared to a figure of 14% before the war.[9] By 1917, 83% of total Government spending was on the War effort. As a consequence, the standard rate of income tax was increased from 6% to 12% in the first War Budget of November 1914 and was progressively raised to 30% by 1918/19. In many respects, the financial problem was assuming more importance than the war on the land. Lord Lansdowne, the Tory Leader of the Lords, in a report shortly after the Battle of Somme, not only lamented the awful loss of life but also said *'the financial burden which we have already accumulated is almost incalculable'*.[10]

These then were the main issues confronting the Government at the end of 1916 and the beginning of 1917. Outside the political world, the main issue for the man in the street and for that matter, even the higher echelons of society, was the shortage of food. So with austerity growing and people experiencing real change in their life style and increasingly affected by Government dictate, how did the citizens of Tunbridge Wells dealt with the challenges of 1917 and 1918?

---

[8] David Stevenson: *1914-1918 The History of the First World War* p.124
[9] AJP Taylor: *Op.Cit.* p124
[10] Stephen Bates: *Asquith* p123

1917 - A YEAR OF AUSTERITY

With little in the way of personal recollections aside from Lady Matthews's diaries, the *Kent and Sussex Courier* and the *Advertiser* are the main sources of local news for the researcher. The social life of the town was recorded in great detail and did not appear to be interrupted to any real degree. The old maxim that 'Life Goes On' certainly applied. Letters to the Editor, and particularly those from people who were prepared to speak out, occasionally provide real glimpses of the underlying situation while reports on news from the many churches and schools events, clubs of many types, and council meetings all combine to paint a picture of daily life.

The shortage of food was creating a mood of frustration and a degree of anger within the community. Despite the growing problem there was little or no control over food distribution, although retailers were imposing a form of rationing for sugar, restricting purchases to 2lb at a time. However, this voluntary code did not prevent people shopping and queuing elsewhere. If there were any people still unaware of the seriousness of the situation, Lloyd George made things very clear in his New Year speech. After pointing out how much land had been lost to pasture over the previous fifty years and that 70-80% of staple cereal was being imported, he concluded by saying *'and I want you to know that our food stocks are dangerously low'*.

Various letters to the Editors of the local papers on the problems of queuing and shortages, indicate a degree of friction between those living in Tunbridge Wells and those in the outlying areas. A letter to the Editor of the *Courier* in early December complains about the weekly scramble for tea, margarine and butter and how often residents of the town are left empty-handed, due to visitors from the outlying districts who arrive by car or by rail and 'grab everything they can'. The writer goes on to suggest that the Food Control Committee, in order to stop tea, margarine and butter being taken out of the town, should require grocers to demand to see the National Registration Cards of suspicious purchasers. *'We would then no longer require the assistance of the police to protect food retailers from bombardment. Signed 'Householder'.*

There were some angry responses to this letter. A letter signed 'Farm Labourer' said ' *Its hardly likely that people from around would come into Tunbridge Wells to shop, often spending hours going from place to place if the village shops could supply their needs. Then there are railway fares, few trains and every inconvenience. Householder, do stop and think before rushing into print again'.*

Queueing in the High Street

A real insight into the difficulties people were experiencing in obtaining food (apart from pictures of food queues) can be gleamed from the diaries of Lady Matthews. In November 1916, she writes about a visit to Sainsbury's:

'I went to fetch 1lb of margarine and 1lb of lard which they had put aside for me, as they no longer deliver. When I got to the door I found a swaying crowd, attempting to crush in the narrow entrance. It was a bitterly cold day and I realised I could not stand for long, so I decided to go to the Food Controller's office and I told him to come with me and see the queue for himself and then went off for a policeman. As a result there was a meeting and the margarine has been commandeered and placed at various grocers around the town.'

A related situation occurred at the Maypole Dairy in Calverley Road on a Saturday in November, when the Food Controller swooped at 9am to exercise his new powers to commandeer food; and he re-allocated more than half of a large consignment of margarine which had been delivered, to other retailers.

On the 2nd March, there was a meeting of the Tunbridge Wells Grocers' Federation, the purpose of which was to prevent panic buying. It was reported that there was great difficulty in making a fair distribution of sugar because selfish people were hoarding.

On the 9th March the *Courier*, responding to a statement by the Prime Minister, wrote:
'Everyone can help to fight the submarine menace – eat less bread.' In the same article the *Courier* requested that those who can afford the more expensive substitutes should do so, in

order that poorer people may not be deprived of bread. There was also a strong message from H.W.Forster, a member of the Tunbridge Wells Food Economy Campaign:
'The Germans are attempting to starve us into surrender. Times will be hard, but it is to bring the truth home to everybody that the Food Economy Campaign has been started'.

Food hoarding was undoubtedly a real problem. Under a Food Hoarding Order dated April 5th 1917, powers were given to officials to enter homes. If more than one-month's provisions were held (excluding potatoes and tomatoes), people were liable to prosecution. Not surprisingly, the Ministry of Food began to attract criticism for its lack of progress in finding a solution to the hoarding issue. The Ministry is on record in a speech by Mr. Clynnes, Parliamentary Secretary at the Ministry (who later was appointed Food Controller and Leader of the Labour Party) that it was experiencing difficulty from minorities of businesses, traders and the consuming public who sought by devious means to undermine the policies of the Ministry. In Mr.Clynnes's opinion:
*'Hoarders and some traders schemed in a most unashamed manner to attain their selfish ends and....***conscientious objectors were self-respecting citizens compared to them.***'*

Despite the best efforts of the *Courier*, it seems that earlier calls in March for people to eat less bread had fallen on deaf ears. On 4th May an editorial commented: *'There must be a more rigid, sustained and purposeful economy in the consumption of bread-stuffs than has yet been seen'*. Quoting the Parliamentary Secretary of the Ministry of Food, the paper went on to say *' the average consumption of bread was still 50% above the limits laid down under the Government's scheme of voluntary rationing – consumption was 6lb a head (last week) instead of 4lb. If consumption does not fall then we are sure that if the unpopular and undesirable alternative becomes necessary, it will be promptly and drastically applied'.*

A similar appeal was made by the Mayor, Charles Emson. He called on the townspeople to live within the requirements laid down by the Food Controller, which were:
        Meat - 3½ lbs per head per week
        Bread - 4lbs per head per week (Includes flour)
        Sugar - ½ lb per head per week

In the same speech, the Mayor said that Empire Day (May 25th) would also be a National Food Savings Day. On that day, he intended to read the Kings Proclamation on the Lower Cricket Ground. In the meantime, he earnestly called on those who could do so, to limit their bread allowance to 3lbs per head. Yet a further policy to reduce bread consumption was the establishment of school canteens, the prime objective being to save on the amount of bread being used in children's lunches.

The shortage of bread led to much correspondence, but perhaps the most bizarre letter was printed in the Courier on the 1st June:

If the present population of Tunbridge Wells at 36,000, ate 2 oz of bread less daily, the saving in one week would be no less that 31,500 lbs, equal to 15,750 ordinary 2lb loaves. This would be a cash saving of £400 a week.'

An equally bizarre letter was published on the 28th December, from a Mr. Edward Taylor of Broadwater:

Why have the Government not been constructing the Channel Tunnel over the last three years. There would be no queues, no shortages of provisions, and much lower prices if they had had the sense to realise this investment would have secured victory by this time, as over 60,000 tons per twenty four hours would have been sent through releasing the transport and naval help on convoys. The question is if they have not done it, is it even now 'too late'.

With sugar becoming even scarcer, the authorities took the first step towards rationing. On the 24th August, the Courier reported on the proposed issue of sugar tickets. The tickets would be perforated and the householder would retain one half and the grocer, who would become that person's registered retailer, would keep the other half. On the householder's half would be the name, number of persons in family, and the amount of sugar that household would be entitled to. At the same time, shopkeepers needed to be registered with their Local Authority. However, the limitations of this scheme were quickly exposed and it was then proposed that householders should be forced to state their name and age in a sealed envelope and which would be given was given to the retailer, who would then pass this on unopened to the proper officials. It is self-evident why this system became known as the "Sugar Muddle".

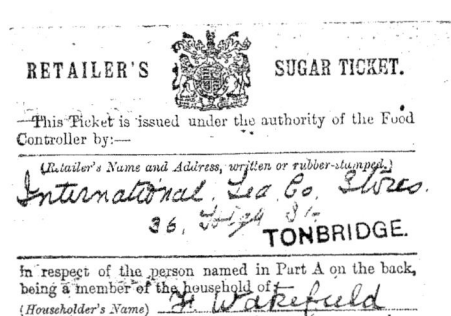

It was not only bread and sugar in short supply. Meat was becoming a luxury and around this time the Tunbridge Wells Meat Order (1917) was issued, detailing the maximum price that could be charged by butchers for all cuts of meat. Meanwhile, requests from local milk farmers to the Food Controller for higher prices met with little sympathy. In their appeal the farmers pointed out that with the cost of cereal foodstuffs having increased by 68%, a lack of labour due to the military requirements and with the price of dairy stock having risen by 100%, their position was untenable. In response the Food Controller said: *'it was the farmers' duty to carry on – if not, heavy fines would be imposed under DORA'.*

Whilst there is considerable reporting about the shortage of food, surprisingly there is little said about the rising cost of food. Clearly, shortages would have led to higher prices, but the extent of the rise in foodstuff prices would have been a serious problem for most household budgets. For towns like Tunbridge Wells with a population under 50,000, the general increase in the price of such products as meat, bacon, fish, bread, milk and butter was of the order of 83% between July 1914 and March 1917.[11]

A natural consequence of food shortages was an increase in the use of land for allotments. Under powers introduced under DORA, the government could take over land when it felt it was necessary to do so. By the end of 1918, Britain had an extra 3 million acres of farming land. Much of the labour needed to work on this land came from the newly formed Women's Land Army and also from Conscientious Objectors. Many appeals were made by the *Courier* for men to find more time to take on allotments. In February Tunbridge Wells had 6,648 rods of land under cultivation, equal to 54 acres – a total of 805 allotments, worked by 85 holders. Of these, 379 were temporary allotments under the Cultivation of Land Order, and 426 were permanent. The number of allotments had increased to 939 allotments by May, of which 598 were permanent and 341 temporary, on 75 acres. By comparison, the pre-war number of allotments was 211 on 15 acres.[12]

The call for more land to be used for the cultivation of potatoes led to members of the Nevill Golf Club approaching the Food Controller. The Courier praised the club members for their patriotic action.[13] On the 30th January, the club members were advised that the land was not worth working – too much gorse and heather – many of today's members would say that little has changed.

AIR RAIDS/LIGHTING RESTRICTIONS
Whilst the main pre-occupation of the townsfolk by mid-1917 remained the shortages of food, there was now the threat of a resumption of the bombing campaign. On the 1st June, the *Courier* reported on an air raid on 'a South-East Town'. The paper's response was typically true to form:
These air raids have no effect in deciding the issue of the struggle. In the use of aircraft as an engine of war for causing panic and the demand for

---

[11] National Records of Scotland HH31/27/56 p.96
[12] *Kent & Sussex Courier* – 9th February and 3rd May 1917
[13] The author is a member of the Nevill and would like to think that this was a spontaneous gesture. However he has found a letter in the *Courier* of 15th January 1917 which may have influenced their decision. A letter signed *Pro Patria* called on all classes and particularly women, and not just artisans, to take up an allotment for the national good. 'In times, like this, the spade is more honourable than the golf club or tennis racquet'.

surrender among the civilian population, the Germans may be said to have "shot their bolt". *'The failure of the Zeppelins on which the overweaning Teutonic mind has placed inordinate hope, has shown that a "German Peace" cannot be won in the sky.'*

Immediately below this article was a copy of a letter sent to the Times by the Hon. A.E.Gathorne-Hardy[14] who happened to be in Folkestone at the time, and which provides an eye witness account of this very raid. The publication of this letter seems somewhat at odds with the decision by the Editor not to publish the name of the town concerned in their report, but maybe it was an oversight by the censor.

Bombing practice by the military was also a matter of concern to many residents, who in letters to the Editor, complained that they were unnecessarily alarmed by this practice taking place late at night. The Courier was of the opinion that in a town with so many invalid and elderly residents, the unexpected sound of bombs, until one becomes accustomed to them, would give rise to complaints. However, the paper in a valiant effort to appease everyone, goes on to say that 'Tunbridge Wells is far too inland to be seriously disturbed by the enemy and any action by the military was necessary and we should probably not be permitted to offer any further criticism.

On the 16th March, there was a modification to the lighting restrictions so that motorists in Tunbridge Wells would now be subject to the rules on headlights which applied in the surrounding County. It is not clear from the article what the difference between these had been.

Strict rules were in place regarding the showing of lights in buildings and many cases are reported of people failing to adhere to the regulations. One such case concerned the Rev. Canon Keating of St. Augustine's Church, who was summoned for contravening the Lighting Order of 28th July. Writing to the Bench in mitigation, he admitted full responsibility and went on to provide a somewhat humorous account of the incident:

'I admit that for a few seconds the lights were not effectively obscured. In palliation of the offence let me plead: The room was in darkness, with the doors and windows wide open, when the amorous cats of my neighbours began in my garden their evening concert. One of the maids passing the door recognised the squeals of her own particular Tabby, evidently in dire straits. Without a moment's hesitation, she rushed to the offending window, switching on all the lighting she could command on the way and gallantly joining in the fray, brought peace once more to my distracted household by emptying the contents of the water jug she was carrying in her hand. That all the town might acclaim her triumph, she left the lights on until my arrival a few moments later. Alas, by the time I had switched off the lights, the faithful guardian of our lives and liberties, like Captain

---

[14] A member of the family of Viscount Cranbrook and related to the Abergavenny family.

Cuttle, had found and made a note. I plead for merciful consideration on account of my appreciation of those we miscall 'our dumb friends'. May I add for those interested in my cat that, at the corner of Calverley Parade, may be seen a fair picture of Pussie as she emerged from the Homeric fight.'

The Bench nonetheless imposed a fine of 10s.

A CALL TO ARMS

A National Service meeting was held at the Opera House in March 1917 increasing yet further the pressure on those who had not come forward. By the spring of 1917, several more rules and restrictions were introduced both at National and Local Level of Government. Under the DORA legalisation, notices were served on Employers that monthly returns were required of all persons employed between the ages of 18 and 42. At the same time Lord Harris, former Chairman of the Kent Tribunal in a letter to the *Courier*, was most critical of young men working in Government offices doing women's work. A further meeting on National Service took place at the Opera House on the 6th April 1917, with an address given by Sir George Reid MP, former (or ex-) Prime Minister of Australia, ex-New South Wales Prime Minister and ex-High Commissioner. Opening his talk he said:

Tunbridge Wells was one of the loveliest spots in England for the residence of any man who had been ex-anything'.

Reports were appearing by July of military representatives rounding-up those eligible but who had so far escaped the military net, at places of amusement in Tunbridge Wells. Clearly, life was becoming pretty unpleasant for those who remained in civilian life. Meantime, employers were under increasing pressure to operate with fewer workers and appeals to the Military Tribunals were increasing and these were reported on weekly. On March 2nd, the *Courier* reported the case of two editors of local newspapers applying for continuance of exemption of indispensable employees. The tribunal found against the appeals, stating that under present Government policies where two local newspapers exist, they should amalgamate to release men for the front.

The need for more manpower to cover for the men at the front was an issue the *Courier* was only too happy to promote with calls for the young women of the town to join the Women's Auxiliary Army Corps (WAACs). The paper expressed its disappointment at the response in Tunbridge Wells to the national appeal for women to work on the manufacture of aircraft parts. It went on to say in a further edition of 12th October, that if women were finding it difficult to travel, then a factory should be built in Tunbridge Wells.

By November it was reported that a Women's Volunteer Reserve was established in Tunbridge Wells and was training women as guards to protect forage depots. The paper noted there was a considerable female labour force in the town and called for the women of Tunbridge Wells to step forward and join the WAAC –'*it was their patriotic duty*' - the recent appeal by Viscountess Hardinge must not fall on deaf ears'.

FUEL SHORTAGES

The middle of the year saw numerous power failures occurring. In one incident, a woman had died whilst undergoing an operation. In the words of the *Courier*, '*she was a victim of Hun brutality*'. One of the immediate side effects of these power cuts was to create a large demand on the gas company from people who had switched from gas to electric lighting and were now demanding that their gas supply be re-instated.

The problem of fuel shortages can be seen from a letter sent in July by the Tunbridge Wells Co-operative Society to the Tunbridge Wells Council: it refers to the serious position of coal supplies in the town pointing out that practically no reserves were available for the coming winter. The Council referred the matter to the Finance Committee, but interestingly no response has been found or record of action taken.

Perhaps the words of contemporary writer, Michael MacDonaugh, aptly reflect the general mood of the people by the end of 1917:

'We are living under a Government that rules practically by dictatorship. It compels its citizens to join the Army and fight the Germans: it restricts the citizens to the kind and quantity of food they eat – not to speak of the other numerous bans imposed upon our movements by the Defence of the Realm Regulations. Are we not to be pitied?'. [15]

---

[15] *King and Country* p.373

Many must have shared this view. Yet despite all the austerity and hardships, the year had seen an upsurge of political support for the war effort. Much of this is thought to be due to the efforts of the National War Aims Committee. In essence their policy was focused on maintaining patriotic consciousness and support for the war, by achieving peace through victory and in rejecting compromise. [16]

1918 'THE DARKEST HOUR'.

'Calmness: it's the only glut in the British market. If the Germans were at Margate, they would still be playing golf at Tunbridge Wells.'[17]

While the British may have remained calm, the shortages of food and fuel and the problems of queuing for food continued to be the dominant issue exercising the minds of the public at the start of 1918. This state of affairs is touched on by Lady Matthews in her first diary entry for 1918: *'during the last month, the food problem has grown cruelly ...and the seriousness of the situation is the queuing'*.

However, despite all the hardships there was no serious opposition to the conflict. Indeed with skilled workers in war-related industries receiving wages in line or above the relatively low inflation rate, and the move by some retailers to impose some form of food rationing, the effect on morale was not so worrying for the Government as the shortage of money to finance the war.

Funding the War

Lending money to the Government was now the most important issue of the day and for the *Courier* it was a matter of civic pride. Throughout the year, the paper was well to the fore in urging the citizens of Tunbridge Wells 'to save and lend'. To this end, a giant thermometer showing the amount of money raised had been erected on the summit of Mount Pleasant during the latter part of 1917. In early 1918 the Tunbridge Wells Savings Committee, clearly concerned over a lack of new investment by the townspeople, was in direct communication with Mr. Bonar Law in order to clarify (in their words) a misapprehension about the possibility of a new loan to be announced in the New Year. This communication was passed to the Chairman of National War Savings Committee who replied:

---

[16] David Stevenson *Op.Cit.* p.459
[17] *Evening Standard/Courier* 18th March 1918

in regard to the suggestion that a higher yielding loan will be issued in the New Year this, in my opinion, is most unlikely, but even if it were true it forms no reasonable excuse for withholding money now.

In his New Year Address, the Prime Minister appealed to the nation to save and lend to the Government: in his words *'money was essential for victory'*. But it would seem that he was talking to the converted for there had been a remarkable rise in the level of weekly investment in 5% National War Bonds during the first three weeks of December with a weekly sum of a little over £22m being invested. Clearly, the various War Savings Committees were proving very adept in their appeals to the public.

Local Traders used their advertising to encourage people to invest in War Loan as well as promoting their goods.

This was part of a concerted policy by the Tunbridge Wells Committee of the War Bonds Campaign to widen the net of potential savers and which proved very successful. At a meeting of this Committee in late 1917 it was stated *'that further propaganda has been decided upon in the shape of pulpit references, lantern lectures, speeches at local places of amusement, appeals in Parochial Magazines and local solicitors are to be invited to invest in War Bonds'.*

Each week the *Courier* printed a table showing National War Bond sales for several towns which might be considered similar to Tunbridge Wells. The table below appeared on the 18th January 1918:

	Population No.	Total £	Per Head £
Harrogate	33,706	260,870	7.73
Cheltenham	48,944	242,410	4.96
Bath	69,183	338,394	4.89
Tunbridge Wells	35,697	157,809	4.42
Maidstone	35,477	149,000	4.19

On the 23rd January the *Courier* reported on the public meeting at which the Mayor had stated that Tunbridge Wells had responded admirably to the call. Although the meeting was poorly attended, the Mayor in the typical verbose language of the time said:
'He hoped this was not an indication that people were not taking an interest in the loan but rather that it could be inferred by their absence that they had already done their duty and invested every half-penny they could spare.'

On the 4th March National War Loan Week commenced. Tunbridge Wells tradesmen considered an appeal to raise £100,000 to build a submarine. The *Courier* talks of the generous reputation of the fashionable metropolis of Kent in the past...and finishes *'the wealth of Tunbridge Wells is proverbial'*. And on the 8th March, it proudly announces that the Navy will now get a destroyer (not a submarine) due to £150,000 having been raised. Having congratulated the townspeople for their efforts, the paper in the very same issue, expressed its disappointment on the figures for the sale of War Savings Certificates. It queried why people had not already re-invested the interest they had just received on their War Loan Bonds that week.

WAR LOAN

All the protagonists in the Great War issued debt in order to fight the war. The first interest-bearing War Loan in Britain was issued in November 1914 at an interest rate of 3.5% with terms for repayment in 1925-1928. A third issue was launched in January 1917 paying 5%, a rate Lloyd George described as "penal". Holders of the existing loan were able to convert to the new bond. A Labour politician later wrote "No foreign conqueror could have devised a more complete robbery of the British nation". In 1932 the Government exercised its right to call in the 5% War Bond, by offering cash or a continuing loan at 3.5%. It is worth noting that in 1974 when Britain was in yet another financial crisis, the price of War Loan fell to around 20 which meant a buyer then received a yield of around 17%. Today the yield is closer to 4.2% with the price around 80. Currently, some £2 billion of War Loan remains outstanding.

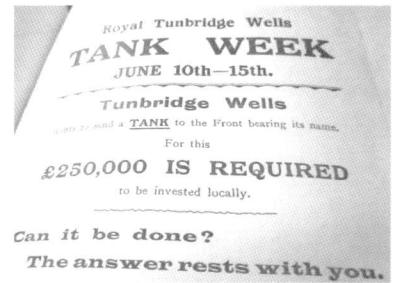

Having raised money for the Navy it was time to do something for the Army and 'Tank Week' was announced in June. The *Courier* in its normal style said the objective was to assist in providing 'the sinews of war' and called on the townspeople to raise £250,000. It went on to say that people would have the satisfaction of knowing, even on the part of those who were only able to lend 15/6d in the purchase of a War Bond, that they would be assisting to render the country all the more secure from the invasion of the Hun. Unlike today, giving investment advice came cheaply with the Mayor pointing out that you could only get 2.5% at the Post Office, whereas a five-year War Bond returned 5%. The Mayor called for a supreme effort saying *'every 15/6d certificate sold meant 125 cartridges for our brave lads'*.

However, on August 23rd the populace received another broadside from the paper – *Must do better – we are below Maidstone!*

FOOD SHORTAGES/ DISTRIBUTION

Despite some voluntary schemes set up by retailers for the distribution of food, the problem of getting enough food remained a major source of worry for most people. Lady Matthew's diaries again provide a real sense of the frustration that people were experiencing:

'The butchers' shops are closed several days a week. We had a dry bit of topside on Sunday – 5 or 6lbs and by the greatest difficulty secured a tiny sirloin for next Sunday – and only that because I pleaded that I had two ladies coming for lunch. But the seriousness of the situation is the queues. Not only in front of the margarine shops, but also the butchers. The shutters are kept closed and the doors locked most of the day.'

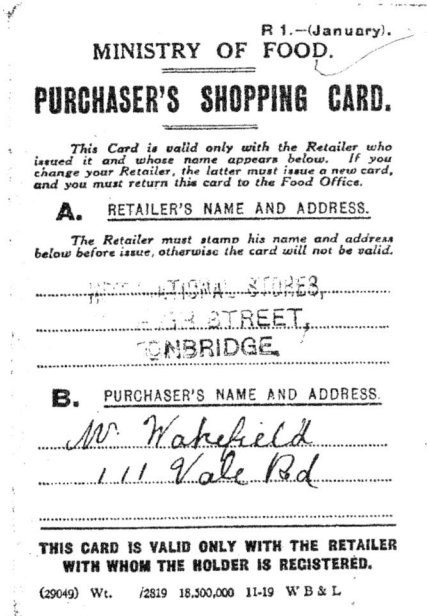

Although the Tunbridge Wells Food Control Committee met to discuss how best to deal with the problems of regulation and distribution they made little progress. This was a national problem and there seems to have been a natural reluctance by the Government to consider food rationing at this time.

However, by early February with reports of malnutrition occurring in poor communities rationing became necessary and householders were required to sign for sugar and margarine.

In February the Borough Council introduced Village School Canteens. Also a communal kitchen was opened at St.Peter's: there were now four kitchens in Tunbridge Wells serving 3,500 meals a week. The opening of a National Restaurant in Tunbridge Wells was reported in the *Courier* on the 8th November. The restaurant had been taken over from the Ministry of Food and catered for all classes. The Mayor in his address said *'he hoped common sense would prevail and all classes will not object to mixing with the masses in a public restaurant.'*

No lunch could be more than 1s. 4d (just under 7p.) or tea 5d (just over 2p.), exclusive of fish, meat or eggs. Tea would be served without sugar. Not only was there a shortage of tea, but there were many complaints to the Food Controller about the quality. Hitherto tea had been carefully blended to suit the waters of a locality and now this was no longer possible as the Government had pooled all supplies. This must have been a worrying problem for the owners of tearooms. (Perhaps even more worrying for them was the advert from International Stores on how to win the war).

The thorny problem of food distribution was in the news again when certain retailers were reported for refusing to sell goods to customers only registered for one item. Such action was illegal and they were liable to prosecution under Ministry of Food regulations. With reports of the sick and children not receiving adequate supplies of milk, the Food Controller moved to deal with distribution. By the Autumn, it was reported that the Food Committee was preparing ration books for issue by the end of October. Rationing covered meat, bacon, butter, margarine and lard. Two cards were issued to every registered consumer, one for meat and bacon the other for fats. Detachable coupons allowed weekly 15 oz. of meat, five oz. of bacon and four oz. of fats, which could be used for purchases, or for meals in restaurants. If you decided to eat out, it was essential to have your coupons with you. Indeed, coupons assumed a greater importance than payment. The following could be bought in a typical teashop: a half coupon for one sausage; or egg and bacon; a whole coupon for stewed steak and carrots, or two sausages, or a plate of cold ham and tongue.[18]

Given this situation, pie lovers would have been in good spirit on reading on the 31st May 1918, that the Tunbridge Wells Food Controller was allowing the National Kitchen operating in the town to sell pies not exceeding six ounces in weight, and not containing more than 20% cooked meat, *without coupons* until the end of June.[19]

FUEL SHORTAGES/DISTRIBUTION

On the 5th July 1918, a Coal Control Order was issued. For a 6-room house, the fuel allowance for one year must not exceed 11,250 cubic feet of gas, or 180 units of electricity. The fuel shortages were now leading to the early closure of shops and the Tradesmen's Association was warned by the Fuel Controller at their meeting in September, that not less than a quarter of the coal used in the past, must now be saved. Larger houses would have to make-up for the lack of saving on smaller houses. Householders were now required to fill in a form, but the Fuel Controller found that 95% of them had been filled in incorrectly. Extra allowances would only be made to those with a Doctor's certificate. Coal could not be taken out of the town and anyone who would be away for over a month, was required to report this to the Fuel Controller.

---

[18] *King and Country* p.373
[19] *Courier* 31st May 1918

Price increases in fuel occurred in January with the Tunbridge Wells Gas Company advising of a rise of 3d per 1000 cubic feet, blaming the increase not only on the higher cost of coal, but also the cost of freighting which had increased from 3/6d per ton to around 14/0d. The company at its AGM, reported that it had complained to the Fuel Controller about the quality of the coal they were buying-in, but had received a terse response along the lines that if you do not want it, just let us know. Council Minutes at that time comment on the concern of some members about the sale of gas for motor cars, which would limit the supply available to households, but it was considered that this was far too difficult a matter with which to deal.

MILITARY MATTERS/TRIBUNALS

On 18th January 1918, the *Courier* commenting on the Military Service Bill said: *'the country will not tolerate young men sheltering in munitions'*. But in April the *Courier* took issue with the regulations of the Man Power Bill, arguing that men in their late forties were of no use to the military – better they continue to run businesses and pay tax. This is the first instance the writer has found where the *Courier* had publicly spoken out against Government policy.

The *Courier* also reported on 19th January a somewhat extraordinary meeing which occurred between a Father and Son on the battlefields of France. The son, Private Reginald Carmen, had emigrated to Australia, joined the Australian contingent and was sent to France and by chance met his father, Private Richard Carmen of the West Kents.

The Need for Manpower in the Forces

An illustration of how every able man, irrespective of occupation, would be called up, can be seen in the records of King Charles' School, which would lose six of its teachers to the Forces. In September 1914, the School Monitor enlisted in the West Kents and in December 1915 Mr. Chamberlain went to join HM forces in London. Later, in May 1916 Mr. Thomas Mann joined the army and was followed in September by Mr. Hargrave. Finally, the Headmaster Mr. John Malden was called up in March 1917 and a student teacher, Mr. A. Bootes, followed the next month. In March 1919, both Mr. Malden and Mr. Mann returned to their previous roles in the School, following demobilisation.

The need for military manpower was still, even as late as August, as insatiable as ever, with the Military Tribunal still meeting weekly and they were now assessing men over the age of forty. One interesting case (2nd August 1918) concerns W. Hearn of Nevill Cottage, Warwick Park who was the groundsman at the Nevill Cricket and Athletic Ground. The appeal from his employer stated that this man worked from 6am to 9pm and also cultivated a 30-rod allotment. In addition, he kept 32 rabbits, 23 fowls and two pigs. Notwithstanding his considerable effort in the local community, it seems that Mr. Hearn was a good catch in the eyes of the Tribunal and he was deemed fit for service, although given a three months exemption. (With the war ending within this time frame, we can probably assume that Mr. Hearn never had to go to War.)

On 27th December 1918, the final meeting of the Military Tribunal was held. During its four years of existence, it had met 95 times and dealt with 2,499 cases. There had been 194 appeals against their decisions and in 137 instances the Tribunal's decisions had been upheld.

MAJOR FRANK WIDENHAM GOODDEN (1889-1917)

Major Goodden, RFC

In January 1917 the Courier reported the death of Major Frank Goodden, RFC. A former pupil of King Charles' School, Major Goodden started his flying career in balloons and airships and had taken part in the Hendon Air Show. He became one of the first airmen to loop the loop and held the record for 14 loops in a row and was reported to have performed aerobatics over Tunbridge Wells.

His flying skills led to him being appointed in 1915 as chief test pilot for the Royal Aircraft factory at Farnborough. Major Gooden was killed in a crash at Farnborough whilst flying one of the first prototype S.E.5s, which broke up in flight. In his short career, and aged just 26 when he died, he had been responsible for making the first flight in six new prototype planes. He is buried in Aldershot Military Cemetery.

OTHER NEWS/EVENTS
The following brief extracts from the *Courier* reflect other events in the town in 1918:

JANUARY
3rd A call from all church denominations for pubs to be closed on 6th January – the day appointed by the King for national prayer. The Licensed Traders Association said it would be resented by their members.
11th A meeting of the War Emergency Workers called for rationing. Letters from the National Union of War Emergency Workers were read out which complained about profiteering. One example was the cost of clothing where it was considered that the quality had fallen by 50% and the price had increased by a similar percentage. The Union had sent a deputation to the Food Controller in which they had expressed consternation at the dangers of shortages of meat and called on Government to assume immediate control over all farms.
A meeting of the Tunbridge Wells Branch of the National Union of Women Workers chaired by the President, Lady Coote, reported on the work carried out in the town by women in the various canteens and in the town

laundry. It was reported that in the previous year the laundry had washed the clothes of 40,000 soldiers.

MARCH
15th Royal Society for the Protection of Birds (RSPB) raiseds concern at vanishing woodlands. It was reported that members of the Canadian Forestry Camp were busy planting trees to replace the ones they had cut down.

APRIL
26th A meeting of the Workers' Educational Association was held at the Town Hall to discuss 'After War Reconstruction'. Not surprisingly the talk had a strong political message with the speaker, a Mr. Henderson Pringle from the University of London, saying there were three essentials that needed to be put in place - there must be an increase in real wealth; there must be a better distribution of wealth and the system of wealth production and distribution must be more democratic.

MAY
10th Due to concern over measles and whooping cough, Empire Day celebrations for children cancelled.
Appeals were lodged by local butchers to Military Tribunal that no further men be taken by the military, given the shortage of butchers capable of cutting meat efficiently. One company had already closed shops and threatened a further closure. Some sympathy was expressed by the Tribunal, but only to the extent that the men in question were given a further three months' deferment.
Culverden Golf Club offered 8½ acres of the course to the Allotment Holders Association.
Letter to Editor explaining the role of Women Patrols for the benefit of those who had been critical of the scheme. These patrols were recognised by the Home Office and the Chief Constable. A subsequent letter complained of the high-handed attitude of the women police of Tunbridge Wells. The gentleman in question had been sitting on a bench on the Common with a well-known and respectable young lady resident, and when approached by the constable, they were ordered to sit further apart as they could be seen from the road. The letter was signed Yours truly, Doing his bit. The Editor's response was however far from sympathetic.

JUNE
1st Military cricket match on the higher ground – Royal West Kent v. Buffs.
Tunbridge Wells Council meeting raised question as to why three women policewomen had been appointed. The simple answer was – there were no men left. They would be paid 35 shillings weekly plus war bonus, which meant 43/6d a week and would have the same duties as men. However, they could be dismissed with a week's notice and were not entitled to a pension.

14th A meeting at the Town Hall, called by the Mayor, was reported by the *Courier* on the 14th June. The purpose of this meeting was to discuss the possibility of forming a Utility Rabbit Club. It was generally considered that every working man should breed rabbits. The Mayor commented on the large profit that could be gained from the sale of rabbits and thought that if this scheme was a success, they could move on to form Pig and Goat Clubs. It would be a remunerative business to those that joined. If for example the 3,000 present allotment holders took up the scheme, they could breed 15,000 rabbits every year which would produce £11,000 on the market. There was great support for the scheme and one speaker said that, if the council gave some of the spare land at the North End Farm and they planned in the next two weeks, by October they could grow 20 tons of swede for feed purposes.

21st Baseball introduced by Canadian military on Lower Cricket Ground. The *Courier* also records that the 'Invicta' magazine had a report of a military football match in India between a Tunbridge Wells team and a Folkestone team. The game was said to be hardly of a professional standard, but the 'Ancient Pantyles Town' team did win 3-2.

Major ERIC STUART DOUGALL VC, MC (1886-1918)

In Hawkenbury Cemetery

Born in Tunbridge Wells, lived at 'Brookside', Upper Grosvenor Road, went to Tonbridge School and Pembroke College, Cambridge, where he read Mechanical Sciences and was an Athletics Blue. He worked for the Mersey Docks & Harbour Board and Bombay Harbour Trust, joining the Bombay Light Horse in 1914 and returning to Britain in 1915 where he was commissioned in the Royal Field Artillery (Special Reserve). He was won his VC on 10th April 1918 when in command of 'A' battery, 88th Brigade RFA for 'most conspicuous bravery and skilful leadership' in the field', firing his battery of field artillery 'over the sights' at point-blank range at the advancing enemy. Maj. Dougall was killed four days later while continuing to direct the fire of his battery. He is buried at Mont Kemmel but he is also remembered on the grave of his parents, Andrew and Emily Elizabeth Dougall, which is in the Tunbridge Wells Borough (Hawkenbury) Cemetery.

JULY

By the beginning of July it was reported that the National Kitchens was running at a loss of £5 a week. Councillors discussed whether they should take over and aim to achieve a self-funding outcome. By August it was felt that the kitchens should close as they were still running at a loss. Chairman's casting vote was in favour of take-over and the kitchen and equipment were valued and purchased for a sum of £700.

12th Housing Conference held in Tunbridge Wells on the need for Housing Reform. Figures were given for the pre-war cost of an urban cottage – estimated that cost will have risen by 75% - which in money terms was an increase from 6/11d to 14/10d.

AUGUST
2nd Formation of field ambulance for service in Tunbridge Wells and Tonbridge.
Grand opening of the Great Hall. Many events held e.g. flower shows, auctions,
9th Baseball match held at the Nevill Ground between Americans and Canadians in aid of the Red Cross. The Marquis of Camden opened the event and a large crowd was in attendance. The Canadians won 7/5.
23rd At a Red Cross Sale, Lady Henry Nevill conducted an auction and amongst the items was a cloak/hood which had belonged to Florence Nightingale.
Letter from Coal Controller suggesting that evening services in churches should now be held in the afternoon and the building should be unheated. It is not known what impact this suggestion had on church attendance.
The War Records Committee of Tunbridge Wells is collecting the names of people serving their country for the purpose of creating a Town Roll of Honour. Over 3000 names had already been collected, of which 2000 were in HM Forces, the remainder being Red Cross and VAD nurses.

SEPTEMBER
6th Call by Tunbridge Wells Boy Scout Association for volunteers, as all its Scout Masters had been called-up.
13th Mr. Alfred Bishop had been proposing for the last 3 years that leaflets should be dropped over Germany. Such a raid had recently been carried out and had clearly been successful, as it was known that Hindenburg had issued a special proclamation.
Article on how not to deal with aliens. This matter had generated a fair degree of letter writing to the Editor, most of which demanded action. However, the paper did not rise to the bait and pointed out that a recent enquiry in Harrogate had established that the vast majority of aliens employed, proved to be not of enemy origin. Of 700 aliens resident, only 90 were enemy aliens and of those, only 11 were German.
The Tunbridge Wells Laundry felt the need to take an advertisement in the *Courier* to explain to their customers that their reduced collection and delivery service of now only once a week, was not of their doing, but a direct instruction from the Road Transport Board and they reproduced the Order in their advertisement to prove this.

Ration Books were introduced in October

OCTOBER
4th Reported that citizens of Tunbridge Wells have subscribed over £1m for the war through the purchase of National War Bonds.

11th Appeal by the Mayor at Fuel Economy meeting for people to use less fuel. People must shop earlier now that shops would be closing earlier and where possible people should carry their purchases home, so that shop assistants were not kept at work after shop had closed. The town was likely to receive only 75% of the fuel it received last year, so people should be prepared for this and wear more clothes.

18th Visit of Sir. Robert Baden-Powell who addressed a meeting at the Opera House. Sir Robert said he had attended Rose Hill School and remembered with fondness his days there. He spoke of the need for boys who had lost their fathers to be given the best training.

NOVEMBER
8th With the Influenza epidemic having abated in the town the authorities felt that schools should re-open. However, cinemas were still out of bounds for military and auxiliary forces.
In response to the Fuel Controller's suggestion that Sunday evening services should be cancelled, weekly services at churches have been re-arranged so that heating will no longer be used from Sunday night to Friday. This policy did not please the Rev. Parsons of St.John's who queried why places of entertainment were not similarly controlled.

15th The scene in the streets following news of the Armistice is vividly described in the *Courier*. In the view of the Editor, the celebrations did not match those which followed the news of the Relief of Mafeking. (See Chapter 11 for a more detailed description). Town bids farewell to army units as they transfer to garrison centres. Trenches in Calverley Park (used for bayonet training) were filled in.

15th Extract from *Daily Express*. The hilly grounds of Tunbridge Wells had proved difficult for the feet of recruits since the beginning of the war. The Mayor had placed a room of his private residence at the men's disposal and called it 'The Soldiers Foot Room' – here feet were 'bandaged and vaselined'. One day the Mayor looked into the room to be greeted by a soldier who asked 'Art tha t'chap as cuts corns?'

22nd Service of Thanksgiving at Holy Trinity – an estimated 2000 present.

CHRONOLOGY OF EVENTS (1918-1919)

1918

6th February — British Representation of the People Act 1918 enfranchised women over the age of 30 who had a minimum property qualification. Representation of the People Act 1928 extended the voting franchise to all women over the age of 21.

3rd March — Peace Treaty (of Brest-Litovsk) signed by *Soviet* Russia and Germany.

21st March — Start of the Kaiserschlacht (Kaiser's Battle) offensive which overran Allied defences by 40 miles but petered out in early April.

29th March — Marshal Foch appointed as Allied Commander on Western Front.

15th July — Start of Second Battle of the Marne. German Army begins to collapse.

4th October — Germany asks Allies for an Armistice.

29th October — German Navy mutinies at Wilhelmshaven and Kiel.

30th October — Turkey makes peace with Allies.

3rd November — Austria makes peace with Allies.

9th November — Kaiser Wilhelm II abdicates and is given sanctuary by neutral Holland. Proclamation of the new German Republic.

11th November — Germany signs Armistice with Allies – the effective end of the War.

1919

4th January — Peace Conference starts at Versailles.

6th February — German government and parliament is moved from Berlin to Weimar.

21st June — The surrendered German Navy scuttles itself where it is moored at Scapa Flow in the Orkney Islands.

28th June — Peace Treaty signed at Versailles. The Peace saw :
- the creation of new independent States - Austria, Hungary, Czechoslovakia and Yugoslavia;
- dismantlement of the Ottoman Empire and creation of new Middle-Eastern states: Turkey, Saudi Arabia, Iran, Iraq, Jordan, Syria, and Lebanon, Palestine (as a Protectorate) and Egypt;
- the restitution of independence to Poland, Finland, Latvia, Estonia, Lithuania and Alsace-Lorraine;
- the demilitarisation of the Rhineland, with very heavy financial reparations by Germany.

11th August — New constitution – the Weimar Constitution – announced for Germany.

Chapter 11
THE BEGINNING OF THE END - AND THE END
by Brian Lippard

The Course of the War

The collapse of Imperial Russia and its replacement by Soviet Russia, effectively led to peace between Germany and Russia. The Russian Revolution of 1917 meant that Germany now only had to fight on one front. As a result, Germany was able to withdraw over one million soldiers and 3,000 guns from the Eastern Front at the beginning of 1918 and send them to the Western Front, with the hope that this would break the stalemate which had existed for over three years.

Germany knew that it had to break the French and British lines before the flow of American troops would make this impossible and so a quick action was needed.[1] The German High Command started to plan their attack well in advance and fixed the date for it to begin as 21st March 1918. The plan was to attack on a 50 mile front and particularly at the point where the British and French Army boundaries met. The Germans were not to know until it was too late that the French were to hand over the most northerly 25 miles of their Front to the British at the end of January 1918. So the German attack would become one directed entirely at the British. The German Spring Offensive of 1918 would come to be known by a number of names. To the Germans, it was Die Kaiserschlacht (the Kaiser's Battle) and the actual Battle Plan was called Prinz Michael's; to the British, it was variously the German March Offensive, the Battle of Picardy or the Second Battle of the Somme.

The March 1918 Offensive did not come as a surprise to the British, but its scale and nature did – the sheer number of German troops, coupled with a change in their battle tactics from frontal attack on strongholds to deliberately bypassing and then surrounding them, was a new development. Further, the very heavy fog on that day favoured the attackers. The Germans swept through and gained up to 40 miles – a very large advance by the standards of the previous three years. The battle was to continue for 16 days until 5th April, when the tide was stemmed and subsequently turned.

---

[1] While the USA had entered the War in April 1917, it took a long time for it to gear up its forces and send them to Europe. On 20th March 1918, there were just six US divisions on the Western Front, compared with 98 French Divisions, 47 British, 10 British Empire and 2 Portuguese - a total of 169 Allied Divisions against 192 German Divisions. By 1st March 1918, some 290, 000 US soldiers had landed in France, but few were as yet in the front-line. By October 1918, the number of US soldiers in France had increased to 1,760,000.

For the whole period of this Battle, British casualties were estimated at 160,000 - 22,000 killed, an unprecedented 75,000 taken prisoner by the Germans and 63,000 wounded – while German casualties were estimated at 250,000, with a much higher proportion of dead, which is inevitable for any attacking force.

Following the failure of Prinz Michael's Plan, the Western Front became a much more fluid battlefield; and helped by the arrival of US Forces, the end of the War would come in just seven months. Afterwards, the 20th March, the day before the battle commenced, was widely described as *'the last day of trench warfare in the First World War'*. This is not strictly true, but is true enough, in the sense that the War on the Western Front would never be the same again.

However, the inhabitants of Tunbridge Wells were not to know that the War would end within seven months, nor should it be said, were the Allied Generals aware of this either. All the inhabitants knew was that
- there were food and fuel shortages;
- a previously unheard-of and complicated restriction called 'rationing' had been introduced;
- the regulations imposed by DORA were still in force, as were lighting and other restrictions;
- and they had fears (absolutely unfounded in reality) that they would be bombed into oblivion by Zeppelins or the new Gotha GIV bombers.

The Spanish 'Flu'.
The other major but largely-not-understood intrusion into the lives of the populace of Tunbridge Wells up to the Armistice (and beyond), was the unexpected arrival of what was a particularly virulent and previously unknown form of the influenza virus, which would subsequently become popularly known as "the Spanish 'flu'", although this name was not widely known or used at the time.

It was an unusually deadly influenza virus which would become a worldwide pandemic and last from January 1918 - December 1920, making it one of the deadliest natural disasters in history. It is now estimated that it killed between 50-100 million people - 3-5% of the world's population at the time – which was many times more than **all** the casualties of the First World War. Unlike the War, it would continue into 1919 and 1920.

It is also estimated that 10% - 20% of those who were infected died. To maintain morale, wartime censors minimized early reports of illness and mortality in Germany, Britain, France, and the United States.

In Britain, the pandemic had largely died out by April 1919, but it has been estimated that as many as 250,000 died of it; 4,496 of these were in Kent; but Tunbridge Wells seems to have got away with much lower figures, both absolutely and proportionately, as the following Table extracted from the Annual Reports of the Town's Medical Officer of Health, (with a comparison for pneumonia), shows:

Year	No. of deaths*	From Influenza	From Pneumonia	'Flu as % of Deaths
1917	465	10	31	2.1
1918	544	97	23	17.8
1919	479	31	23	6.5
1920	450	19	25	4.2

* among civilian residents

Certainly there was a significant increase in the number of civilian deaths in 1918 and there was also a significant increase in *the proportion* of deaths due to 'flu. However, it was a relatively minor hiccup in the long-term demographics of the town.

It is clear that Tunbridge Wells residents did not appreciate at the time that they were part of a world-wide pandemic; they thought that they were suffering from a particularly nasty 'overdose' of what was a regular feature of the town's illnesses. In Tunbridge Wells, this surge lasted approximately five weeks – 74 of the 97 deaths from 'flu in 1918 occurred between the weeks ending 26th October and 9th December. The numbers of deaths in each of these weeks was twenty, thirty, twelve, four and eight.

Hence it is probably not surprising that there was comparatively little comment on it at the time. There is no reference to the epidemic in any Council minutes of 1918 or 1919, although they did issue an advisory leaflet in October (see next page for a copy). Neither were there many articles in the press. Whilst individual notifications of death in the *Courier* might include a reference to influenza, there was nothing to suggest that this was anything out of the ordinary, unless the sharp-eyed reader spotted this sentence tucked away in the *Courier* of 26th July 1918 under the heading "Skinners' Day at Tonbridge": *"There was not so large a gathering as in former years, the prevalence of influenza no doubt having an effect in this direction".* The topic as such was not mentioned in the News sections until 18th October 1918 and, even then, it simply said: *"The Elementary Schools of the borough have been closed for a fortnight as a precautionary measure against the influenza infection. The Sunday Schools will also be closed for two Sundays".* The Opera House was forced to advertise that it would be closed until further notice at the beginning of November. However, it was able to re-open a week later.

"Spanish Flu"

(Prevention is better than Cure).

Doctor Mackenzie's
INFLUENZA TONIC

Is a sure Preventative of this distressing Malady and will also cure and relieve the worst cases of Influenza, Cold in the Head, Shivering, Feverishness, Running at the Eyes and Nose, Pains in the Back and Limbs, Prostration and General Weakness.

Only obtainable at

PEARMUND,
Chemist,
17, Calverley Rd., Tun. Wells.

Price 1/1½, 2/9, 4/6 per bot.

Courier, 25th June, 1918.

Influenza

Bovril Ltd. wish to express their regret at the shortage of Bovril during the recent Influenza epidemic.

The proprietors of Bovril, recognizing that those who are deprived of the body-building powers of Bovril may more easily fall victims to the epidemic, have done their utmost to increase the supply, but the lack of bottles has seriously hampered—and still hampers—their endeavours. Efforts are being made to collect empty bottles, and it is hoped that supplies will soon be increased by the release of men for the bottle factories.

It is suggested that those consumers who have a stock of Bovril should avoid purchasing at present, and thus leave the available Bovril for those who have more pressing need of it at this critical time.

Courier 29th November 1918.
A somewhat subtle advertising approach, relating to the 'Spanish 'Flu'.

BOROUGH OF TUNBRIDGE WELLS.
INFLUENZA.

WARNING.—The Person attacked by INFLUENZA who does not take precautions runs grave risks himself and may be a source of danger to others.

INFLUENZA IS A SERIOUS DISEASE AND IS HIGHLY INFECTIOUS. Infection is always caught through DIRECT CONTACT with a person suffering from the disease. A very severe attack may be caught from a person who has it in a mild form. The patient is MOST INFECTIOUS AT THE BEGINNING OF THE ILLNESS.

PRECAUTIONS. TRY TO PROTECT YOURSELF AND OTHERS.

HOW TO AVOID ATTACK.

General Rules.

(1) **Protect Your Health.** Remember if you protect your health, your health will protect you.

(2) **Cleanliness and Moderation.** Lead a clean, simple, natural life. Avoid excesses of all kinds; the immoderate drinker stands a poor chance if Pneumonia follows Influenza.

(3) **Fresh Air and Ventilation.** Be in the open air as much as possible, and get all the fresh air that can be got into the living and sleeping rooms by opening the windows wide and often.

Special Rules.

(1) **Follow the General Rules.** When Influenza is prevalent remember these three Rules.

(2) **Avoid Overcrowded Places.** The risks are greatest where there are crowds of people and ventilation is poor. Keep away from crowded meetings and places of amusement. Walk rather than travel in crowded trains, trams or 'buses.

(3) **Avoid Infected Houses and People.** Avoid altogether as much as possible any house where there are cases of Influenza. Keep at as great a distance as convenient when talking to anyone suffering from a cold in the head or a feverish cold.

(4) **The Path of Infection.** Remember the infection gets into the body by the mouth and nose, and when Influenza is prevalent there is risk of breathing-in infection in most places of public resort.

(5) **A Clean Mouth and Teeth.** At these times be careful to keep the mouth clean. See that the teeth are sound. Use the tooth-brush night and morning. Wash out the mouth and gargle the throat.

(6) **A Mouth Wash.** Warm water containing a little salt and Condy's Fluid may be used.

(7) **Keep the Nostrils Clean.** The nostrils may also be washed out by snuffing the mixture from the palm of the hand and expelling it through the mouth.

P.T.O.

HOW TO PROTECT YOURSELF IF ATTACKED.

Pneumonia, Heart Failure, and Consumption often follow Influenza

(1) **Isolation**. Every new attack is a source of danger to yourself and others. Go to bed at once in a well-aired room and send for the Doctor.

(2) **Avoid Draughts.** The influenza patient should be kept warm and protected from draughts. The mouth and nose may be covered as described.

(3) **The Doctor and the Nurse.** In bad cases medical advice is essential, careful nursing may be necessary. In such cases the patient should be as completely isolated as arrangements in the home allow.

(4) **Prevent Complications.** After the illness and fever have gone, chill and exertion should be avoided.

HOW TO PROTECT OTHERS.

The Infected Person can and must Avoid Spreading Infection.

(1) **Remain Indoors.** The proper place for a person with Influenza is indoors. He is a source of danger to others. Public places and meetings should be avoided as far as possible.

(2) **Sneezing and Coughing.** When he sneezes or coughs, the infected person discharges infection that others may breathe, especially if the material coughed up is carelessly spat out.

(3) **Shield the Mouth.** In coughing and sneezing the mouth and nose should be shielded with a handkerchief or otherwise. The handkerchief should not be carelessly left about and should be kept out of the reach of children.

(4) **Destroy Expectoration.** Material coughed up should be received in a special vessel and afterwards disinfected or burned.

All these Rules apply equally well to a "Cold in the Head." When Influenza is prevalent any feverish cold may be Influenza and for the sake of the Sufferer and the Public should be considered Influenza.

Further information may be obtained from the undersigned.

5, Calverley Parade,
Tunbridge Wells,
October, 1918.

WM. STAMFORD,
Acting Medical Officer of Health.

SHAW & SONS, Printers and Publishers, 7 & 8 Fetter Lane, London, E.C.4

The Armistice and shortly after

In common with the rest of the country, Tunbridge Wells had very little warning of the Armistice. Technically, it was only a suspension of fighting but everybody knew that it was the End of the War. It was signed between 5.12 and 5.20 am in a railway carriage in Compiegne and its first condition was that fighting would cease at 11am on Monday 11 November 1918, _Paris time_. At 10.20am GMT the British Prime Minister issued the official communique saying "hostilities are (sic) to cease on all fronts at 11 a.m".

Lady Matthews' Diary records _"This has been a truly Great Day....in a very few minutes...the town burst mysteriously into bunting. Flags and banners were showing everywhere – the children were all released from School, the soldiers freed from drill and everyone greeted everyone else with smiles and sometimes tears. It was the gayest and most thrilling time. The Mayor proclaimed Peace from the Town Hall at midday"._

'Quick off the mark' advertising by Waymark

The crowds began to collect, mainly in Calverley Road. Church bells were rung, bunting appeared, flags were waved, the choruses of popular songs were sung and the boys in blue from the V.A.D hospitals organised their own procession. In the evening the arc street lamps were lighted in the main thoroughfares, regardless of any views the Fuel Controller might have had. A number of coloured fires were lit and rockets were discharged. Many squibs and crackers were let off in the crowd, but there were no reports of any injuries.

Quiet prevailed in other parts of the town and lighting restrictions remained in force, although the Pantiles was able to benefit from one bright spot in the Y.M.C.A headquarters. Apparently the nearby inhabitants were relieved that no "mafficking" took place.

Large crowds gathered throughout the day at the _Courier's_ office to read the terms of the Armistice which had been telephoned from London.

The Mayor invited the populace to observe the following day, Tuesday 12th as a public holiday; and to join in a service of thanksgiving at the Lower Cricket Ground on that day. Despite the short notice, a procession was hurriedly organised to leave from the Town Hall in Calverley Road.

The Crowds on 12th. November 1918 in Tunbridge Wells

"The favourite chorus of "the boys" (young soldiers) appeared to be "Old soldiers never die; they only fade away" but these exuberant lads displayed no signs of evanescence. In fact, one section of "the boys" who took up a position immediately behind the Mayor and Corporation proved so exuberant that, coupled with a recalcitrant donkey in a coster's barrow, which also asserted a right to join in the tail of the procession, there was some danger of civic dignity being gravely compromised but for the tactful persuasion of Chief Constable Prior."

It was reported that thousands of people - a bigger crowd than even for the Coronation or Jubilee celebrations at the same place - packed into the natural amphitheatre around the platform on the Lower Cricket Ground. This memorable occasion concluded with the band playing "Rule, Britannia" and the National Anthem into which the vast concourse loyally joined.

However, in one family, the news was greeted with proper decorum. One Tunbridge Wells inhabitant recalls how her mother, aged six at the time, met the telegraph boy in the road who told her the news. She ran home where her siblings were being taught by their nanny in the nursery. She burst into the room with `the War's over`. Nanny said: `Go out, shut the door, knock and come in properly`. Manners must not to be ignored!

Churches held thanksgiving services on Sunday 17th November; with the Mayor and Corporation attending at Holy Trinity Church.

Other local organisations marked the Armistice. The Y.M.C.A's Anniversary gathering took place on the afternoon of 27th November. The Mayor took the chair and said that on behalf of the town he desired to express the utmost appreciation of the work accomplished by the YMCA. He had been struck with the enjoyment of the soldiers of the entertainments provided. On the same day Dr. Barnado's organised a Grand Bazaar.

Castle Hotel, London Road

The first Victory Dinner in Tunbridge Wells was that organised by the Farmers' Club held on 29th November at the Castle Hotel. In pride of place stood a plough with the caption "The weapon that helped the home front!!" This was sold on the evening with the proceeds going to the British Farmers' Red Cross Sale Fund. It was a curious auction in that everyone who bid had to pay what they had bid, whether they won or not. The President claimed ownership with his bid of 20 guineas. £114 6s was raised.

The toasts and resolutions proposed, and the vocabulary they used, at this Dinner are indicative of the mood of the time, which may seem a little 'over the top' one hundred years later.

The Mayor proposed the first toast: *"The Imperial Forces of the Crown, our Allies and the United States of America"* and immediately confessed he couldn't find the appropriate words which were sufficiently adequate to express our feelings towards the soldiers and sailors.

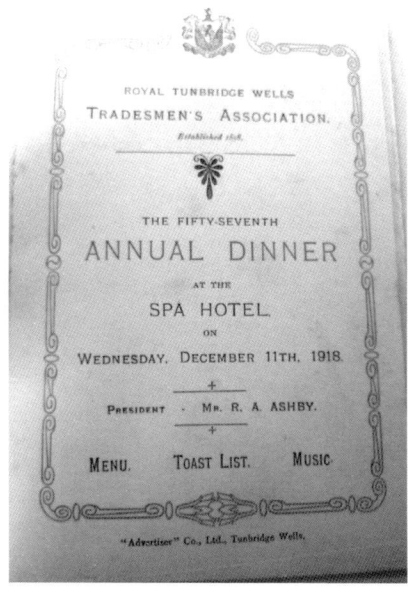

The President then moved two resolutions:
That this meeting begs to offer to your beloved Majesty their heartfelt loyalty and warm congratulations on the successful termination of hostilities and to echo the hope you expressed on the occasion of your visit to the French capital that the union of hearts and mutual trust amongst the Allies may co-ordinate with and secure the future peace, happiness and prosperity of the world.

That this meeting begs to tender its hearty congratulations and grateful thanks to the Prime Minister, Admiral Beatty, Sir Douglas Haig and the President of the Board of Agriculture for the increasing care, trouble and interest they have at all times evinced during the great war, for the exceedingly valuable part they have taken in moulding the defence of the Empire and on the successful and victorious termination of hostilities.

Colonel H. H. Spender-Clay CMG, MC, JP, prospective parliamentary candidate, was present. Whether this had anything to do with many of the subsequent speakers pleading the case for agriculture is unclear.

The Tunbridge Wells Tradesmen's Association decided to celebrate the war's end by reviving its Annual Dinner at the Spa Hotel on Wednesday 11 December at 5.45pm. Its President was R(eginald) A(rthur) Ashby, who owned butcher's shops at 54 Calverley Road, 45 Church Road and 9 Ye Pantiles. Shortly before it was due to take place, the secretary, Mr H O Gilliam, became aware of a potential embarrassment and issued a dire warning to all its members. The *Courier* of 6th December 1918 reported:

> "A wartime difficulty has arisen in connection with the revival of the annual dinner of the Tunbridge Wells Tradesmen's Association next week. The members had been notified that they must send one half-coupon for meat with their application for a dinner ticket, but it now transpires that under the National Rationing Order, each member must produce his ration book at the dinner table. The possibility of an absent-minded member of the Association immersed in public affairs sitting down to dinner minus his properly filled up ration book in his swallow-tail and having to feast in Barmecedian style was so distressing that the Secretary has specially notified every member through the post of what he must do if he would dine adequately next Wednesday."

The speeches after the dinner were all about thanksgiving, rather than celebration. After the usual loyal toast, the Ven. Archdeacon A T Scott, Vicar of St. James's Church, set the tone. *The Advertiser* reported:

> "He rose to propose no toast, and in accord with no precedent, for they were living in unprecedented times, and in accord with no custom. Such times of rejoicing were never known, not only for the mighty things done for them and the Allies, under the providence of God, but also for what they had been delivered from; but great as their rejoicing was, there was a cloud. The victory was great, the cost had been great; great in money, great in the setback to civilisation all wars caused, great in the cost of life; and at this time he asked them to think of those who had lain down their lives that they might live, and whose name would be revered for evermore. He would ask them to rise in a moment, "lest we forget".

Many societies such as the Oddfellows, the Druids (Ancient Order of) and the Buffaloes (R.A.O.B) continued with their regular weekly, fortnightly or monthly meetings. Newspaper reports of their activities are limited, but some at least are known to have stood and remembered those of their number who were no longer with them. For others, life appeared to continue as usual, which is indicated by the following selection of the *Courier's* reports from the last three Fridays in November 1918:

- The lady members of the Nevill Golf Club called a special meeting at 86 High St., to elect a new Honorary Secretary.

- The University Extension Association decided to proceed with its lecture about the USA on the afternoon of 12th November at the Technical Institute (now the Adult Education Institute), despite few attending due to so many townspeople celebrating outside.
- The Workers Educational Association held a talk at the Town Hall on the League of Nations.
- The British Women's Temperance Association held a pleasant gathering to discuss "Women's Work in National and Local Government".
- The Women's Citizens Association met in the Town Hall. After rapidly reviewing the marvellous progress of women's enfranchisement during the four years of the war, they drew attention to the fact that three local Women's Societies – the Women's Suffrage Society, the National Council of Women and the Women's Citizen Association – were forwarding to the candidates for Parliamentary election in the constituency, sets of questions specially touching on the interests of women, and that it was intended to insert the replies in the local Press.
- The Natural History and Philosophical Society held a lecture entitled "Modern Poetry" at the Literary Society's rooms in the Pantiles.
- The Mount Pleasant Young Peoples' Union held a lecture on the life of Christina Rossetti.
- The Gardeners' Association held their fortnightly meeting; W. Schmidt was awarded 1½ points for a dish of turnips. Two weeks later he was awarded 2½ points for a dish of leeks.
- The Shop Assistants' Association met at the Town Hall where unity was urged, as this was felt to be the best way to re-attain the level of pre-war wages.
- The Fanciers Association met at the Friendly Societies Hall where Mr. Young won several prizes including "Likeliest layer, not pure bred" and "Best 4th hen".
- A farewell military whist drive and concert was held at King Charles' Church Hall under the auspices of the 4th Queen's. This taxed the building's capacity to the utmost.
- The Nevill Golf Club organised a smoking concert in aid of club funds in the spacious billiard room of the Kent & Sussex Club. "True conviviality and complete enjoyment" marked the gathering. "The jollity and abandon which was manifest created the welcome atmosphere of pre-war days".
- The Hairdressers' Association met at the Friendly Society's Hall. As a thanksgiving offering for the termination of the war, they decided to give a donation to the "Wilson Benevolent Fund". They also agreed to suspend business on Boxing Day as well as Christmas Day.

The 1918 General Election

The General Election took place on Saturday 14th December 1918. It had been planned before the end of the War was known and would be the first election in which all men, and also women over the age of 30 who met a minimum property qualification, could vote.[2]

As can be seen from his poster, the Coalition candidate was not afraid to use the war to further his candidacy.

The result of the election was
Colonel Spender-Clay	(Coalition)	14,622
Jack Palmer	(Labour)	5,006
T F Buxton	(Liberal)	1,851

Herbert Henry Spender-Clay, born 1875, was first elected in 1910 as the MP for what was then the Tunbridge division which included Tunbridge Wells. Boundary changes in 1918 meant this division was replaced by the Tonbridge Division which Spender-Clay would represent until his death in 1937.[3]

---

[2] In 1928 the voting franchise was extended to all women over the age of 21.
[3] Tunbridge Wells would not become an independent Parliamentary constituency until 1974.

Declaration of Peace

Whilst the Armistice had become effective on 11th November 1918, Britain was still formally at war with Germany until the Treaty of Versailles was signed on 28th June 1919. The Mayor, Robert Gower read the official Proclamation of Peace on 3rd July 1919, standing on a Russian armoured car outside the Town Hall in Calverley Street.

**Reading the Proclamation of Peace.
Note the Macebearer in full regalia (below).**

PEACE CELEBRATION, JULY 19th, 1919.

HIS WORSHIP THE MAYOR.
(ALDERMAN R. VAUGHAN GOWER, O.B.E.)

THE MAYORESS.

Peace Day and the Peace Procession

In May 1919, as it became clear that the declaration of peace was imminent, the government started to give thought as to how the country should celebrate the formal cessation of hostilities. They decided that there would be a Peace Day which was to be held on Saturday 19th July 1919. The central event would be a Victory Parade through London. Other cities and towns were encouraged to celebrate in whatever way they saw fit. Tunbridge Wells decided to hold a Peace Procession through the town with many other activities occurring throughout the day.

- 8am — Bell ringing in all churches
- 10.30am — A Monster Grand Procession culminating in a service on the Lower Cricket Ground
- 11am — Kent v Hampshire cricket match at the Nevill Ground
- 2 – 4pm — Children's entertainments
- 2.30pm — Athletic Sports and Gymkhana in the grounds of the Rusthall V.A.D hospital
- 2.30pm — Old English sports on the Lower Cricket Ground
- 4.30pm — Children's tea
- 6pm — Grand concert and Festival of Song in the Great Hall Grounds
- 8.30pm — Grand Fancy Dress Carnival
- 10pm — Monster Beacon Bonfire on the Common near the Queen's Grove (by official instruction, the Beacon fires were to be lit throughout the Kingdom at the same hour)

The arch erected at the top of Mount Pleasant

The Peace Procession at the bottom of Mount Pleasant

At 6pm, competitors in the carnival were due to assemble near the Spa Hotel. Although by now it was raining in torrents, many brave contestants, including some in the flimsiest of fancy costumes, put in an appearance. The Mayor said he couldn't risk injuring competitors' health so he announced that judging would be postponed until Wednesday and suggested entrants went home immediately to change. The rain then ceased for a short period, so it was decided that the procession and judging of the cars could take place.

With the premature end of the carnival, there seemed a danger that the events on the common would fall flat. However, the Town Band started to play and three of the Day's organisers were inspired to suggest an impromptu dance. The Band agreed to play dance music and in no time at all a ring was cleared and couples were tripping to the strains of the Band. Many deck flares were lit as it grew dark and towards 11o'clock, Verey lights and rockets were fired in large numbers. At 11 o'clock, the Beacon was lit, those at Frant and Crowborough being already clearly visible.

Hurrah for England!
A Patriotic Song
Tune: British Grenadiers

Hurrah! hurrah! for England,
Till woods and valleys ring,
Hurrah! for good old England,
Hurrah for England's King.
Strong ships are on her waters;
Firm friends upon her shores,
Peace, peace within her borders,
And plenty in her stores.

Right joyously we're singing,
We're glad to make it known
That we love the land we live in,
And our King upon the throne.
Then hurrah! for merry England;
And may we daily sing
The triumphs of our country
And praises of our King.

Originally written for children by M A Stodart in Queen Victoria's reign.

The concert took place on the following Wednesday in the Calverley Park Meadow. The *Courier* reported that "The children's choir alternated with the Peace choir in patriotic selections which floated in musical cadence across the valley". Just before the Mayor gave his speech, "See the Conquering Hero Comes", and **"Hurrah for England"** were sung. The crowd joined in the two concluding anthems: "The Hallelujah Chorus" and the National Anthem.

The Peace Procession programme announced that "A Handsome Souvenir Medal with special design, embodying the Arms of Tunbridge Wells, will be presented to each child, but it is regretted that owing to the shortness of time it will be impossible to present them on Peace Day, but it is hoped to do so in the near future." It is not known when they were actually issued, nor how many and to whom.

A photo of the medallion issued, is shown right. It was made of gilt bronze and bears a maker's mark of 'JRG'[4]. The obverse depicts the figure of Britannia standing frontal with

---

[4] J. R. Gaunt & Son Ltd (1899-2013) were medallists, bronzists, silversmiths, enamellists, die-stamping, manufacturers of badges, buttons, swords, and souvenirs.

her right hand holding an olive branch and her left hand holding a dove with 'Peace' below. The allied nations of 'Britain, France, Italy and Belgium' are given around the edge. On the reverse is the title "Borough of Royal Tunbridge Wells" "Vaughan Gower Mayor" and the Coat of Arms of the town with the motto "Do Well Doubt Not" and "1919".

To

The Mayor, Aldermen & Inhabitants
of the
Borough of Royal Tunbridge Wells
welcome you home after your service with his Majesty's Forces in the Great European War.

It is due to the self-sacrifice and gallantry of you and your Comrades in Arms that the British Empire and its Allies have been victorious, and this memento is presented to you as a token of the appreciation and the regard in which you are held by your fellow townsmen.

Dated this Nineteenth day of July, One Thousand Nine Hundred and Nineteen.

Mayor.

The programme also announced that the entertainment of wounded and disabled sailors and soldiers was postponed due to the shortness of time. However they would be entertained, along with other returning servicemen, at a 'Welcome Home' Reception, Banquet and Entertainment which had to be given four times, on 19th, 20th, 21st, and 22nd August 1919 to accommodate them all, since the Pump Room where it was held, could only accommodate 600 at a time. All those attending were given a personalised Certificate of Appreciation from the Mayor, Aldermen, and Inhabitants of Tunbridge Wells. (See left).

One of the four Banquets. Note the Japanese flag in the background, which was there because Japan was an ally of the West in the First World War.

A Drumhead Memorial Service[5] was held on Sunday 17th August 1919 on the Lower Cricket Ground. A big muster of wounded, discharged and demobilised members of His Majesty's Armed Forces were led by the Veterans' Band which marched from the Town Hall to the Common. The Advertiser reported there was a "Great Gathering on the Common".

Remembrance Day and Remembrance Sunday
The first Remembrance Day, which was initially known as Armistice Day, is now recognised as having occurred on 11th November 1919. On 7th November 1919, King George V issued a proclamation asking that "…..all locomotion should cease, so that, in perfect stillness, the thoughts of everyone may be concentrated on reverent remembrance of the glorious dead."

The first Remembrance Sunday as we now know it, i.e. at 11am on the second Sunday in November, with a Service and March Past at the Cenotaph, did not actually take place until 1945. From 1919 until 1945 the Remembrance Service was held on Armistice Day itself. However, a Remembrance Sunday took place on Sunday 4th August 1918 when special services were held at churches to mark the anniversary of the *outbreak* of the war. In Tunbridge Wells there was a Civic Procession to and from Holy Trinity Church. This consisted of the Mayor, the Deputy Mayor, Aldermen and Councillors, the Town Clerk and borough Officials, the Borough Magistrates, Detachments of the Military Regiments stationed in the town, the local Corps of Kent Volunteers, the Borough Police, Firemen and Ambulance Corps, a detachment of the W.A.A.C., representatives of Friendly Societies and other local Associations, together with the Band of the Royal West Kent Regiment.

Remembrance Day is now only known in its role of honouring the fallen in the First World War and subsequent conflicts. This was not always the case. In 1921 some ex-servicemen, angry at the lack of opportunity and support they had received since returning home and disagreeing with continued concentration on the dead when survivors needed help, disrupted the service at the Cenotaph and this was repeated throughout the 1920s. At the same time, some young people began holding celebrations on November 11th to celebrate the fact that the war was over and they could have fun once again, although this had begun to decline in favour of more sombre events by the mid-1920s. From the poster shown on the next page, it would seem that Tunbridge Wells saw the first

---

[5] A Drumhead Service is a church service held "in the field" during armed conflict, where no church is available and where drums grouped together served as the altar.

anniversary of the Armistice at least as an occasion for Celebration, rather than one of Remembrance. The significance of Remembrance came later.

BOROUGH OF
ROYAL TUNBRIDGE WELLS

Armistice Day

November 11th, 1919.

THE MAYOR

(Sir Robert Gower, O.B.E.), and

THE MAYOR-ELECT

(Councillor H. A. Latimer, M.D.)

Appeal to the Public to Display

FLAGS AND BUNTING

on their Houses and Business Premises on the Anniversary of the Signing of the Armistice, November 11th.

Saunders, Tun. Wells, Ltd.

The Presentation Tank

The preceding chapter mentioned the Town's War Savings Campaign to raise £250,000 for tanks. In 1919 the Government was faced with the problem of what to do with its surplus tanks. It decided to give one to each of the 265 towns on a "Silver List". These were the ones who had raised the most money per capita in the 1918 Tank Week. It is not recorded how many the government gave away, but estimates suggest about 400.

Not everyone in Tunbridge Wells was thrilled at the prospect of receiving such a present and some towns declined it, although others not on the original list were given one. At its meeting on Wednesday 4th June 1919, the Royal Tunbridge Wells Council debated the proposal to accept a tank and where to position it. The first two speakers made clear their positions:

> Councillor Emson (the Mayor from 1913-1917) said it was not in the best interests of the town that the Tank should be placed opposite the Post Office. It was a very ugly thing, and he thought the Grove would be a far better place for it.

> Councillor Brown: *'Better have it buried, sir.'* (laughter); and later in the debate: *'It would be one of the biggest mistakes if they had this horrible creature in the Grove. It would necessitate another Grove attendant to keep the children off it.'*

The Presentation of the Tank took place at 3pm on Wednesday 30th July and was astutely linked in as part of a further War Savings Week to raise

more money for the Government. Tunbridge Wells was given an ex-training "female" tank (meaning it had no machine guns), no. I 31, the Roman I indicating that it had been with I Battalion of the newly-formed Tank Corps. [6]

The Tank made a disappointingly uneventful journey into Tunbridge Wells. It set off at 1 pm from Goods Station Road, where it had been unloaded, and went by Norman Road, Stanley Road, Camden Road, Monson Road, York Road and London Road as far as Richmond Terrace. It had performed no circus tricks. It had not even butted any civic dignitary marching in front of it. In view of this, the Mayor asked the officer in charge if it could demonstrate its ability to climb any obstacle in its path. "Why certainly" came the reply and the tank immediately proceeded to climb the steep bank up to the Common scattering all before it and vanished from sight. It then reappeared at the top of the slope; a gap in the crowd opened, the tank poised itself on the skyline before plunging down the precipitous slope to reach its final resting place.

The Tank on the Common

As its detractors predicted, the tank was largely ignored and inexorably deteriorated to become a rusting eyesore. It was sold for scrap in 1937.

But it had become a tourist souvenir for Tunbridge Wells.

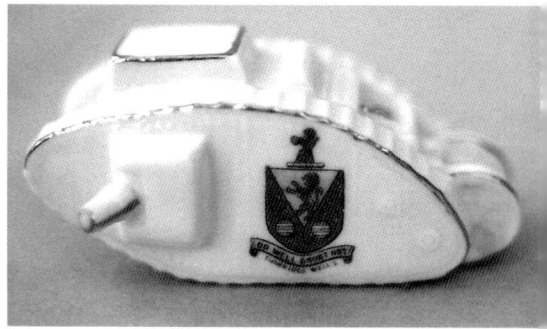

---

[6] I Battalion subsequently became the 9th Bttn, of the Tank Corps and in the Second World War, the 9th Royal Tank Regiment.

The War Memorial

By the end of January 1919, much thought had been given as to what form the town's memorial should take. Ideas ranged widely and were not restricted to a stone and/or sculpted War Memorial. The six principal proposals were:
- An extra ward to be added to the General Hospital.
- A special commemorative tower be incorporated into the new YMCA building at Ye Fiveways.
- A Public Library.[7]
- A Regular Memorial.
- Houses for the widows and orphans of the men who had fallen.
- A Winter Garden, or a Band Pavilion.

The Council convened a public meeting on Wednesday 2nd April 1919 to discuss how to proceed. By then, only the first five of the above ideas were put forward for consideration. Each option had its passionate supporters. During the debate, Cllr. Dr. Latimer made what was to become the crucial argument which resulted in the subsequent choice of a Regular Memorial. He said "Excellent schemes had been advocated but they failed in one point. They were memorials to the Great War, but not memorials to the men who had served in the Great War".

In May 1921 the Council decided to have a Memorial built and invited interested architects to submit their ideas. The design chosen for the monument was by the architect Stanley Nicholson Babb (1874-1957), which consisted of a stone plinth upon which was mounted a bronze statue of a WW1 soldier carrying a rifle, with an inscription placed on the plinth. Extending from its central position in the overall monument was a back wall upon which the bronze plaques bearing the names of the fallen from WW 1 were mounted, with a left and right wing of stone extending out towards the pavement of Mount Ephraim.

The memorial was unveiled by Colonel Viscount Hardinge on 11th February 1923 with the Guard of Honour being provided by the 4th Battalion, The Queen's Own Royal West Kent Regiment. From the roof of a house in Calverley Parade, buglers sounded the Last Post and Reveille. The event was attended by well over 1,000 people.

On 9th June 2011, British Heritage gave the monument a Grade II listing.

---

[7] The Town Council took over the Dudley Institute (a reading room on the southern corner of Dudley Road and Mount Pleasant) as a public Library on 21st May 1921.

The Unveiling Ceremony, 11th February 1923

St. Augustine's Church with the Crucifix War Memorial on outside wall

Many other memorials were placed in churches and schools. One of these, on the outside wall of St. Augustine's Church (which was then in Grosvenor Road opposite the hospital) was possibly the first Memorial in the country to be unveiled following the Armistice. It caused considerable controversy. On 7th July 1918, the parish priest, Canon Keatinge, had asked for donations so that a Memorial could be erected on the outside church wall. This was quickly oversubscribed and a large wooden Crucifix, which is what the Memorial was, was delivered on 17th November.

The Low Church/anti-Catholic element in the Town expressed grave concerns about it and said (amongst other things) that it "would frighten the horses". The unveiling and dedication were fixed for 11th December 1918, just one month after the Armistice. Threats were made to set the memorial on fire. The Canon astutely invited the Mayor, whose wife was a Catholic, to unveil the Memorial knowing that the attendance of the Mayor would automatically ensure a police presence. Although the event passed off without any trouble, it was not the end of opposition.

A detailed petition was presented to the Council in May 1919 requesting "the removal of the image purporting to be part of a war shrine". Five key arguments were put forward which are summarised below:
- The image was a breach of God's Commandment about 'graven images';
- It was an offence against a law of 1822 and a Proclamation by Queen Victoria in 1852;
- It constitutes a scandal, offence and public insult to Protestants;
- It was liable to cause a breach of the peace and destruction of property;
- It was likely to cause a depreciation in the value of adjoining properties.

The Mayor thanked Canon Stather Hunt (Vicar of Holy Trinity Church)[8] for what he said was the extremely moderate way in which he had presented his case. He felt sure they would acquit him of any discourtesy

---

[8] A full transcript of the petition and Canon Hunt's address to the meeting can be viewed in the Gower Scrapbook for May 1919, which is held in the Tunbridge Wells Reference Library.

when he ruled that the matter was not one on which the Council could pass any resolution.

Cllr. T. Edwards managed to interject *"It is a deliberate insult to every Protestant in the town"* before the Mayor moved the meeting onto the next item of business. However, Cllr. Edwards was in no mood to give up and at the next meeting when the Minutes of the previous Meeting came up for approval, he demanded the right to address the Council on the issue – an action which the Council and the media said was unprecedented. Cllr. Foster joined Cllr. Edwards in protesting. It must have been a dramatic occasion. The Mayor asked Cllr. Edwards no less than four times to sit down and Cllr. Edwards refused, so the Mayor adjourned the meeting and when it reconvened about ten minutes later with Cllr. Edwards absent, the Minutes were approved unanimously and without comment.

Lieutenant Richard Prankerd – the last resident of Tunbridge Wells to be killed in action in the First World War.

Photo:
Courtesy: Repton School

Born in 1895, Richard lived with his widowed mother and aunt at Fairlawn, St. James Road. In 2014, although much altered and extended, this house still stands and is now the Firtree Nursing Home.

He was educated at Repton School from 1909 to 1912 and at Clare College Cambridge from October 1914 to March 1915 before he left to join the army.

In 1916 he became a member of the 100th battalion of the Machine Gun Corps (MGC) having previously served with the 1st Warwickshire Yeomanry as a Second Lieutenant. He was killed on 10th November 1918 near Pont-sur-Sambre, which is about 18 miles south of Mons, and is the location where the last VC to be awarded in the War was won on 6th November.

In its short history the MGC gained an enviable record for heroism as a front line fighting force. During the latter part of the war, as tactics changed to defence in depth, it commonly served well in advance of the front line. It had a less enviable record for its casualty rate. Some 170,500 officers and men served in the MGC with 62,049 becoming casualties, including 12,498 killed, earning it the nickname of 'the Suicide Club'.

CHAPTER 12
TUNBRIDGE WELLS AFTER THE WAR
by John Cunningham

Five years is a short period in the life of any town and so under normal circumstances, one would not expect to see too much change. But the events of five years of War had been overwhelming by the usual standards and pace of life in Tunbridge Wells and so, in hindsight, the surprise is that the changes which did occur, were not greater.

For less than five years during the First World War, Tunbridge Wells had ceased to be a peaceful and relatively quiet town with an overwhelming female and retired population; a town whose principal occupation was genteel tourism; a town which ruled itself by strict and fundamental Christian standards; and which was ruled by men who were quite sure of their God-given right to do so.

It became a bustling town, with its population swollen by about a quarter to a third, nearly all of whom were men and above all soldiers, who were there either in transit to, in training for, or in recuperation from the Western Front. While as far as the needs of these newcomers were concerned, Tunbridge Wells could have been any town, provided that it served their purpose; for the inhabitants of Tunbridge Wells it would create a major re-orientation of the focus of their lives, at least for the duration of the War.

Much of the activity in the town now became directed towards providing for these newcomers, who would however be only transient, whatever their condition, and would never settle there in the long-term. Bearing in mind the reputation which soldiers can have, these men seem to have been generally well-behaved. There are no significant reports of Military Police activity, although this may not be surprising, since possibly half of those potentially involved were convalescent and not capable of being 'up to mischief.'

It became a town, which although well-supplied with medical services, would still have to treble that capacity, to cope with the thousands of wounded who 'arrived', as they also did in many other areas and towns, and who could not be 'turned away'.

These services understandably would be 'switched off', but somewhat abruptly within 3-9 months of the end of the War, leaving many of their staff, who were mainly women, unemployed.

It is also became a town which had to learn for the first time along with many other towns in Britain about how to cope with the direct impact of War on its life: with all sorts of people with whom it had never had to deal with before, particularly soldiers and refugees; and with circumstances such as the irrational paranoia created by rumour, the fear of enemy aerial bombing[2], blackout regulations, inflation (particularly of food prices), increasing food shortages, the rationing of food and fuel supplies; and with sudden death, for example, 42 casualties in the Tunbridge Wells area in just one week of the Battle of the Somme; all of which would have been outside its previous knowledge or experience.

So what did all this teach Tunbridge Wells? How much did it change?

The first lesson we can learn in hindsight is the resilience of past behaviour in restoring itself to nearly where it was before. Yes, it had to change, and the clock could not be put back to yesterday, but Tunbridge Wells while accepting that moving from one minute to midnight to one minute after, was not just moving two minutes, but actually entering a new day, a very different day, would nonetheless seek to keep this change of time to the very first hour of today.

The second lesson is that those who are in control are understandably reluctant to give it up. Certainly, except in the most revolutionary of situations, they *never* surrender it, but may make concessions, as minimal as they think unavoidable. But with the example of the Russian Revolution of October 1917 before them, there was a general realisation that the people of Britain were not democratically represented; that many of the soldiers who had fought and died for their country, did not even have the vote; and that all of the women who had done so much to support the War Effort also did not have the vote.

The result was the Representation of the People Act of 1918 which was passed in February, four months after the Russian Revolution and nine months before the Armistice of November and which not only gave the vote to all men, but also women, but not all women - only those *over the age of 30*.

As a result, the electorate tripled from 7.7 million in 1912 to 21.4 million by the end of 1918. Women now accounted for about 43% of the electorate, but if women had been enfranchised upon the same criteria as men, they would have been in the majority. The first election held under

---

[2] A fear which probably would not have existed, but for the futuristic writings of Jules Verne and H. G. Wells in the late 19th and early 20th centuries.

the new Act took place on 14th December 1918. just 33 days after the end of the War.

The Act gave about 8.4 million women the vote. The Eligibility of Women Act of November 1918 also allowed women to stand for Parliament and it is ironic that the only female candidate actually to be elected in the 1918 election - a number stood, but were not elected - represented the Sinn Féin party in Dublin, and chose not to take her seat at Westminster.[3]

The position of women in society and their role in the economy had changed irrevocably and this would never be reversed, but it would be still constrained by previous attitudes and behaviour. It would however be dealt with by Evolution rather than Revolution - and this can be much more drawn-out and frustrating. Even today, 100 years later, there are still major issues about 'glass ceilings'.

The right of women to vote would have come inevitably from the activity of the Suffragists and Suffragettes without any War, but there is no doubt that the contribution of women to the War effort accelerated this considerably. But it was not until the Representation of the People Act of 1928 that the voting franchise for all women was finally extended to all over the age of 21, which at last put them on a level-pegging with men.

Tunbridge Wells had had several very active and outspoken women in its community and a number of these have been covered in detail in Chapters 6 & 7. In the governance of the Town, three are of particular note.

Amelia Scott and Susan Power were elected in 1920 as the first women Councillors. Rosamund Baker succeeded Amelia Scott in 1923 and would become Tunbridge Wells' first Lady Alderman in 1935. There were never more than two female Councillors out of the 24 until after the Second World War and it is probably significant that they were always unmarried – there would be no married female Councillors until after the Second World War.

---

[3] The first woman to take her seat in the House of Commons would be Nancy Astor on 1st December 1919, having been elected at a by-election.

POPULATION (See also Appendix 2)

Somewhat surprisingly, the population of Tunbridge Wells would remain virtually static from the Census of 1911 (35,697) to that of 1931 (35,365) which is actually a drop of 332 (-1%) over the period, 129 by 1921 and a further 203 by 1931.

This was in marked contrast to the population trend over the same period of 1911-1931 in Great Britain (+10.8%), in Kent (+16.6%), and also in all the neighbouring towns of Tunbridge Wells; and it can only be defined as stagnation. The causes of this are debateable: whether it was economic or social or a mixture of the two is arguable, but the fact remains that it was real. It may have been that the town already had a reactionary image which did not appeal to potential inhabitants, but, whatever the explanation, there is no doubt from the statistics that something must have put them off. Ostensibly nothing had changed. It was still 35 miles from London; one could still travel from Tunbridge Wells to five London termini (Charing Cross, Waterloo, London Bridge, Cannon Street and Victoria) without changing train and in 50-70 minutes, which was not possible from any other 'dormitory' town of London.

The irony is that those in charge in Tunbridge Wells would almost certainly have been largely oblivious to the static population, since the proof of it would only be revealed in hindsight by the ten-yearly Census data.

Maidstone which was fractionally smaller than Tunbridge Wells in 1911, had a increase of 6,805 (+19.2%) in the 20 years. Although remaining smaller than Tunbridge Wells, Tonbridge had an increase of 1,537 (+10.4%), Sevenoaks an increase of 1,302 (+14.2%), and even Southborough had 349 (+5.0%).

While there was no Census in 1941 because of the Second World War, the next Census in 1951 showed a population for Tunbridge Wells of only 38,397, an increase of only 2,700 on 1911, or 3,032 on 1931 – both well below the growth of the Kent County population and the towns surrounding Tunbridge Wells.

The very strong bias towards women in the breakdown of the town's population by sex in 1911 would continue, dropping by only one percentage point from 60% to 59% by 1931. What is most interesting is the information which the three Censuses of 1911, 1921 and 1931 provide about the married/unmarried status of the female inhabitants of Tunbridge Wells and whether they were 'occupied' i.e. working. While the total number of women in Tunbridge Wells remained virtually static for twenty years, as the table below shows, the number of married women rose from 30% to 36%; unmarried women declined from 62% to 53%; and the widowed and divorced rose from 8% to 11%.

In terms of female employment, the long-term trend remained fairly even – 35% were employed in 1911 and 36% in 1931, but there was a distinct hiccup in 1921 when the figure dropped to 31%, no doubt reflecting men returning to their civilian jobs, and the fall in domestic indoor employment caused by the war, but it was still above the National and Kent averages.

What was however significant between 1911 and 1921, was the change in the nature of women's employment. Domestic Indoor Service declined from 60% of female employment to 46% in 1921, as did Textiles (which included the ambiguous 'dress-maker' category) from 14% to 7%, while Commercial/Finance, Professional, Nursing and Teaching rose from 12% to 31%. It is a pity that the 1931 data for Tunbridge Wells is not available for further comparison – no doubt it was collected and analysed, but it does not seem to have ever been published.

The available data is probably best presented as a Table:

Status and Occupation of Women in Tunbridge Wells						
	1911		1921		1931	
Status	No.	%	No.	%	No.	%
Married	6,275	30	7,013	33	7,554	36
Unmarried	13,101	62	12,012	57	10,987	53
Widowed/Divorced	1,771	8	2,151	10	2,169	11
Total	21,147	100	21,176	100	20,710	100
Not working/Retired	13,581	65	14,490	69	11,669	64
Working	7,196	35	6,601	31	9,041	36
		100		100		100
Employment						
In Personal Service	4,721	65	3,985	60	n/a	
Domestic Indoor	4,345	60	3,015	46	n/a	
Textiles	1,013	14	493	7	n/a	
Teaching	273	4	302	5	n/a	
Nursing (all)	261	4	308	5	n/a	
Commercial/Finance	147	2	714	11	n/a	
Professional	116	2	648	10	n/a	

POLITICAL PARTIES
One aspect of the post-War change nationally was in the control of local government, where the national political parties began to take over control of local government. Political parties had been present in local government before the War, but they had not been in overt control, which had rested in a somewhat disorganised way among a melange of difficult-to-define Independents, Ratepayer Associations, Tradesmen's Associations and other groupings of what were essentially local interests.

There was an inexorable move to more and more control and funding of local government responsibilities by central government, because local government could not afford to fund the ever-increasing cost of providing schools, social services and roads. So it was inevitable that in due course the political parties involved in national government, would take over control of local government as well.

GOVERNMENT OF THE TOWN
The War did not however bring any change in the government of Tunbridge Wells. The controls created by War - the Food Controller, the Fuel Controller - did vanish very quickly, but the Old Guard, which was temperamentally very conservative, were still firmly in control and when the Conservative Party began to become more prominent in local affairs, the Old Guard remained in place, just changing the label of their provenance/affiliation.

William Charles Cripps who had been the Town Clerk since its Incorporation as a Borough in 1889, would continue as the Town Clerk until he finally retired in 1925 at the age of 70.[4]

Seven of its eight Aldermen in 1914 were still in place in 1919, one (Colonel Sladen) having gone off to fight a war; and five of them were still in office in 1924, a further two having died. Such 'continuity' is not altogether surprising when Aldermen were 'elected' by their fellow-Councillors, not by the general electorate, for terms of six years at a time. Being an Alderman was a 'job for life', which was normally only ended by Death. Aldermen aged 93 and dying 'in office' were not unknown – William Delves did so in 1922, when he was still Chairman of the Finance Committee, and it happened on the day before he was due to move in Council the adoption of the next year's Borough Rate. He had been an Alderman since 1892 – some 30 years.

Councillors, of whom there were 24, lacked the *gravitas* and also the security of tenure of an Alderman and were a more variable bunch who changed more often, probably because they were only elected for a three

---

[4] On retirement, he became a Freeman of the Borough, and subsequently was elected a Kent County Councillor at the age of 74, and an Alderman of KCC at the age of 85.

year term and also by the general electorate, who could express in the polling booth any displeasure they felt. Nonetheless, despite the upheavals of the intervening 10 years, 13 of the 24 in 1911 were still Councillors in 1921.

While individual Aldermen and Councillors changed slowly, their political beliefs changed not at all. The Borough Council would be firmly Conservative in name and behaviour until the 1990s.

That does not mean that they were necessarily reactionary, but they were inclined to be cautious and hesitant about change, and change was something which could not be denied or avoided. They seem to have lost the thrusting vision and vigour of the Founding Fathers of the Borough which had been there twenty years before. It would seem that they were no longer forward-looking, but had become indecisive and unwilling to change their ideas.

Two examples illustrate this. The first concerns the bandstand in Calverley Grounds. For many years since the 1890s, there had been considerable but indecisive debate of the need for Tunbridge Wells to have an indoor Winter Garden which was considered essential for any respectable Victorian resort. A part of any Winter Garden was a Bandstand to entertain visitors. However, the nature of public entertainment was changing fast – cinema and radio were growing and cars, charabancs and buses were changing the nature of travel and the nature of visiting resorts. The day-trip rather than the one-two week stay was beginning to develop. The bandstand concept was ideal, as a major relaxing entertainment for the days when there was no cinema or radio, and when the visitor was staying a week rather than the inside of a day,

but it was definitely on its way out. So it was at the end of the era of the bandstand, that the Borough Council finally decided in 1926 to have a Bandstand, but without a Winter Garden in Calverley Grounds, and they provided one with room for a huge audience of 2,400 – 1,200 under cover and 1,200 outside[5].

The second example concerns the current Civic Centre, housing the Town Hall, the Museum and Art Gallery, the Assembly Hall theatre and the Police Station and Magistrates' Courts. The original Town Hall, Police Station and Courts had been together in Calverley Road since the 1830's and there is no doubt that by the end of the War the premises were no

---

4 It would be destroyed by a German bomb in 1940, but was rebuilt after the War and demolished yet again in 2010, this time by the Council.

longer 'fit for purpose' and a new site was needed. It would however take the Borough Council some 20 years before it was built and part of it opened in 1939[6]. The site – Calverley Terrace (now Civic Way) - was purchased in 1922, not demolished until 1931, the plan was not chosen and approved until 1935-6 and the building was incomplete when War came in 1939.[7]

SO WHAT HAPPENED TO THE TOWN AFTER THE WAR?

At the immediate level, there were adjustments to be made – soldiers were being demobilised and expected to return to their jobs. For example, B. Warren, a tailor who had closed his shop in the High Street and gone to war, returned to reopen it and hoped to recover his old custom. Women were also losing their jobs as their menfolk returned, war work such as munitions ceased and the VAD hospitals closed down.

Ad in the Courier in 1919

But longer term, there would be consequences which would be less immediately obvious. The War had been a huge shock (as, admittedly, it was for nearly every other town), but it was particularly for Tunbridge Wells with its female/male imbalance, its older population, its strong Low Church view of the values of life and its strong masculine control of its government.

It therefore withdrew in on itself, wishing to restore previous standards, values and behaviour and it became much more introspective as a result of its exposure to the War. There is always safety and reassurance in retreating into the past and maybe this was an instinctive 'gut' reaction. It was still the same old town which depended on genteel tourism and upper-middle class retirees and that profile does not/cannot change or disappear in just five years. The fact that the Old Guard seemed to be still very much in control was reassuring and Tunbridge Wells would not have anything which even slightly resembled a revolution.

---

[6] It was bad luck that the Second World War then intervened and delayed the completion of the Museum, Art Gallery and Library section until 1952.
[7] There have been contemporary parallels with this example, in the demolition of the Ritz cinema site which took 13 years (until 2014) to implement.

No doubt Tunbridge Wells post-War still thought of itself as a progressive town, as it had seen itself pre-War. In many respects it still was. It appeared to have an open approach to new initiatives and technology, but in reality it was only open to them within the relatively narrow framework of its existing social structure, which it could see no cause or reason to change.

However there were signs of change. It did elect its first female Councillors and its first female JPs, but so did everywhere else and it would have been hard-pressed not to do so, in view of both the very strong female individuals who had contributed so much in the previous four-five years, as well as the mass of women who had done so much in filling men's jobs, and laundering their clothes.

It also started to address the social problems of which it had been aware from before the War but had done nothing, such as working–class housing. In the 1920s, the first Council houses were built and by 1974, the year that the Borough of Royal Tunbridge Wells was replaced by the much larger and wider Borough of Tunbridge Wells, it had 16 housing estates with a total of 2,782 houses and 12,000 (over a quarter of the population) living in them. The estates were concentrated in four areas – Rusthall (which was the first in 1926); Powder Mill Lane; High Brooms and Sherwood; and Ramslye and Showfields.

There was also the beginning of what would be a long-term trend in property and housing. Society and lifestyle was changing radically and this affected the type of property people wanted, or could afford.

The employment market in Britain ended the First World War with 743,702 fewer employees, since that was the number of British men who had been killed[8]. During the War, women had learnt to take the place of men in many industries and services; and that meant that there were at least three-quarters of a million women who did not need or want to take domestic service, when they could have better pay and/or more satisfying jobs, with more regular hours.

Prior to the War, domestic service had been the only employment choice for most women. After the War, they had many more choices. This had an obvious impact on the domestic employment market. With fewer staff available, it created a small but nonetheless inflationary increase in wages, which in turn led to lower levels of domestic staff employment – a vicious circle (or even a downward spiral). It meant that if you already had a large house (and grounds), you became increasingly aware that

---

[8]Hansard, 9th. March 1923. There was also a similar number of disabled.

you did not have enough help to run it (even if you could afford to pay for it).

The problem would become progressively more acute in the late 1920s and 1930s, despite the Depression; and the only solution, in the absence of sufficient staff, was either to keep on and let everything - house, grounds - deteriorate slowly, often so slowly that you might not realise that it was happening; or move to smaller, more manageable properties, which is what those without previous commitments were already doing.

There was a clear trend in the late 1920s and 1930s towards to smaller, more manageable houses and gardens, which could be run with less or no domestic help and this would accelerate after the Second World War. This led over the next 30-40 years to three developments:

- large houses being divided into smaller houses/ flats;
- large houses being demolished to allow more, smaller houses/flats to be built on the site;
- large plots (i.e. particularly gardens) being sub-divided to accommodate more houses/flats (currently known as 'garden–grabbling').

Sometimes all three developments could occur on the same site, as many sites in Tunbridge Wells can demonstrate.

There was also one other major development, which at a distance of 100 years has been largely overlooked and that is the introduction of gas and electricity, both of which we take for granted today in our houses. Today, we assume that the supply of both is complementary, with one being used mainly for lighting and power and the other mainly for heating and cooking.

But it was not always so. They started as deadly rivals, since each saw themselves as the only means of power for both lighting and heating. In the early days and even in the 1920s when many houses still did not have electricity, each of them battled to be the only supplier of light to the domestic household. Electricity obviously won out but Gas had been the first to come to Tunbridge Wells in 1843 and was produced by a private company until it was nationalised in 1948. Electricity came much later in the late 1880s and in Tunbridge Wells was provided by the Borough Council which had its own generating station, until it too was nationalised in 1948. It is somewhat ironic that William Delves, the Chairman of the Tunbridge Wells Gas Company for 33 years, was also an Alderman of the Borough for 36.

THE IMPACT OF DEVELOPING COMMUNICATIONS

A major development post-war was in communications which progressively would have a major impact on public awareness and knowledge of and attitudes towards, international, national and local issues.

Printed media such as newspapers and magazines had existed for a long time. The abolition of Stamp Duty on newspapers in 1855 had increased circulation considerably; as did the Education Act of 1870 which increased literacy significantly; as did the introduction of popular, illustrated and cheap newspapers, such as the Daily Mail and the Daily Mirror in the 1890s.

But prior to the War, most communication had still been essentially personal and individual - that is word-of-mouth, or the very efficient Royal Mail. The telephone had not yet really established itself as a means of communication and by 1914, it was installed in fewer than 10% of households.

It was only after the War that the era of mass-communication would begin.The growth of the cinema which had developed during the War from being a 'Music Hall' down-market entertainment medium into a news, information and propaganda medium as well, had widened the means of mass-communication and this would be increased further by the post-War development of radio. The BBC would be created in 1923 as the first radio broadcasting station in the world.

But these developments, which were considered 'wonders' at the time, were nonetheless relatively slow to take off. They needed further stimuli in the form of sound (1927-8) and colour (1935-7) for the cinema, and television (1936) for the BBC before they were fully established.

Finally, since this monograph is about what happened to the people of Tunbridge Wells during the First World War, there is one final question which needs to be answered.

HOW MANY MEN FROM TUNBRIDGE WELLS ACTUALLY DIED? AND WHEN?

On the Tunbridge Wells War Memorial, there are inscribed 801 names of Tunbridge Wells men who died in the First World War. Since in the 1911 Census, there were only 14,550 men in Tunbridge Wells, 801 is 5.5% of this total, which is somewhat higher than the 4.2% usually calculated for the United Kingdom.

The figure of 801 should not however be taken as a definitive number for the Tunbridge Wells dead, since it is now known that in some cases, families never got round to submitting a name, or just did not wish the name to be on the Memorial; and in others, the names of men who did not actually come from Tunbridge Wells were put forward by their relatives who did, and who wished to create some public recognition and record of the sacrifice of their relation.

More precise figures do exist for smaller, more clearly defined groups, such as the Skinners' School where 522 Masters and Old Boys served and 87 died. This was 16.7% of those who served, and 7.2% of its 1,200 Old Boys since its foundation in 1887.

Ed Gilbert has made a detailed analysis of the 801 and while establishing the year of the death for many of them, he has also been able to create 'biographies' for about 600. Of the names on the memorial, his research shows an interesting ebb and flow in the number of deaths by year:

Year	No. who died
1914	27
1915	125
1916	92
1917	167
1918	156
1919	15
Uncertain	84
	666

The figure of 125 for 1915 is not surprising in view of the Hythe disaster that year, when 129 local men from Southborough, Tunbridge Wells and Speldhurst were drowned in the Dardanelles.

The figure of only 92 for 1916 is however somewhat surprising in view of the carnage of the Battle of the Somme that year which probably produced the highest casualties of any year for the British Army, but it may reflect a relative absence of local regiments in the Battle.

The 1916 figure of 92 should be put in the context of a higher number of deaths in subsequent years: 167 in 1917 and 156 in 1918 (which was not a year as such, but just over 10 months).

CONCLUSION

The First World War would probably never have occurred if the participants had known what the consequences would be. At the start, it was thought that it would be another short and relatively local war of which there had been many in Europe in the previous 100 years – which produced the 'over by Christmas' attitude – but it escalated into what would be called 'The War to end all Wars' because of the personalities and ambitions of their leaders, coupled with a major change in the strategy and tactics of warfare created by new weaponry, such as the machine-gun, much-improved artillery, the aeroplane and during the War, the tank.

Despite the widespread belief that it would 'Never Again' happen, 'The War to end all Wars' would lead to another World War in twenty years, but there has not been another *World* War for the past 70 years and we're still counting.... Wars still continue, but their nature has changed yet again. They are no longer set-piece confrontational battles, with every one wearing a uniform, but they have become local and relatively limited 'guerrilla' warfare where many of the fighters, regardless of their sex, look no different from the rest of the population.

With this change, it seems unlikely that Tunbridge Wells will ever be directly involved in a War again, for which we should all be very grateful. Nonetheless, the two World Wars in which the Town was involved were watersheds in the history of the World, of the United Kingdom and also of tiny Tunbridge Wells; and the lives of all of us would never be the same again.

The outcome of these Wars could never be reversed. For Tunbridge Wells, the Shock of the First World War was enormous and produced a catharsis which at first stunned the Town, but seems in the end to have made it stronger to cope with the Second World War, when it began some 7,600 days later.

GREATER LOVE HATH NO MAN THAN THIS,
THAT A MAN LAY DOWN HIS LIFE FOR HIS FRIENDS.
(John, 15:13)

Appendix 1   Sir John and Lady Matthews

Sir John Bromhead Matthews (1865-1934) and his second wife, Lady Annette Amelia Matthews (neé Kitson, 1873-1957) were both prominent Tunbridge Wells citizens during the First World War. In addition to her public work, Lady Matthews kept a journal throughout the war as a record of events and how they affected the family, written specially for her children who were too young at the time to fully realise what was happening. This journal, now in the Archives at the Imperial War Museum, provides a unique insight into the wartime life of a wealthy, but politically-committed wife and mother.

Sir John in 1910

Sir John was born in Hull in 1865 and was educated a Doncaster Grammar School. He became a solicitor and later a barrister, and then entered the colonial service as acting solicitor-general of the Straits Settlements in Singapore. After serving as attorney-general in both the Bahamas and the Straits Settlements, he finished his colonial career in 1910-11 as Chief Justice of the Bahamas. He was made a King's Counsel in 1909 and was knighted in the New Year's Honours List two years later.[1] On retirement – still in his forties - he moved to Tunbridge Wells and quickly became involved in local affairs as a Justice of the Peace for Kent and chairman of the local Charity Organisation Society.

Lady Matthews in 1934

Lady Matthews married the widower Sir John in 1910. She was born in Leeds in 1873, the youngest child of a self-made locomotive manufacturer and ironmaster, James Kitson, who was already in his sixties by the time of her birth. Indeed, Lady Matthews' half-brother, also called James, (later the first Baron Airedale) was nearly forty years older than her. The Kitson family were not only commercially successful but politically active: James Kitson senior was a Mayor and Alderman in Leeds as well as a magistrate, and James junior was elected the Liberal MP for Colne Valley in 1892, before being made a peer by the Liberal government in 1907[2] and one of his sisters, Miss J.B. Kitson, would be the first woman

---

[1] *Times*, 2nd January 1911; 6th August 1934.
[2] *Oxford Dictionary of National Biography*.

to be Lord Mayor of Leeds, in 1942. His youngest sister, Annette Amelia, was no exception in this politically engaged family. She did volunteer work in a women's settlement and nursed children. Then in 1905 she entered local government as a Poor Law Guardian in Scarborough. As is proudly stated in her self-penned obituary notes, 'from its inception she acted as secretary of the Scarborough Women's Suffrage Society'.[3]

Stephen, Bryan & Esther, c.1919, for whom the War Diaries were written

By the outbreak of war in 1914 Lady Matthews and her husband had two young children, a boy and a girl. But she had not neglected her political activities in her new home town, having been made a Vice-President of the Tunbridge Wells Suffrage Society. During the war she gave birth to her youngest child, Bryan (her 'war baby', as she called him) and was involved in a wide range of volunteer work (see main chapter). Her wartime diary also shows that she kept in close touch with relatives in Yorkshire, where her deceased brother's stately home, Gledhow Hall, had become a VAD hospital, and she was a keen observer of the progress of the bill to enfranchise women as it went through Parliament. She also supported her husband as Sir John was also busy with war work. He spoke from public platforms in support of Lord Derby's voluntary army recruitment scheme in 1915 and later was an Assistant Food Commissioner under the rationing schemes introduced in 1917-18. He also adjudicated at local tribunals under the National Service Act, where men who sought exemption from military service would put their case. In 1916 a hosier, questioned whether a woman could do his job, asked Sir John if he would like his inside leg measured by a woman! The tailor's appeal was dismissed.[4] It is hard to imagine that Sir John was very sympathetic even to conscientious objectors, but no doubt his legal and judicial training was an asset in making impartial assessments.

After the end of the War, the Matthews' carried on their shared life as pillars of the community from their base in Molyneux Park, involving themselves in a range of committees and activities. Lady Matthews continued to campaign for feminist causes, for example as a self-proclaimed 'ardent supporter of women police'. She was president of the local Equal Citizens Society and was 'a keen executive member' of the National Council of Women branch run by Amelia Scott, becoming its

---

[3] Imperial War Museum, 09/36/1, 'Notes for obituary if required'.
[4] *Kent and Sussex Courier*, 6th October 1916.

president in 1928.[5] In the early 1920s she became very concerned about the so-called 'servant problem', and alleged that young women were being paid unemployment benefit while potential employers were 'genuinely suffering' because of their inability to find domestic help. A letter to the *Times* from Lady Matthews was followed by her appearance giving evidence to the Ministry of Labour's Domestic Service Enquiry in 1923. She claimed that domestic work was women's 'highest profession', that cookery was 'applied chemistry', and that domestic science should be taught in all schools.[6]

Like many wealthy former Liberals, Lady Matthews drifted towards the Conservative Party, probably during or soon after the First World War when the Liberal Party went into a steep electoral decline. She became a member of the Conservative and Unionist Women's Association, but her family's liberal roots are perhaps evident in her backing of the League of Nations Union, which had vigorous support in interwar Tunbridge Wells. She was also involved in civic affairs as a co-opted member of the local education committee, and from 1929 as a magistrate. Like many women JPs of this era she took a special interest in the juvenile court and the probation committee.[7]

8 Mayfield Road in the 1950's

Sir John died in 1934, aged sixty-nine. His wife continued to live in Tunbridge Wells, and although deafness caused her to resign from the magistrates' bench in 1945, she remained active in the local Conservative Association until well into her eighties, only resigning in 1956, just over a year before her death. She died at her house, 8 Mayfield Road.

A draft obituary, which appears to have been written by Lady Matthews herself, recalled that 'it was a great satisfaction ... to learn that on September 4th 1944, two trained policewomen, who were to be in uniform, and fully attested had been appointed onto the Borough Police Force'. Thus she had witnessed and celebrated the culmination of a feminist campaign which had begun long ago, back in the days of 'khaki fever' at the start of the First World War.[8]

AL

---

[5] 'Notes for obituary'.
[6] *Times*, 20th December 1922; 16th June 1923; 10th October 1924.
[7] 'Notes for obituary'
[8] *Ibid.*

	Sex	1891 No.	%	1901 No.	%	1911 No.	%	1921 No.	%	1931 No.	%
England and Wales	Male	14,052,901	48	15,728,613	48	17,445,608	48	18,082,220	48	19,133,485	48
	Female	14,949,624	52	16,799,230	52	18,624,884	52	19,803,022	52	20,819,508	52
	Total	29,002,525	100	32,527,843	100	36,070,492	100	37,885,242	100	39,952,953	100
Index 1891 = 100		100		112		124		131		138	
Admin. County of Kent	Male	383,849	49	471,136	49	506,780	48	542,088	47	584,336	48
	Female	401,825	51	489,703	51	538,721	52	599,578	53	634,938	52
	Total	785,674	100	961,139	100	1,045,591	100	1,141,666	100	1,219,273	100
Index 1891 = 100		100		122		133		145		155	
Tunbridge Wells MBC	Male	11,538	41	13,656	41	14,350	40	14,360	40	14,655	41
	Female	16,357	59	19,717	59	21,147	60	21,191	60	20,710	59
	Total	27,895	100	33,373	100	35,597	100	35,551	100	35,365	100
Index 1891 = 100		100		120		128		127		127	
Southborough UDC	Male			3,145	45	3,090	44	3,091	44	3,276	45
	Female			3,832	55	3,911	56	4,011	56	4,074	55
	Total	5,409		6,977	100	7,001	100	7,102	100	7,350	100
Index 1891 = 100		100		129		129		131		136	
Cranbrook UDC (incl. Hawkhurst)	Male	6,776	49	6,303	49	6,710	49	6,108	47	6,160	48
	Female	6,954	51	6,641	51	6,979	51	6,801	53	6,767	52
	Total	13,720	100	12,944	100	13,689	100	12,909	100	12,927	100
Index 1891 =100		100		94		100		94		94	
Tonbridge UDC	Male	6,009	49	6,207	49	7,163	48	7,810	50	7,698	47
	Female	6,134	51	6,529	51	7,640	52	8,158	50	8,635	53
	Total	12,143	100	12,736	100	14,803	100	15,968	100	16,332	100
Index 1891 = 100		100		105		122		131		134	
Sevenoaks UDC	Male			3,424	42	3,898	43	3,828	42	4,562	44
	Female			4,682	58	5,284	57	5,232	58	5,922	56
	Total	7,610		8,106	100	9,182	100	9,060	100	10,480	100
Index 1891 = 100		100		107		121		119		138	

Source: Census Returns
Note: England & Wales have been taken as UK figures prior to 1921 included Ireland

APPENDIX 2 - TABLE 2 — POPULATION BY EMPLOYMENT

	England and Wales						Kent						Royal Tunbridge Wells					
	1911		1921		1931		1911		1921		1931		1911		1921		1931	
	No.('000)	%	No.('000)	%	No.('000)	%	No.	%	No.	%	No.	%	No.	%	No.	%	No.	%
MALES																		
Employed *	11454	66	12112	67	11564	60	324400	64	352846	65	364026	62	9489	65	9312	65	na	na
Not working/retired	5992	34	5962	33	7567	40	182570	36	189240	35	220309	38	5061	35	5048	35	na	na
TOTAL MALES	17446	100	18075	100	19133	100	506970	100	542086	100	584336	100	14550	100	14360	100	14655	100
Index 1911 = 100	100		104		110		100		107		115		100		99		101	
FEMALES																		
Employed *	4831	26	5065	26	5123	25	125700	23	136993	23	138014	22	7296	35	6601	31	na	na
Not working/Retired	13795	74	14746	74	15696	75	413021	77	462585	77	496924	78	13851	65	14590	69	na	na
TOTAL FEMALES	18625	100	19811	100	20819	100	538721	100	599578	100	634938	100	21147	100	21191	100	20710	100
Index 1911 = 100	100		106		112		100		111		118		100		100		98	
PERSONS																		
Employed *	16,284	45	17177	45	16687	43	450100	43	489839	43	502040	41	16785	47	15913	45	na	na
Not working/Retired	19786	55	20709	55	22665	57	595491	57	651825	57	717233	59	18912	53	19658	55	na	na
TOTAL PERSONS	36070	100	37886	100	39952	100	1045591	100	1141664	100	1219273	100	35697	100	35551	100	35365	100
Index 1911= 100	100		105		111		100		110		117		100		100		100	
In Indoor Domestic Service **																		
Male	30	2	62	5	***262	***	1530	3	2753	5	***		207	6	137	3	na	na
Female	1208	98	1149	95	1119	95	51440	97	49261	95	48196		3357	94	3985	97	na	na
Total	1238	100	1211	100	1381	100	52970	100	52014	100		100	3564	100	4122	100	na	100
Index 1911 = 100	100		98		114		100		98				100		77			

na Not available
* Minimum school leaving age was 10 in 1911, 12 in 1921 and 14 in 1931
** Private, not commercial domestic service
*** Data not comparable as it includes outdoor domestic workers
Source : Census Returns

ACKNOWLEDGEMENTS

The Publishers would like to express their appreciation of, and offer their thanks to:

General (for more than one Chapter)
The Executors of the estate of Lady Matthews and the Imperial War Museum, for permission to refer to, and quote from Lady Matthews' Diaries.
The Curator of the Liverpool Scottish Regimental Museum and Archive for permission to reproduce a number of regimental photographs.
The Ed Gilbert Archive
The Keith Hetherington Archive
LSE Library Collections: Papers of Amelia Scott, 7ASC.
Tunbridge Wells Museum and Art Gallery for advice, assistance and permissions.
Tunbridge Wells Reference Library for providing such a wide range of relevant information.
www.womenshistorykent.org

Chapter 7
LSE Library Collections: Papers of Amelia Scott, 7ASC.

Chapter 8
Michaël Amara (General Archives, Brussels, Belgium)
Geoffrey Copus
Christophe Declerq (UCL)
Francoise Faulkner –for information about the Meeus family
Rodney Hall – for information about his grandfather, Paul van den Kerckhove
Edward Hertogs (Local History Circle, Lint, Belgium) for information about Abbé Jos. Peeters
Steve Parlanti –for information about Paul van den Kerckhove
Leo Spaepen (Local History Circle, Wijnegem, Belgium)
Peter Vandenabeele, for information about the Baes family and the Mayor of Herent.
Barbara Vesey (Archivist, Society of the Sacred Heart, Roehampton)
Ivo Wynants (Mayor of Wijnegem, Belgium)

Chapter 11
Forces War Records website
Machine Gun Corps Old Comrades' Association
Repton School
Tunbridge Wells Reference Library: Gower scrapbooks

ABBREVIATIONS/ ACRONYMS USED IN THIS BOOK

CFC	Canadian Forestry Corps
DORA	Defence of the Realm Act 1914 and subsequent additions
KCC	Kent County Council
NUWSS	National Union of Women's Suffrage Societies
NUWW	National Union of Women Workers
RWK	Royal West Kent Regt.
RTWBC	Royal Tunbridge Wells Borough Council
VAD	Voluntary Aid Detachment (of Red Cross/St. John's Ambulance)
WAAC	Women's Auxiliary Army Corps
WAG	War Agricultural Committee
WAHIV	Women's Agricultural & Cultural International Union
WEA	Workers' Educational Association
WEC	Women's Emergency Corps
WI	Women's Institute
WVR	Women's Volunteer Reserve
YMCA	Young Mens' Christian Association

SOURCES AND BIBLIOGRAPHY

PRIMARY SOURCES
General (for more than one Chapter)
Amelia Scott Papers : Women's Library @ LSE
British Newspaper Archive online
Gower 'Scrapbooks' 1916-1920 (10 bound volumes: Tunbridge Wells Library).
Kelly's Directory for Tunbridge Wells 1900-1925
Kent & Sussex (Tunbridge Wells) Courier, passim
Lady Matthews's Diaries 1914-1919: IWM
Pelton's Directory for Tunbridge Wells, 1900-1920
The Times Archive, *passim*
Tunbridge Wells Advertiser, passim
Tunbridge Wells Borough Council - Minutes of Council & Committees, *passim*
Tunbridge Wells Medical Officer of Health: Annual Reports 1905-1920
UK Census returns: 1881-1931 for England & Wales, Kent and Royal Tunbridge Wells: National Archive and University of Essex (hist.pop.org)
www.womenshistorykent.org

For Chapter 7
Newspapers:
Birmingham Daily Mail ; *Daily Express*, 22nd April 1915 ; *Daily Mirror*, 26th July 1919;
The Times, 31st December 1914; 24th October 1916 ;
Whitstable Times and Herne Bay Herald 5th Sept 1914

Printed sources:
The Times History of the War, part 221, Vol 17, 12th November 1918
    pp. 448-9.
Parliamentary Recruiting Committee poster 1915 (Art.IWM PST 5160)
Parliamentary Recruiting Committee poster, 1915 Art.IWM PST 4884)
Some War Work in Tunbridge Wells. May 1915- April 1919: *National Council of Women of Great Britain and Ireland (NUWW) 1920*

Archive sources:
Kent History and Library Centre, Maidstone:
    NCW Tunbridge Wells Branch, The First Seventy-five years 1895-1970
Imperial War Museum: *Private Papers of Lady Matthews (17087 1914)*
Public Record Office: 1911 *Census Returns RG14: 4062, 184.*
Women's Library, London School of Economics:
    'Women and War Work', Amelia Scott Papers, 7/ASC/2/1/4/1;
    NUWSS Kentish Federation, (1913) First Annual Report

For Chapter 8

Beechwood Sacred Heart Convent & School Archives:
    Barat House, Roehampton

Belgian National Archives - *Archives de la Guerre:*
T476 Comité Officiel belge pour l'Angleterre (réfugiés belges e Angleterre);
T483 Documents divers relatifs aux réfugiés belges en Grande Bretagne (1914-1920)
T530 Documents et archives transmis par le consulat de Belgique à Folkestone (Grande Bretagne) 1914-1924.

Imperial War Museum : *Women's War Work Archive (BEL):*

Report of the Tunbridge Wells Belgian Refugees Committee, October 1915 - March 1919

Appendix 1
The Times, 2 January 1911; 20 December 1922; 16 June 1923 10 October 1924; 6 August 1934.
Imperial War Museum, 'Notes for obituary if required', Papers of Lady Matthews, 09/36/1

Appendix 2
National Archive and University of Essex (hist.pop.com)

SECONDARY SOURCES
General (for more than one Chapter)

Dictionary of National Biography, 2004. *Oxford University Press*
Ed Gilbert Archive
Keith Hetherington Archive

BIBLIOGRAPHY
General (for more than one Chapter)
The 12 Monographs on Tunbridge Wells local history, previously published by the Local History Group of the Royal Tunbridge Wells Civic Society, 2003-9.
(See website: www.thecivicsociety.com for a detailed listing of all 12 titles)

Chapter 5
Captain C.T. Atkinson: The Queen's Own Royal West Kent Regiment 1914-1919, *Simpkin, Marshall, Hamilton, Kent and Co. 1924.*
John Ellis: Eye-deep in Hell: Trench Warfare in World War I, *Johns Hopkins University Press 1989*
Richard Holmes: The Western Front, *BBC Books, 1999*
Richard Holmes: Tommy: The British Soldier on the Western Front, *Harper Perennial 2005*
Nigel Jones: Peace and War: Britain in 1914, *Head of Zeus, 2013*
John Keegan: The Face of Battle, *Penguin 1976*
John Keegan: The First World War, *Hutchinson 1998*
Paul Lewis: For Kent and Country, *Reveille Press 2014*
Lyn Macdonald: 1914-18: Voices and Images of the Great War, *Michael Joseph 1988*
Lyn Macdonald: 1914, *Penguin 1987*
Lyn Macdonald: 1915: The Death of Innocence, *Penguin 1997*
Lyn Macdonald: They called it Passchendaele, *Michael Joseph 1979*
Robin Neillands: The Old Contemptibles: The British Expeditionary Force 1914, *John Murray 2004*
Julian Putkowski and Julian Sykes: Shot at Dawn, *Leo Cooper 1992*
John Terraine: The Smoke and the Fire: Myths and Anti-myths of war, *Leo Cooper 1980*
Denis Winter: Death's Men: Soldiers of the Great War, *Penguin 1979*

Chapter 7
On-line Resources:
Inspiring Women: Hidden Histories from West Kent
/www.womenshistorykent.org/themes/post-war/index.html

Secondary Sources
National Council of Women of Great Britain and Ireland (formerly NUWW): Some War Work in Tunbridge Wells, May 1915-April 1919: *published 1920:* covers the Soldiers' Central Laundry, the Women's Patrol Movement and the Soldiers' Canteens.
Wollacott, A., (1994) On Her Their Lives Depend: Munition Workers in the Great War, *University of California Press, pp. 1-2.*

Woollacott, A. (1994) '"Khaki Fever" and its Control: Gender, Class, Age and Sexual Morality on the British Homefront in the First World War," *Journal of Contemporary History* 29, 2.
Watson, J.S. K. (1997))'Khaki Girls, VADs, and Tommy's Sisters: Gender and Class in First World War Britain', *International History Review* 19: 1

Chapter 8
Michaël Amara : Des Belges à l'épreuve de l'exil. Les réfugiés de la Première Guerre mondiale en France, en Angleterre et aux Pays-Bas *(Editions de l'Université de Bruxelles, 2008)*
Eric van Schoonenberghe, Erik Houtman, Kristof Evers, Leo Spaepen, Kris van den Berg, Carlo Evers & Vik Werrebroek : De Stokerij Meeus in Wijnegem *(Heemkundige Kring Jan Vleminck Wijnegem, 2011)*
Arthur Marwick : The Deluge - British Society and the First World War *(Palgrave Macmillan, 1965, 2nd edition 2006)*
J.C. Carlile, D.D. (Ed.) : Folkestone during the War (1914-1919): A Record of the town's life & work *(F.J. Parsons Ltd, Folkestone)*
***Fiction:* May Wynne** : Stranded in Belgium *(Blackie and Son Limited, 1918)*

Chapter 10
Stephen Bates: Asquith*: Haus Publishing 2006*
Neil Ferguson*:* The Pity of War*: Allen Lane The Penguin Press 1998*
Lawrence James*:* The Rise and Fall of the British Empire*: Little,Brown 1994*
National Records of Scotland : HH31/27/56
Brian MacArthur: For King and Country: Voices from the First World War: *Abacus 2009*
David Stevenson: The History of the First World War; *Allen Lane ,2004*
A.J.P.Taylor : English History 1914-1945: *Oxford University Press 1965*

BIOGRAPHICAL DETAILS ABOUT CONTRIBUTORS

Lionel Anderson has lived in Tunbridge Wells since 1973 and is a committee member of the Local History Group. He spent most of his working life in the City of London. Since retirement, he has been an investment adviser to a number of charities, including the Charities Aid Foundation (CAF) and has completed a study in Kentish History at the University of Kent. He is a liveryman of the Worshipful Company of Turners and a Freeman of the City of London.

Ann Bates is a member of the LHG Committee. was born and has lived all her life in Tunbridge Wells. She studied Art at the Tunbridge Wells School of Art and also in London at the Central School of Arts and Crafts (now St. Martin's Central School). She worked in London before serving four years in the WRNS in the Education Branch. After working in London and Orpington as a florist, she set up her own flower-shop in Southborough. Since retiring, she has devoted her time to her garden and local and family history, writing Tunbridge Wells in the Second World War and the Years of Austerity for the Local History Group, and contributing several chapters to the RTWCS Local History Group series of monographs.

Stephen Bates read Modern History at New College, Oxford and spent 36 years as a journalist, working for the BBC, Daily Telegraph, Daily Mail and - for 22 years – at The Guardian where he was successively a political correspondent, European Editor and religious and royal correspondent. He retired in 2012 to become a full-time author: his recent books include Two Nations: Britain in 1846 and The Poisoner: The Life and Crimes of Victorian England's most notorious doctor, about the 19th Century murderer William Palmer. His next book, 1815: Regency Britain in the Year of Waterloo, will be published in January 2015. Married, with three children, Stephen lived in Tunbridge Wells for 14 years, but moved to Deal last year.

John Cunningham read History at Peterhouse, Cambridge in the late 1950's. His career was essentially a diagonal progression in marketing and general management in three leading companies in the advertising (J. Walter Thompson), market research (Taylor Nelson AGB) and publishing (Mintel International) industries. He retired in 1996 and since then has been a founder in 2001 of the Local History Group within the Royal Tunbridge Wells Civic Society, was the Chairman of the Society for three years from 2005-2008 and continues to be the Chairman of the Local History Group, during which time the Group has published some 13 Monographs and 3 Occasional Papers. Besides researching and writing for this monograph, he has been the Co-ordinator and the Editor of the project.

Michael Fradd was educated at The Skinners' School and Sheffield University. His career has been teaching Science and then IT. He has lived all his life in the area, except for 6 years in the South Pacific. He is a fanatic about Church bells and bell ringing and since retiring, has been a library volunteer, for the Home Library service and as a 'Computer Buddy'.

Edward Gilbert of **Thunder Bay, Ontario, Canada.** Edward's father, Douglas, was born in Tunbridge Wells, and his mother, Ruth, in Heysham, Lancashire. His father's family moved to Canada from Tunbridge Wells in 1923. He was born in 1950 in Ontario and graduated with honours as a Civil Engineering Technologist and Civil Engineer. In 1975, he joined Bell Canada in Toronto. In 1985, he resigned from Bell Canada to become progressively the President of three property development and management companies, retiring in 1998. Since then, he has devoted his life to researching and writing about his interests, one of the greatest of which is the history of Tunbridge Wells, where he still has living relatives. He has created a website: www.allabouttunbridgewells.com with many of his 400 articles.

Keith Hetherington is a craftsman, now retired from the electricity industry. He has had a deep interest in Local History all his life and has accumulated a considerable archive of material and photographs on the history of Tunbridge Wells. He has written many articles for the monthly '*Bygone Kent*' and is the author of *Old Pubs of Tunbridge Wells and District* and *Yesterday's Bottles*, as well as being the co-author of several other local histories and guides. He was the first to propose the creation of the Victoria Cross Grove in Dunorlan Park, to commemorate those of Tunbridge Wells who had been awarded the Medal.

Roger Kasper is the Editor of the Kent and Sussex Courier and has been a journalist for 31 years, on both local and national newspapers and magazines. His great-grandfather, Joseph Beeson, died in the First World War when his battleship HMS Vanguard exploded at Scapa Flow, in the Orkneys, in 1917 while on routine exercises. His name is on the war memorial on The Great Lines, Gillingham. He is the author of *Just for the Record*, the biography of the Status Quo Group.

Dr. Catherine Lee is an Associate Lecturer and Research Affiliate in History at The Open University. Her book 'Policing Prostitution, 1856–1886: Deviance, Surveillance and Morality', which has a strong local history focus, was published in 2012. Catherine's previous collaborative work with Dr Anne Logan has included 'Inspiring women: Hidden histories from West Kent', an exhibition mounted in the Tunbridge Wells Museum and Art Gallery and on-line. Catherine is currently working on a collaborative project between The Open University and the BBC, entitled 'The World Made by Women', a four-part TV series to be broadcast in 2015.

Brian Lippard read Natural Sciences at Peterhouse, Cambridge in the late 1960's. He then worked for the National Provident Institution (NPI) in a variety of management roles within the Computer Development and Customer Service divisions. Since his retirement, he has volunteered at the local Citizens Advice Bureau where he has been both an adviser and now carries out their IT support. He also helps with the commercial side of the Spa Valley Railway. He very much enjoys bridge and has recently been Chairman of the Tunbridge Wells Bridge Club. He is currently a member of the Executive Committee of the Civic Society. He has lived in Tunbridge Wells since 1981 and is married with two sons.

Dr. Anne Logan is Senior Lecturer in the School of Social Policy, Sociology and Social Research at the University of Kent. Her PhD is from the University of Greenwich where she researched the first women magistrates appointed in England and Wales. She is the author of several publications including the monograph *Feminism and Criminal Justice: a historical perspective* (Palgrave, 2008) and is an editor of *Women's History Magazine*. Anne teaches history and criminology and her research interests include the women's suffrage movement and women's voluntary activity in Kent. She is currently writing a full-length biography of the twentieth century penal reformer and educationalist, Margery Fry (1874-1958).

Alison Sandford MacKenzie lived and worked in Brussels for many years, before settling in East Sussex when her diplomat husband retired. A graduate in French and Drama from Bristol University, she first encountered the Belgian refugees in Tunbridge Wells while working with Claque Theatre on research for "The Vanishing Elephant", a Community Play about the Camden Road area of the town which was performed by 135 local residents in 2009. A passionate family historian, she continues to research the refugees' story with the aim of tracing the history of all those who spent The Great War in Tunbridge Wells. She is currently also developing a project around another
Tunbridge Wells resident, the writer and campaigner for women's rights, Madame Sarah Grand (1854-1943).

Dr. Alastair Tod, after reading English at Wadham College, Oxford, qualified as a town planner, and spent twenty years in local government.; He has a Ph,D degree from the University of Kent. He worked in the voluntary sector in fields including the presentation of military history and the public interpretation of science. In the commercial world, he has represented the renewable energy industry to local authorities and community groups. He has been the Chairman of the Royal Tunbridge Wells Civic Society for two terms of two years, which has combined his interests in local democracy, history and the environment. He has published an autobiography, *Confessions of an Optimist*.

Pat Wilson started his working life on a bicycle as a reporter for the Courier before taking the train to Fleet Street, and a variety of unlikely jobs in radio, television and the murky world of Government communications .He returned to Tunbridge Wells with his wife some years ago to spend his time going to Civic Society meetings and paying builders to help keep his ancient house from falling down.

INDEX

A
Abergavenny, Marquess of 6, 67, 105, 204
Air Raids/Lighting restrictions 215-7
Allotments 215
Ard, Miss Rachel 119, 148
Armistice, The   230, 235-9
Army Meat scandal 60-1
Army pay/allowances 43, 44
Asquith, Herbert 5, 88, 208

B
Babb, Stanley 251
Banks 23
Baseball 108, 227, 228
Bath Parades 44, 82, 105
Belgian Refugees 56, 71, 73, 74, 136, Chap.8
Beechwood Sacred Heart Convent 181, 185
Beer, Rachel 119-120
Bidborough Court VAD 117, 129, 129
Billeting 42, 70-1, 93
Bismarck 3
Blackhurst VAD 125, 129
Black-out/ street lighting 77-8, 193
Blue Hospital uniform for wounded 127-8
Boer War 5, 88
Bredbury VAD 123
Broomlands VAD, Langton Green 123, 130

C
Caley, Ald. H.M. 14, 190, 191
Calverley Lodge VAD 125, 130
Calverley Park/Grounds 63, 79
Camden , Marquess 6, 34, 108
Canadian Forestry Corps 86, 104-8 *(box)*
Candler Sarah 69, 79, 83,134,138,144, 163, 164, 190, 203
Casualties 74, 189, 193-5, 266
Census, 1911, 1921, 1931   6, 258-9
Charing X Railway Bridge189,199-201
Christmas
    For the troops 46-7, 51, 106,136, 206
    At VAD hospitals 127
Chronology of Events 3-5, 30-1, 49-50, 230, 269
Cinemas 22-23
Civic Centre 261-2
Civil defence 77
Clayton's Farm 169, 170, 171
Club Albert 177, 178, 184
Council for Civil Liberties 164
Council housing 263

Congress of Vienna 3
Conscription 83, 195, 196
Conscientious Objectors 197-8
Courier, Kent & Sussex   *passim*
Courier Tobacco Fund 46, 189, 199
Crothers VAD 122, 130, 170
Cripps, WC 10, 36, 71,187, 204, 260

D
Defence of Realm Act (DORA) 63, 72-3, 84, 189, 215
Delves, Ald. W. 13, 68, 260
Denyn, Josef 168
Domestic Service 16-17, 259, 263-4
Dougall, Maj. E.S., VC 227 *(box)*
Doyle, Sir Arthur Conan 18, 86
Dutch, George 83, 163, 197-8

E
Education 18-19
Electricity 264
Elwig, Ald. Henry 102, 190, 191
Emergency Scheme 71-72
Emson, Ald. W.C. 36, 54, 56, 57, 61, 68, 69, 70, 77, 84, 164, 170, 171, 177, 186, 187, 213, 249
Employment 16-17, 259
Eye & Ear Hospital 52, 116

F
Fensibles, Mid-Kent Regt. of 29
Fete du Roi 184-5, 185
Food Control Order 77
Food Controller 84, 85
Food hoarding 213
Food Shortages 210, 211-215, 222-3
Fuel Shortages 76-7, 218-9, 223-4, 229

G
Gallipoli 64, 96, 100,101
Gas Company 68, 78, 264
General Election 1918.   241
General Hospital 21, 46, 61, 62, 110, 114, 128
Goodden, Major F.W. 205 *(box)*
Government advertising 198
Government of Town   260-2
Gower, Ald. Sir Robert 2, 40, 62, 68, 69,
    75, 85, 144, 190, 242, 243, 246
Grand, Sarah 71, 133, 144
Groombridge104, 105

H
Hardinge, Col. Viscount 251
Hargate Forest 106, 107
Health/Health Care 19-22,
Henrietta Maria   6
Herent, Flanders 170
Hoare, Canon E. 13

- 281 -

Homeopathic Hospital 21, 116
Hop-pickers 62-3, 182
Housing 82, 86, 263
Hutchings, K.L.,cricketer, 95, 98, 99
Hythe, HMS, Sinking of 64-6, 101

I
Incorporation of Borough 9, 10

J
Johnstone, Mrs. of Burrswood 169, 170, 171,182

K
Kaiser 4
Kaiserschlacht, Die 231-2
Keating, Canon 170, 177, 181, 216-7
Kent Nursing Institute 117, 130
Kent Volunteer Fencibles 55
'Khaki Fever' 137,138, 270
King Charles I 6
King Charles II 6
King Edward VII 5, 6, 13-14
Kingswood VAD 107, 124, 128, 130
Kingswood Kippers 107
Kitchener, Lord 88, 89, 91, 107
Kosmos Cinema 23, 78,102,109, 191, 192

L
Le Jeune, M.& Mme 175, 185, 187, 188
Lord Derby /Scheme 56, 83, 189, 195-6
Litraps aerodrome 69
Liverpool Scottish Regt. 41, 42, 45, 48, 75, 92
Lusitania, RMS 59
Lydia La Lacheur 133, 135, 149, 163, 170

M
Macquarie VAD 125, 130
Matthews, Sir John & Lady 1-2, 44, 70, 71, 73, 74, 75, 79, 83, 84, 133, 136, 142, 145, 146, 148, 152, 153, 157, 158, 160, 162, 175, 179, 208 , 212, 235 , 269-70
Mayoral Divine Service 69, 202-3
Meeus-de Meurs family 176 (box)
Militia, Local 28-29
Mountain, Rev. J.192
Munition workers 154-5

N
National Council against Conscription 83, 163
National Restaurants 85, 157, 227
National Union of Women's Suffrage Societies (NUWSS) 132-133, 134

National Union of Women Workers (NUWW) 58, 75, 133, 134, 138,139, 145, 156, 160, 161, 163, 185, 225
Nevill Ground 190, 204, 224
Nevill Park, No.8 121, 128, 130
Newspapers, Local 24-5
No Conscription Fellowship 83, 163, 197

O

P
Park House, Southborough 117-8, 130
Parsons, Victor 99
Peace Day & Procession 242-247
Peace Treaty at Versailles 230
Pembury Hospital (Sandhill Infirmary) 116
Pembury Workhouse 116 fn.
Political Parties 12, 260
Population 6, 7, 15-6, 258-9
Portuguese workers 106, 107
Postal Services 25-6
Power, Miss Susan 136, 141, 161, 177, 184, 257
Prankerd, Lt. Richard 86, 254
Presentation Tank 249-50
Prior, Chief Constable 12, 42, 71, 74, 139
Prussian-Austrian War 4
Public Baths 82, 105
Pump Room 109, 246

Q
Queen Victoria 5

R
Rabbit clubs 83, 227
Rail services 24
Rationing 84-5, 222-3
Recruitment 54, 83
Recruitment Appeals Tribunal 83, 189, 196-7
Reich, Ludwig 40, 80, 87
Remembrance Day 247-8
Rendezvous de Réfugiés Belges 73, 178
Religion 13
Representation of the People Act, 1918. 256-7
Requisitioning 73, 177
Royal Engineers 39, 64-6, 71, 92, 136,
Royal Victoria Hall, Southborough 118, 130
Royal Tunbridge Wells 6, 13-14
Royal West Kent Regt. 29, 33, 35, 38, 45, 89, 90, 93, 94, 100,101,103, 121, 224
Rust Hall 119, 128, 130

- 282 -

S

Salomons, Sir David, Bt. 10, 35, 90
Salomons, Capt. 'Reggie' 64-6, 90
Salvation Army 59, 73, 157, 159
Sassoon, Siegfried 97
Scott, Miss Amelia 86, 133,136,139, 140, 144, 157, 160, 161, 181, 184, 187, 257
Second Army HQ 74
Shernfold Park VAD 126, 130
Shops 26-7
Skinners' School 89
Sladen, Ald. Col. Sydney 13, 196, 260
Snell, Ald. J.B. 55, 65, 190, 191
Soldiers' Laundry 140-143
Soldiers' 'Soviet' 197-8
South Coast Railway 6, 24
South East Railway 6, 24,153
'Spanish' 'flu 86, 108, 229, 232-4
Speldhurst, St, Mary the Virgin 129
Spender-Clay, Col. H.H., MP 239, 241
Sports Clubs 28
Stamford, William MOH 20
Starmer, W.W. 168
St. Augustine's Church 35, 115, 176, 177, 178, 180-181, 253-4
St.Mark's Military Hospital 107, 118, 128, 130
St. Paul's, Rusthall 120, 129
Stone-Wigg, Ald. John 9
Strange Ald. C.H. 91
Sunday Concerts for the Troops 73, 78-79, 189-192
Suffragettes/suffragists 18, Chap.7
Sugar 'tickets' 85, 214
'Summer Time' 199

T

Taylor, Mrs. H.A. 207
The Hollands, Langton Green 121, 130
Tonbridge School 194-5
Tourism 17
Troops' Christmas Dinner 47-8, 51
Tunbridge Wells/ Royal Tunbridge Wells *passim*
Tunbridge Wells:
  Belgian Refugee Committee 172, 177, 181, 186, 187
  Cricket Week 32
  Tradesmen's Assoc. 62, 69, 70, 76, 81, 85, 239
  War Memorial 94-95, 96, 251-254, 266
  Volunteer Training Corps 54

U

U-Boats 209-10
Upper Grosvenor Rd, 170, 171, 172, 177
Urban, Joseph, hairdresser 60, 80
Usher, Rev. Dr. 192

V

VAD Hospitals 62, 74, 78, Chap. 6, 155, 198
  Available beds 128-131
  No. of soldiers treated 128-9
Van den Kerckhove, Paul 187-8

W

Wansbon, Ada 149
War Hospital Supply Depots 126-7
War Savings 79, 203, 219-20, 229, 249
Warren, B., tailor 179, 262
Wartime Restrictions 201-2
Waymark 14, 28,177, 235
WEA 86, 226
West Hall VAD 122-3, 130
White Feathers 156, 195
Wijnegem, nr. Antwerp 176
Women and the Peace Movement 163-4 (box)
Women's Auxiliary Army Corps (WAAC) 146, 148, 161, 217, 218
Women's Emergency Corps (WEC) 57, 146
Women's Land Army 148-150
Women's police Patrols143-5, 226
Women, position of , 17-18, Chap.7
Women's Suffrage Society 132
Women's Volunteer Reserve (WVR) 57, 146-8, 218
Women's War Emergency Corps 57

X

Y

YMCA 44, 107, 109, 199, 242, 244, 258

Z

Zeppelin(s), Raid of /concern over, 41, 63-64, 77, 79-80, 207, 232